Karen O'Connor
Editor

Women and Congress: Running, Winning, and Ruling

Women and Congress: Running, Winning, and Ruling has been co-published simultaneously as *Women & Politics,* Volume 23, Numbers 1/2 2001.

Pre-publication REVIEWS, COMMENTARIES, EVALUATIONS . . .

"An excellent resource for courses in women and politics at both the graduate and undergraduate level. . . . Provides a solid overview of the field while exploring both new dimensions of the relationship between gender and political behavior."

Linda L. Fowler, PhD
Director
The Nelson A. Rockefeller Center
Professor of Government
Dartmouth College, New Hampshire

More pre-publication
REVIEWS, COMMENTARIES, EVALUTIONS. . .

"I so thoroughly enjoyed reading this book, and my enthusiasm is so great, that I don't know where to begin praise. It will be an invaluable text in my women and politics class next year and for semesters to come. . . . Bridges the past, present, and future wonderfully. Very well written . . . accessible for students and experts alike."

Joanne Connor Green, PhD
Associate Professor
Department of Political Science
Texas Christian University
Fort Worth

"An impressive collection of original research . . . from an impressive list of scholars. Addresses all of the important issues and questions about the conditions under which women get elected. Must reading for students of Congress, congressional elections, and women and politics."

Jon R. Bond, PhD
Professor of Political Science
Texas A&M University
College Station

"Useful and interesting . . . an effective text for courses on American politics, voting behavior, and/or legislative politics. Each and every chapter contributes significantly to this story of transformation, diversity, and adversity, and does so in ways that are methodologically innovative and effective."

Beth Reingold, PhD
Associate Professor
Department of Political Science
and Institute for Women's Studies
Emory University, Altanta, Georgia

The Haworth Press, Inc.

Women and Congress: Running, Winning, and Ruling

Women and Congress: Running, Winning, and Ruling has been co-published simultaneously as *Women & Politics,* Volume 23, Numbers 1/2 2001.

The *Women & Politics* Monographic "Separates"

Below is a list of "separates," which in serials librarianship means a special issue simultaneously published as a special journal issue or double-issue *and* as a "separate" hardbound monograph. (This is a format which we also call a "DocuSerial.")

"Separates" are published because specialized libraries or professionals may wish to purchase a specific thematic issue by itself in a format which can be separately cataloged and shelved, as opposed to purchasing the journal on an on-going basis. Faculty members may also more easily consider a "separate" for classroom adoption.

"Separates" are carefully classified separately with the major book jobbers so that the journal tie-in can be noted on new book order slips to avoid duplicate purchasing.

You may wish to visit Haworth's website at . . .

http://www.HaworthPress.com

. . . to search our online catalog for complete tables of contents of these separates and related publications.

You may also call 1-800-HAWORTH (outside US/Canada: 607-722-5857), or Fax 1-800-895-0582 (outside US/Canada: 607-771-0012), or e-mail at:

getinfo@haworthpressinc.com

Women and Congress: Running , Winning, and Ruling, edited by Karen O'Connor, JD, PhD (Vol. 23, No. 1/2, 2001). *"Bridges the past, present, and future wonderfully. Very well written . . . accessible for students and experts alike." (Joanne Connor Green, PhD, Associate Professor, Department of Political Science, Texas Christian University, Fort Worth)*

Politics and Feminist Standpoint Theories, edited by Sally J. Kenney and Helen Kinsella (Vol. 18, No. 3, 1997). *"Illuminating . . . This collection will be useful to scholars and students interested in exploring how we should understand the explosion in knowledge generated by feminist projects." (Sandra Harding, PhD, Professor, Education and Women's Studies, UCLA)*

The Politics of Pregnancy: Policy Dilemmas in the Maternal-Fetal Relationship, edited by Janna C. Merrick, PhD, and Robert H. Blank, PhD (Vol. 13, No. 3/4, 1994). *"A valuable resource for teachers or upper-level college students." (Science Books & Films)*

Women and Public Administration: International Perspectives, edited by Jane H. Bayes (Vol. 11, No. 4, 1992). *"A long-awaited important six-nation comparative analysis of women's role in public administration." (Joyce Gelb, PhD, Professor, Department of Political Science, City College and Graduate Center, CUNY)*

Women, Politics and the Constitution, edited by Naomi B. Lynn, PhD (Vol. 10, No. 2, 1990). *"Fresh, new, and challenging. Naomi Lynn has done well in assembling these diverse perspectives on women and the Constitution." (J. Darcy, PhD, Professor, Department of Political Science, Oklahoma State University)*

Feminism and Epistemology: Approaches to Research in Women and Politics, edited by Maria J. Falco, PhD (Vol. 7, No. 3, 1988). *Here is a timely and informative introduction to a new phase of the ongoing feminist dialogue, reflecting the special dimension feminists have added to the debate over the positivist-behavioral paradigm.*

The Politics of Professionalism, Opportunity, Employment, and Gender, edited by Sarah Slavin, PhD (Vol. 6, No. 3, 1987). *Presents a picture of the complex social processes we characterize as "political," and a better sense of the less obvious elements that determine the political process.*

Women as Elders: Images, Visions, and Issues, edited by Marilyn J. Bell, PhD (Vol. 6, No. 2, 1987). *"Recommended for any woman who is interested in the issues of aging . . . and any woman who is attempting to create an empowered, positive identity for herself, at any age." (Common Ground)*

Gender and Socialization to Power and Politics, edited by Rita Mae Kelly, PhD (Vol. 5, No. 4, 1986). *Illustrates how the interaction of childhood socialization and the reality of the adult woman's life produces variations in political attitudes and in perceptions of available options for political behavior.*

Criminal Justice Politics and Women: The Aftermath of Legally Mandated Change, edited by Claudine Schweber, PhD, and Clarice Feinman, PhD (Vol. 4, No. 3, 1985). *"A good introduction to the subject. . . . The book will enlighten readers who may believe that discrimination can be readily eliminated through legal changes alone." (Corrections Today)*

United Nations Decade for Women World Conference, edited by Naomi B. Lynn, PhD (Vol. 4, No. 1, 1984). *Experts assess the progress that has been made, lament the failure of nations to take more steps to improve women's status, and analyze the divisive issues that have been at the forefront of concern and have limited the achievements of the two United Nations conferences on women.*

Biopolitics and Gender, edited by Meredith W. Watts (Vol. 3, No. 2/3, 1984). *"Provocative. . . . Welcomed as a way to broaden discussion of gender beyond an exclusive focus on sex links to oppression and discrimination." (Political Science Quarterly)*

Women in Developing Countries: A Policy Focus, edited by Kathleen Staudt and Jane Jacquette (Vol. 2, No. 4, 1983). *"Recommend[ed] . . . to any reader who would like to learn more about how it is possible, through mismanagement, ignorance, lack of powerful women staff members, and the deliberate ignoring of women's needs, to pour substantial amounts of money into development programs without helping women at all." (International Journal of Women's Studies)*

The Equal Rights Amendment: The Politics and Process of Ratification of the 27th Amendment to the U.S. Constitution, edited by Sarah Slavin, PhD (Vol. 2, No. 1/2, 1982). *An exploration of the attempt to ratify the Equal Rights Amendment and efforts of organizations and individual states to either secure or defeat ratification.*

Women and Congress: Running, Winning, and Ruling has been co-published simultaneously as *Women & Politics*™, Volume 23, Numbers 1/2 2001.

Cover design by Jennifer M. Gaska

Library of Congress Cataloging-in-Publication Data

Women and Congress: Running, Winning, and Ruling / Karen O' Connor, editor.
p. cm.
"Co-published simultaneously as Women & politics, Vol. 23, nos. 1/2, 2001."
Includes bibliographical references and index.
ISBN 0-7890-1670-2 (alk. paper) – ISBN 0-7890-1671-0 (pbk. : alk. paper)
1. Women in politics–United States. 2. Women legislators–United States. 3. Political campaigns–United States. I. O'Connor, Karen, 1952- II. Women & politics. v. 23, nos. 1/2 2001 (Supplement)
HQ1391.U5 W62 2002
328.73'0082–dc21 2002001688

Women and Congress: Running, Winning, and Ruling

Karen O'Connor
Editor

Women and Congress: Running, Winning, and Ruling has been co-published simultaneously as *Women & Politics*, Volume 23, Numbers 1/2 2001.

The Haworth Press, Inc.
New York • London • Oxford

Indexing, Abstracting & Website/Internet Coverage

This section provides you with a list of major indexing & abstracting services. That is to say, each service began covering this periodical during the year noted in the right column. Most Websites which are listed below have indicated that they will either post, disseminate, compile, archive, cite or alert their own Website users with research-based content from this work. (This list is as current as the copyright date of this publication.)

Abstracting, Website/Indexing Coverage . . . . Year When Coverage Began

- *ABC POL SCI: A Bibliography of Contents: Political Science & Government, ABC-CLIO <www.csa.com>* 1992
- *Academic Abstracts/CD-ROM* 1993
- *Academic Index (on-line)* 1992
- *Academic Search: data-base of 2,000 selected academic serials, updated monthly: EBSCO Publishing* 1995
- *Academic Search Elite (EBSCO)* 2000
- *America: History and Life, ABC-CLIO, Inc. <www.abc-clio.com>* . . . 1992
- *BUBL Information Service: An Internet-based Information Service for the UK higher education community <URL: http://bubl.ac.uk/>* 1995
- *CNPIEC Reference Guide: Chinese National Directory of Foreign Periodicals* 1996
- *Contemporary Women's Issues* 1998
- *Current Contents/Social & Behavioral Sciences <www.isinet.com>* 2000

(continued)

- *Current Legal Sociology <www.iisj.es>* . . . 1992
- *Expanded Academic ASAP <www.galegroup.com>* . . . 2000
- *Expanded Academic Index* . . . 1996
- *Family Index Database <www.familyscholar.com>* . . . 2001
- *Feminist Periodicals: A Current Listing of Contents* . . . 1992
- *FINDEX <www.publist.com>* . . . 1999
- *GenderWatch <www.slinfo.com>* . . . 1999
- *Handbook of Latin American Studies* . . . 1999
- *Historical Abstracts, ABC-CLIO, Inc. <www.abc-clio.com>* . . . 1992
- *IBZ International Bibliography of Periodical Literature <www.saur.de>* . . . 1995
- *Index Guide to College Journals (core list compiled by integrating 48 indexes frequently used to support undergraduate programs in small to medium sized libraries)* . . . 1999
- *Index to Periodical Articles Related to Law* . . . 1992
- *InfoTrac Custom <www.galegroup.com>* . . . 2000
- *International Political Science Abstracts/Documentation Politique Internationale* . . . 1992
- *LEGALTRAC on INFOTRAC web <www.galegroup.com>* . . . 2000
- *MasterFILE: Updated Database from EBSCO Publishing* . . . 1995
- *OCLC Public Affairs Information Service <www.pais.org>* . . . 1999
- *Periodica Islamica* . . . 1994
- *Periodical Abstracts, Research I (general and basic reference indexing & abstracting data-base from University Microfilms International (UMI)* . . . 1993
- *Periodical Abstracts Research II (broad coverage indexing & abstracting data-base from University Microfilms International (UMI)* . . . 1993
- *RESEARCH ALERT/ISI Alerting Services <www.isinet.com>* . . . 1999
- *Social Sciences Citation Index <www.isinet.com>* . . . 1999
- *Social Sciences Index (from Volume 1 & continuing) <www.hwwilson.com>* . . . 1999
- *Social Scisearch <www.isinet.com>* . . . 1999
- *Social Services Abstracts <www.csa.com>* . . . 1992
- *Social Work Abstracts <www.silverplatter.com/catalog/swab.htm>* . . . 1992
- *Sociological Abstracts (SA) <www.csa.com>* . . . 1992
- *Studies on Women Abstracts* . . . 1992

(continued)

- ***Women Studies Abstracts*** **1992**
- ***Women's Resources International Abstracts*** **1998**
- ***Women's Studies Index (indexed comprehensively)*** **1992**
- ***Worldwide Political Science Abstracts (formerly: Political Science & Government Abstracts) <www.csa.com>*** **1988**

Special Bibliographic Notes related to special journal issues (separates) and indexing/abstracting:

- indexing/abstracting services in this list will also cover material in any "separate" that is co-published simultaneously with Haworth's special thematic journal issue or DocuSerial. Indexing/abstracting usually covers material at the article/chapter level.
- monographic co-editions are intended for either non-subscribers or libraries which intend to purchase a second copy for their circulating collections.
- monographic co-editions are reported to all jobbers/wholesalers/approval plans. The source journal is listed as the "series" to assist the prevention of duplicate purchasing in the same manner utilized for books-in-series.
- to facilitate user/access services all indexing/abstracting services are encouraged to utilize the co-indexing entry note indicated at the bottom of the first page of each article/chapter/contribution.
- this is intended to assist a library user of any reference tool (whether print, electronic, online, or CD-ROM) to locate the monographic version if the library has purchased this version but not a subscription to the source journal.
- individual articles/chapters in any Haworth publication are also available through the Haworth Document Delivery Service (HDDS).

Women and Congress: Running, Winning, and Ruling

CONTENTS

ABOUT THE EDITOR

Karen O'Connor, JD, PhD, is Professor of Government in the School of Public Affairs at American University in Washington, DC. She is Director of the Women & Politics Institute and Editor of *Women & Politics*. Dr. O'Connor has written or co-authored numerous books, including *No Neutral Ground: Abortion Politics in an Age of Absolutes; American Government: Continuity and Change* (7th edition, with Larry Sabato); and *Women, Politics and American Society* (3rd edition, with Nancy E. McGlen, Laura van Assendelft, and Wendy Gunther-Canada). Dr. O'Connor has published numerous monographs, book chapters, and articles in leading social science and political science journals and law reviews. She is also a member of several editorial boards including *Law & Policy*.

In 1998, Dr. O'Connor received the Erica Fairchild Award from the Women's Caucus of the Southern Political Science Association as the outstanding mentor of women in the political science profession. In 1999, she was named a mentor of distinction by the American Association of University Women. She is also an active member of the American Political Science Association, Past Chair of its Law and Courts Section, and Past President of the Women's Caucus for Political Science. She is also Past President of the Southern Political Science Association and President of the National Capital Area Political Science Association.

∞ ALL HAWORTH BOOKS AND JOURNALS ARE PRINTED ON CERTIFIED ACID-FREE PAPER

Introduction

Karen O'Connor, American University

When I became editor of *Women & Politics,* I quickly learned how far the study of women in legislative bodies–especially at the level of the United States Congress–had evolved. Emmy Werner (1966) pioneered the quantitative study of women in Congress. Still, given that few women have served in Congress, most early systematic analyses of women and legislatures–especially work on the important question of whether having women elected in those positions made a difference–were concentrated on state level analyses (Dubeck 1976; Kathlene 1994; Kirkpatrick 1974; Reingold 1992; Thomas 1997). Some, including Diane Kincaid (Blair) (1978), examined how women became members of Congress (often, in Kincaid's phraseology, "Over His Dead Body"); others tried to access the electability of women candidates (Bullock and Hays 1972; Darcy and Schramm 1977; Deber 1982). Still, until 1992, the small number of women serving in the U.S. Congress, especially at the Senate level, made empirical analyses difficult. The year 1992, however, not only saw the election of record numbers of women to the House and Senate, it also ushered in a new era of research on women in Congress, as is reflected in this special volume.

The diversity of the nature of research questions now being asked about the women who run for, or serve in, the U.S. Congress is well illustrated by the breadth of articles collected in this volume. Before women can make a difference in a legislative body, they must seek elective office and win. A growing key to election, especially at the national

[Haworth co-indexing entry note]: "Introduction." O'Connor, Karen. Co-published simultaneously in *Women & Politics* (The Haworth Press, Inc.) Vol. 23, No. 1/2, 2001, pp. 1-5; and: *Women and Congress: Running, Winning, and Ruling* (ed: Karen O'Connor) The Haworth Press, Inc., 2001, pp. 1-5. Single or multiple copies of this article are available for a fee from The Haworth Document Delivery Service [1-800-HAWORTH, 9:00 a.m. - 5:00 p.m. (EST). E-mail address: getinfo@haworthpressinc.com].

level, is money. The development of scores of women's political action committees (PACs) has contributed significantly to the success of female candidates for national office. As Peter L. Francia notes in this volume, the huge success of pro-Democratic women's PACs such as EMILY's List, which provides critical early money to women candidates it assesses to be viable, has translated into a significant advantage for Democratic women candidates. Not only do these PACs provide critical initial funds, thereby allowing women to establish themselves as viable candidates, they also help those same women to raise crucial funds later in the campaign cycle. This phenomenon, in turn, says Francia, has fostered the election of a disproportionate number of Democratic women to the U.S. House of Representatives.

Women's PACs are not the only factor that has enhanced the number of women in elective office at the national level. A wide range of other factors have been found to influence the outcome of women's races for Congress. Many of those factors are addressed by articles contained in this volume.

In "Electoral Context, Issues, and Voting for Women in the 1990s," Kathleen Dolan, building on the work of Sapiro and Conover (1997), analyzes the 1992, 1994, and 1996 elections for the House of Representatives. She finds that 1992 offered a unique environment not present in subsequent elections. This environment facilitated the election of so many new women to the House and the Senate that it was hailed as "The Year of the Woman." Ronald Keith Gaddie, Kim U. Hoffman, and Carrie Palmer also examine the 1992 election, but do so in the context of analyzing House open seat elections since 1982. Interestingly, unlike Dolan, in "Candidate Sex and Congressional Elections: Open Seats Before, During, and After the Year of the Woman," Gaddie, Hoffman, and Palmer find that the partisanship of the district is key to understanding women's electoral success.

Also examining congressional elections in this volume are Barbara Palmer and Dennis Simon in "The Political Glass Ceiling: Gender, Strategy, and Incumbency in the U.S. House Elections, 1978-1998." With data collected from all primary and general House elections from 1978 to 1998, Palmer and Simon conclude that incumbency fosters a general lack of competitiveness in both primary and general elections, which in turn serves as a political glass ceiling for women. Without term limits or other factors to produce major exits from the House, the authors see the opportunities for women's progress to be hindered considerably.

While money, PAC support, partisanship, structural variables, open seats, and incumbency are critical to the outcome of elections, as highlighted in the first four works in this volume, so is the extent and nature of media coverage of candidates for public office. Martha E. Kropf and John Boiney build on the work of Kahn (1992, 1994a, 1994b, 1996) and others to assess the effects of print and television news coverage of the electoral viability of women candidates for the U.S. Senate. They provide evidence to show that discrimination in television coverage of women Senate candidates exists and call for additional research on the role that the media continues to play in the election process.

Scholars long have asked the question of whether differences matter, or, as Michele Swers in this volume asks: What is the policy impact of women in the national legislature? The fact that a record number of women–thirteen–now serve in the U.S. Senate will go far to open up even more areas of inquiry for scholars. These women not only form a critical mass, they also, when acting as a bloc, have the potential to wield significant power in the Senate, which is closely divided on the party lines in the 107th Congress.

In this volume, Dena Levy, Charles Tien, and Rachelle Aved, in "Do Differences Matter? Women Members of Congress and the Hyde Amendment," attempt to answer the question of whether or not women in the House of Representatives make a difference by analyzing floor debates on the Hyde Amendment. The authors find that not only do women frame the abortion debate differently, but their numbers have fostered a change in the nature of the debate over time.

Colleen Shogan analyzes the public statements of House members in the 105th Congress and finds that Republican and Democratic female members invoke women in their public statements at similar rates, but that Republican female members discuss women in the context of very different issues than do their Democratic counterparts.

Shogan's work, which explores the role of women as legislators by measuring public statements entered in the *Congressional Record,* raises interesting questions about how these women legislators present themselves to their constituents as well as to the media. Thus, as David Niven and Jeremy Zilber point out in "How Does She Have Time for Kids and Congress?," not only are women candidates treated differently by the media, but women representatives are, too, despite how they attempt to package themselves and their areas of expertise. One need only look at the talking heads on television to recognize that male legislators are far more likely to be called upon to discuss the issues of the day than are their female counterparts.

How women candidates are perceived by the media, especially the print media, as well as by the electorate, has been the focus of excellent analyses. Most scholars have found pervasive discrimination in the coverage of female candidates, as did Kropf and Boiney in this volume. Niven and Zilber take this work in a new direction by exploring the degree to which the press offices of women members of Congress project their members to the media and the public as "special" representatives of women. The authors find that women representatives do not highlight the fact that they are women, yet the media continues to see them in that vein and not as more general policy experts.

In the last article in this volume, "Research on Women in Legislatures: What Have We Learned, Where Are We Going?" Michele Swers surveys the literature on women and Congress and points out directions for further research suggested by the articles presented here and elsewhere. As new books, including those by the nine women Senators in the 106th Congress, and Swers's work underscore, it is only a matter of time before women other than Representative Nancy Pelosi (D-CA) move into more leadership positions in both Houses and continue to increase their impact on policy and on both legislative bodies.

REFERENCES

Bullock, Charles S., III, and Patricia Lee Findley Hays. 1972. "Recruitment of Women for Congress: A Research Note." *Western Political Quarterly* 25: 416-423.

Darcy, Robert, and Sarah Slavin Schramm. 1977. "When Women Run Against Men." *Public Opinion Quarterly* 41: 1-12.

Deber, Raisa. 1982. "The Fault Dear Brutus: Women as Congressional Candidates in Pennsylvania." *Journal of Politics* 44: 463-479.

Dubeck, Paula J. "Women and Access to Political Office: Comparison of Female and Male State Legislators." *Sociological Quarterly* 17 (winter): 46-48.

Kahn, Kim Fridkin. 1992. "Does Being a Male Help? An Investigation of the Effects of Candidate Gender and Campaign Coverage on Evaluations of U.S. Senate Candidates." *Journal of Politics* 54: 497-517.

Kahn, Kim Fridkin. 1994a. "The Distorted Mirror: Press Coverage of Women Candidates for Statewide Office." *Journal of Politics* 56: 154-173.

Kahn, Kim Fridkin. 1994b. "Does Gender Make a Difference? An Experimental Examination of Sex Stereotypes and Press Patterns in Statewide Campaigns." *American Journal of Political Science* 38: 162-195.

Kahn, Kim Fridkin. 1996. *The Political Consequences of Being a Woman: How Stereotypes Influence the Conduct and Consequences of Political Campaigns.* New York: Columbia University Press.

Kathlene, Lyn. 1989. "Uncovering the Political Impacts of Gender: An Exploratory Study." *Western Political Quarterly* 42: 397-421.
Kathlene, Lyn. 1994. "Power and Influence of State Legislative Policymaking: The Interaction of Gender and Position in Committee Hearing Debates." *American Political Science Review* 88: 560-576.
Kincaid, Diane. 1978. "Over His Dead Body: A Positive Perspective on Widows in the U.S. Congress." *Western Political Quarterly* 38: 96-104.
Kirkpatrick, Jeane. 1974. *Political Women.* New York: Basic Books.
Reingold, Beth. 1992. "Concepts of Representation Among Female and Male State Legislators." *Legislative Studies Quarterly* 17: 509-537.
Sapiro, Virginia, and Pamela Johnston Conover. 1977. "The Variable Gender Basis of Electoral Politics: Gender and Context in the 1992 U.S. Election." *British Journal of Political Science* 27: 497-523.
Thomas, Sue. 1997. "Why Gender Matters: The Perceptions of Women Officeholders." *Women & Politics* 17: 27-53.
Werner, Emmy E. 1966. "Are Women More Liberal Than Men in the U.S. Congress?" *Legislative Studies Quarterly* 10: 125-134.

Early Fundraising by Nonincumbent Female Congressional Candidates: The Importance of Women's PACs

Peter L. Francia, University of Maryland

SUMMARY. This study investigates the effects of early contributions by women's PACs to female nonincumbent U.S. House candidates. The results show that women's PACs give early money disproportionately to female Democrats. This advantage provides female Democrats with greater success in raising later funds and in gaining electoral support than nonincumbent female Republicans. *[Article copies available for a fee from The Haworth Document Delivery Service: 1-800-HAWORTH. E-mail address: <getinfo@haworthpressinc.com> Website: <http://www.HaworthPress.com> © 2001 by The Haworth Press, Inc. All rights reserved.]*

Throughout the past several decades, female candidates running for the U.S. Congress have become increasingly competitive and successful. Women have more than doubled their numbers in the U.S. House since 1975 and now raise comparable sums of money to men after controlling for political experience and incumbency status (Burrell 1985, 1994; Uhlaner and Schlozman 1986). The growth of women's political action committees (PAC) is one of the reasons for the improved fortunes of female congressional candidates, particularly challengers and open-seat candidates (Seltzer, Newman, and Voorhees Leighton 1997; Witt, Paget, and Matthews 1994).

[Haworth co-indexing entry note]: "Early Fundraising by Nonincumbent Female Congressional Candidates: The Importance of Women's PACs." Francia, Peter L. Co-published simultaneously in *Women & Politics* (The Haworth Press, Inc.) Vol. 23, No. 1/2, 2001, pp. 7-20; and: *Women and Congress: Running, Winning, and Ruling* (ed: Karen O'Connor) The Haworth Press, Inc., 2001, pp. 7-20. Single or multiple copies of this article are available for a fee from The Haworth Document Delivery Service [1-800-HAWORTH, 9:00 a.m. - 5:00 p.m. (EST). E-mail address: getinfo@haworthpressinc.com].

One of the most significant forms of assistance provided by women's PACs is their willingness to provide female candidates with early money, or what is also known as "seed money."[1] Seed money purchases pollsters, helps develop campaign plans, and prepares campaigns for attacks by opponents (Nelson 1994). Seed money is particularly important to nonincumbents who need to establish credibility and improve their name recognition with voters quickly.

Most women's PACs, however, are liberal and contribute their money mainly to Democrats. This raises the possibility that the partisan leanings of women's PACs provide fundraising and electoral advantages for Democratic women that do not exist for Republican women. This study tests that hypothesis and presents evidence that seed money from women's PACs helps Democratic female nonincumbents raise greater sums of campaign money and gain increased electoral support compared to Republican females.

THE IMPORTANCE OF EARLY FUNDRAISING

Fundraising is often very difficult for challengers. Numerous contributors follow access strategies, giving money to incumbents to secure influence (Sabato 1984; Sorauf 1992). Nonincumbents, on the other hand, are forced to rely on contributors who follow ideological or electoral strategies. These contributors give money for the purpose of electing the maximum number of candidates who support the group's agenda and will be agreeable to their concerns on legislative issues (Eismeier and Pollack 1988; Gopoian 1984; Humphries 1991).

Women's PACs typically follow electoral strategies. Many contribute money to nonincumbents and most require candidates to take a pro-choice stance. PACs such as the Women's Campaign Fund routinely give the majority of their contributions to nonincumbents (Nelson 1994). Women's PACs such as EMILY's List are committed to electing promising women candidates and protecting the Supreme Court's *Roe* v. *Wade* (1973) ruling, which guarantees abortion rights. The position of most women's organizations is that abortion is a fundamental human and reproductive right of all women that should be guaranteed by law. Over the past several decades, abortion has been one of the nation's most intense political issues. Pro-life activists have successfully led the charge to limit abortion. They have won several battles such as *Webster* v. *Reproductive Health Services* (1989) and *Planned Parenthood of Southeastern Pennsylvania* v. *Casey* (1992), which upheld the right of states to pass laws restricting abortion, such as informed consent and twenty-four hour waiting periods. With abortion under attack and no guarantee of its preservation, electing candidates who pledge to protect abortion rights is frequently a top priority for women's PACs (Thomas 1994). Because Democratic candidates tend to support abortion rights more often than Republicans do, women's PACs such as EMILY's List give their money exclusively to women who are pro-choice Democrats.

This is problematic for Republican women, particularly those who are conservative and pro-life, because they must compete with male candidates for money from traditional GOP financial sources, such as businesses and socially conservative organizations. Liberal Democratic women, by contrast, do not have to compete with men for money from most women's PACs. More significantly, however, women's groups such as EMILY's List are particularly helpful in assisting Democratic women in raising money in the early stages of a campaign. Its name is an acronym for Early Money Is Like Yeast. Early money helps campaigns because it provides challengers with the resources to communicate their campaign message and to overcome the lack of name recognition (Jacobson 1997; Mann and Wolfinger 1981; Squire and Wright 1990).

Nonincumbents also depend on seed money to hire pollsters, media consultants, and other campaign advisors (Biersack, Herrnson, and Wilcox 1993). These specialists handle advertising, conduct polls, and assemble "PAC kits" to help convince potential contributors of the viability of a particular campaign (Herrnson 1992). Furthermore, seed money is often a factor in determining whether party committees will assist nonincumbents. Party committees often set targets for early fundraising and will withdraw party aid to those who fail to meet those targets (Biersack, Herrnson, and Wilcox 1993).

For all of these reasons, those who raise seed money are the same candidates who raise more total monetary contributions (Biersack, Herrnson, and Wilcox 1993). This is significant because a nonincumbent's success is strongly related to the total amount of money raised and spent in the campaign (Jacobson 1990, 1997). Nonincumbents typically raise far less money than incumbents and are thus very dependent on groups motivated by electoral strategies that invest seed money. Women's PACs, which follow electoral strategies and give mainly to women, thus play an important role in the campaigns of nonincumbent female candidates.

DATA AND METHODS

Campaign finance data for this study comes from the Federal Election Commission (FEC). The analysis includes female challengers and open-seat candidates who ran for a seat in the U.S. House during the 1994 general election.[2] It excludes male nonincumbents because they are less often the recipients of women's PAC support.

The data analysis relies on seemingly unrelated regression equations (SURE).[3] The first equation estimates the factors that affect total seed money from women's PACs. The second equation analyzes whether nonincumbent Democratic women receiving seed money from women's PACs are more likely to raise greater sums of total receipts than nonincumbent Republican women. To test that hypothesis, the model includes an interaction variable that multiplies Democratic Party affiliation and seed money from women's PACs. This study defines women's PACs as a "committee whose primary purpose is to elect women to political office" (see Nelson 1994; see also Appendix A for a complete list of how all variables were defined and coded, and Appendix B for a listing of women's PACs used in this study).

The control variables are political experience, whether the race was for an open seat, incumbent vulnerability, the partisanship of the district, and the existence of a primary opponent. Those with previous political experience are typically the strongest candidates and consequently raise more money and receive more support than those without it (Biersack, Herrnson, and Wilcox 1993; Jacobson 1997). Open-seat candidates are usually in more competitive races than challengers, and have an easier time building name recognition among voters due to preferential treatment by the media (Herrnson 1998; Jacobson 1997). Strong challengers tend not to enter races against incumbents who have won their districts by large margins in the previous election. An incumbent's most effective strategy is to discourage serious opposition by avoiding "slippage at the polls" (Jacobson 1997, 43). A poor showing by an incumbent in one election was a strong predictor of seed money for the challenger in the next (Biersack, Herrnson, and Wilcox 1993). The partisanship of the district is another important factor in determining a nonincumbent's ability to raise money and wage an effective campaign against an incumbent.[4] Nonincumbents are more likely to perform better in districts where their party's presidential nominee performs well. Candidates facing a primary challenger also have a greater urgency to raise early funds than those running unopposed. These control variables also test whether Democratic women receiving seed money from women's PACs received additional electoral support. Electoral support is based on the percentage of the district vote received by the candidate in the 1994 general election.

THE EFFECTS OF SEED MONEY FROM WOMEN'S PACS ON LATER FUNDRAISING AND ELECTORAL SUPPORT

Female Democrats raised more seed money and received greater support from women's PACs than female Republicans. Democratic women raised an average of $86,876 in seed money from all sources compared to $43,423 for Republican female nonincumbents (see Table 1). Women's PACs helped Democratic women gain that early advantage by giving to them almost eight times more than to Republicans.

The wide financial gap separating women in the two parties during the early stages of the election is partly explained by the importance of EMILY's List, an exclusively Democratic donor. Direct contributions from EMILY's List accounted for roughly 18% of all seed money donations by women's PACs to female nonincumbents who participated in the 1994 general election. However, because a campaign finance law limits PAC contributions to $5,000 per candidate in each election, EMILY's List requests that its members make individual donations directly to female candidates. EMILY's List collects these checks and then physically presents them to the candidates. This technique, known as "bundling," allows groups to funnel more money to the candidates they support. In 1994, EMILY's List had more than 33,000 members who contributed roughly $6.2 million.[5]

The Women's Campaign Fund (WCF) was also a significant source of early money for female candidates. The WCF gave $92,688 in direct seed money contributions to nonincumbent female candidates. Seventy-nine percent of that amount went to Democrats.

The WISH List, a pro-choice Republican PAC, attempted to counterbalance the Democrat's advantage, but simply could not compete with EMILY's List or the WCF. WISH List's direct contributions were less than half the amount that EMILY's List or the WCF gave to female nonincumbents in 1994.

Democratic women who received the most money from women's PACs were the most successful fundraisers (see Table 2). Female Democrats who took in between $1 and $2,999 in seed money from women's PACs raised roughly 2.4 times more money in total contributions than Democratic women who failed to raise any seed money from women's

TABLE 1. The Average Amount of Seed Money Raised by Democratic and Republican Female Nonincumbents

	Democrats			*Republicans*		
	Challengers	Open Seats	All	Challengers	Open Seats	All
Seed Money Receipts	$44,003 (58,621)	$206,921 (145,854)	$86,876 (113,878)	$23,541 (26,972)	$132,885 (110,045)	$43,423 (65,707)
Seed Money From Women's PACs	732 (1,530)	7,982 (8,150)	2,640 (5,323)	194 (961)	917 (2,010)	326 (1,209)
(N)	28	10	38	27	6	33

Note: Standard deviation in parentheses.

TABLE 2. The Estimated Effects of Early Contributions from Women's PACs

	Total Receipts		*Vote Percentage*	
Women's PAC Seed Money	Democrats	Republicans	Democrats	Republicans
$0	$136,901 (180,004)	$303,625 (427,786)	30.2%** (7.2)	38.4%** (11.9)
$1-2,999	330,037* (140,746)	360,864 (297,090)	37.7** (6.4)	44.5** (10.6)
$3,000 and up	578,991* (268,149)	312,030 (381,278)	48.8** (14.9)	38.5** (7.8)
N	38	33	38	33

Note: Standard deviation in parentheses. $^{**}p < .01$, $^{*}p < .05$

PACs. Female Democrats who raised more than $3,000 in seed money from women's PACs raised roughly 4.2 times more money in total receipts than Democratic women who failed to raise any seed money from women's PACs.

By comparison, Republican women who received seed money from women's PACs did *not,* on average, raise significantly more money than other Republican females. These patterns remained consistent when analyzing vote percentages. Democratic women who received the most seed money from women's PACs did the best on Election Day, while seed money from women's PACs showed no relationship with the electoral success of Republican women. Democratic women are able to tap the major women's PACs, such as EMILY's List and the WCF, and consequently receive benefits from the early money those PACs provide. Republican female candidates get no such benefit.

The multivariate model confirms that Democratic Party affiliation is a significant predictor of seed money receipts from women's PACs (see Table 3). The results also show that the disproportionate share of seed money from women's PACs to female Democrats helps them raise more total money during their campaigns than female Republicans. Democratic women who received the average amount in seed money from women's PACs (roughly $2,640) raised an estimated $50,075 more in total contributions than Republican women who did not receive seed money from women's PACs.[6] Political experience, open seat contests, and district partisanship were also statistically significant predictors of total receipts.

Two Michigan candidates bring these numbers to life. In different campaigns, Democrat Lynn Rivers (MI) narrowly won her race with 51% of the vote and Republican Meagan O'Neill (MI) narrowly lost her election with 47% of the vote. While both elections were close, Rivers raised substantially more money than O'Neill. Rivers raised $640,417 and O'Neill raised $302,158 in total receipts. Rivers ran in an open-seat contest, and O'Neill faced an incumbent. This gave Rivers a clear advantage. Open-seat candidates are more successful, particularly for women candidates (Dabelko and Herrnson 1997). The model confirms that open-seat candidates have an advantage and estimates that it earned Rivers an additional $185,189.

There are other important factors, however, that explain why Rivers was more successful in raising money. Rivers was in a district where the partisanship was slightly more favorable than for O'Neill, and that factor translated into an additional $14,380 for Rivers. Rivers' ability to raise $5,500 in seed money from women's PACs helped her earn an estimated $199,865 in additional total receipts compared to O'Neill, who

TABLE 3. The Effects of Seed Money from Women's PACs and Other Determinants on the Total Receipts and Electoral Success of Female Nonincumbents

Characteristics	Women's PAC Seed Money	Total Receipts	General Vote Percentage
Political experience	1,099 (1,180)	156,495** (90,515)	1.07 (1.83)
Open seat	4,099*** (1,122)	185,189** (92,464)	6.79*** (1.87)
Incumbent vulnerability	−67** (36)	3,090 (2,789)	.20*** (.06)
District partisanship	52 (44)	7,190** (3,384)	.45*** (.07)
Primary opponent	1,034 (916)	−42,786 (69,883)	1.42 (1.41)
Democrat	2,492*** (832)	−88,192* (68,284)	−6.26*** (1.38)
Women's PAC seed money (per $1,000)	–	−41,188 (37,711)	−1.66** (.76)
Democrat X women's PAC seed money (per $1,000)	–	52,374* (38,000)	2.13*** (.77)
Intercept	1,201 (1,432)	186,737** (108,841)	32.48*** (2.20)
N	71	71	71
R^2	.36	.44	.81

Note: Standard error in parentheses. Coefficients are based on seemingly unrelated regression estimates. ***p < .01, **p < .05, *p < .10.

raised no seed money from women's PACs. The model thus predicts that Rivers should raise $399,434 more in total receipts than O'Neill, which comes close to the actual difference of $338,259.

Women's PACs do not simply support candidates who are already well financed or have the best chance at victory. Representative Zoë Lofgren (D-CA), for example, began her campaign as a distinct underdog in the primary election for the seat representing the sixteenth district of California. In February 1994, *Congressional Quarterly* listed San Jose Mayor Tom McEnery as the favorite to win the election (Elving 1994). *The San Francisco Chronicle* reported that McEnery held a 19 point advantage over Lofgren, but added that Lofgren's early support from EMILY's List made her a potentially serious candidate (Simon 1994). Lofgren received ten of her first eighteen donations from women's organizations, or $26,069 of her first $30,000, in campaign receipts. Other PAC donations poured in after that initial support. Lofgren became one of the most successful female fundraisers in 1994, raising over $600,000. She defeated McEnery in the primary and won the general election. Her success highlights the fact that women's PACs, such as EMILY's List, often invest in underdogs like Lofgren and provide them with the critical early resources that establish credibility for the campaign and trigger later contributions.

Conservative female challengers and open-seat candidates who do not receive assistance from women's PACs often have a difficult time raising early funds from traditional sources. Corporate PACs typically invest in likely winners and will often avoid contributing money to risky nonincumbents. Party committees, likewise, often contribute later in the process when the primary election has passed. Conservative ideological groups such as the Family Values PAC exist, but they do not exclusively focus on female candidates as do women's PACs. Conservative female candidates must compete with male candidates for the same sources of seed money. In contrast, women's PACs are among the few venture capitalists that contribute money early in an election, and Democratic women have near exclusive access to these critical funds.

Women's PACs also played a role in influencing electoral support. Female nonincumbent Democrats received an additional .32% of the vote after raising $14,000 in seed money from women's PACs.[7] For each additional $1,000 after the $14,000 threshold, there was an increase in the vote of .47%. This result demonstrates how the relative lack of seed money for Republican women puts them at an electoral disadvantage. For example, Republican female challengers Sherill Morgan (NC) and Lynn Slaby (OH) lost by less than 3%. Morgan and Slaby each raised under $65,000 in seed money, which was below the mean amount raised by general election female candidates. Neither received any financial contributions from women's PACs. In contrast, Democrats such as Lofgren and Sheila McGuire (IA), who were in competitive races, received over $19,000 in seed money from women's PACs. If Morgan and Slaby had received the same support from women's

PACs as Lofgren and McGuire, their electoral support would have improved by almost 3%, and may have turned their narrow defeats into narrow victories.

The control variables indicate that open-seat races, incumbent vulnerability, and district partisanship are significant predictors of higher vote percentages for female nonincumbents. All three factors are related to an increased likelihood of a competitive race. The strongest nonincumbent candidates are strategic and run only when the circumstances point to a competitive election. They challenge only vulnerable incumbents, or simply wait for the seat to become open when they have the best chance of winning.

A variety of factors, therefore, influence the fundraising and electoral success of female candidates. Of these factors, the ability to raise seed money from women's PACs is one of the most important. Women's PACs give money disproportionately to female Democrats, which places female Republicans at a comparative disadvantage.

DISCUSSION

Raising money is a critical element to any nonincumbent's campaign. Candidates who receive the most money usually wage the strongest campaigns. However, to be a successful fundraiser, candidates need to develop a strong base of support early in the campaign. For female candidates, women's PACs provide the early support that establishes a campaign's viability and signals other contributors. Because the majority of support from women's PACs flows to Democratic women, Republican women face a more daunting task of establishing early viability.

Whether this unequal situation will continue in future elections is difficult to ascertain. What is clear is that Republican women need to find financial networks that are committed to helping them early. Democratic women currently enjoy the early benefits provided by women's PACs. Republican women need to find comparable counterparts or they risk losing races that could otherwise be won with early support.

NOTES

1. Previous research defines seed money as the total "receipts recorded in the first two reports filed by a candidate" (Biersack, Herrnson, and Wilcox 1993, 538).

2. I use 1994 because of its favorable environment to conservatives. I believe that the results of the article are made stronger by showing that women's PACs provided an

early fundraising advantage for female Democrats in a Republican year. I exclude third party candidates because the focus of the article is to compare Democrats and Republicans. Also not included are those who lost in the primaries because such candidates did not raise later receipts or compete in the general election. I include Representative Patricia Slocumb (R, LA) even though she did not compete in the general election. This exception was made because there were no 1994 U.S. House general elections in Louisiana. Due to the unique way that Louisiana conducts its elections, the primary is essentially equivalent to the general election.

3. I use SURE because it is likely that the error terms in my equations are correlated. Zellner (1971) suggests estimating the equations simultaneously to avoid the problem of "contemporaneous correlation." Zellner found that estimating the equations separately improved the efficiency of the estimators.

4. The variable for the partisanship of the district subtracts Clinton's nation mean (43%) from his district performance for Democrats, and subtracts his district performance from his national mean for Republicans. This creates a positive score for Democrats and Republicans in elections where their nominee was stronger, and a negative score where their nominee was weaker.

5. The communications office of EMILY's List provided the information of its membership in 1994 and the amount of "bundled" money its members contributed during the 1994 elections.

6. The number is computed by multiplying the interaction coefficient of $52,374 by 2.64 (for $2,640) which equals $138,267. That number is then subtracted by the coefficient for Democrat, which is 88,192. The difference equals $50,075.

7. The number is computed using the following formula: $[(2.13 - 1.66) * 14] - 6.26$.

8. Emma's List, the National Abortion and Reproductive Rights Action League, the National Federation of Business and Professional Women's Clubs, Susan B. Anthony Fund, WISH List, Women . . . for a Change, Women for Life, Women for Washington, Women in Energy, Women in Leadership, Women Running, Women's Action for New Directions, Women's Action for Nuclear Disarmament, Women's Business Coalition, Women's Business Owner's PAC, Women's Democratic Coalition, Women's Leadership Network, Women's Power Campaign Delegate Committee, and Women's Victory Campaign are not included in the Nelson listing. I include them because I believe they fit the definition of a women's PAC.

REFERENCES

Biersack, Robert, Paul S. Herrnson, and Clyde Wilcox. 1993. "Seeds for Success: Seed Money in Congressional Elections." *Legislative Studies Quarterly* 4: 535-551.

Burrell, Barbara. 1985. "Women's Campaigns and Men's Campaigns for the U.S. House of Representatives, 1972-1982: A Finance Gap?" *American Politics Quarterly* 13: 251-272.

Burrell, Barbara. 1994. *A Woman's Place Is in the House*. Ann Arbor: University of Michigan Press.

Dabelko, Kirsten La Cour, and Paul S. Herrnson. 1997. "Women's and Men's Campaigns for the U.S. House of Representatives." *Political Research Quarterly* 50: 121-135.

Eismeier, Theodore J., and Philip H. Pollack III. 1988. *Business, Money, and the Rise of Corporate PACs in American Elections*. New York: Quorum Books.
Elving, Ronald D. 1994. "Special Report–Rolling the Dice: California." *CQ Weekly*, February 19.
Gopoian, J. David. 1984. "What Makes PACs Tick? An Analysis of the Allocation Patterns of Economic Interest Groups." *American Journal of Political Science* 28: 259-281.
Herrnson, Paul S. 1992. "Campaign Professionalism and Fundraising in Congressional Elections." *Journal of Politics* 54: 859-870.
Herrnson, Paul S. 1998. *Congressional Elections: Campaigning at Home and in Washington*. Washington, DC: Congressional Quarterly.
Humphries, Craig. 1991. "Corporations, PACs, and the Strategic Link Between Contributions and Lobbying Activities." *Western Political Quarterly* 44: 353-372.
Jacobson, Gary C. 1990. "The Effects of Campaign Spending in House Elections: New Evidence for Old Arguments." *American Journal of Political Science* 34: 334-362.
Jacobson, Gary C. 1997. *The Politics of Congressional Elections*. New York: Addison Wesley Longman.
Mann, Thomas, and Raymond Wolfinger. 1981. "Candidates and Parties in Congressional Elections." In *Congressional Elections*, ed. L. Sandy Maisel and Joseph Cooper. Beverly Hills: Sage.
Nelson, Candice J. 1994. "Women's PACs in the Year of the Woman." In *The Year of the Woman*, ed. Elizabeth Adell Cook, Sue Thomas, and Clyde Wilcox. Boulder: Westview.
Planned Parenthood of Southeastern Pennsylvania v. *Carey*. 1992. 505 U.S. 833.
Roe v. *Wade*. 1973. 410 U.S. 113.
Sabato, Larry J. 1984. *PAC Power: Inside the World of Political Action Committees*. New York: W.W. Norton.
Seltzer, Richard A., Jody Newman, and Melissa Voorhees Leighton. 1997. *Sex as a Political Variable*. Boulder: Lynne Rienner.
Simon, Mark. 1994. "Stanford May Expand Med Center," *San Francisco Chronicle*, 17 February, Section A.
Sorauf, Frank J. 1992. *Inside Campaign Finance: Myths and Realities*. New Haven: Yale University Press.
Squire, Peverill, and John R. Wright. 1990. "Fundraising by Nonincumbent Candidates for the U.S. House of Representatives." *Legislative Studies Quarterly* 15: 89-98.
Thomas, Sue. 1994. "The National Abortion Rights Action League PAC: Reproductive Choice in the Spotlight." In *Risky Business? PAC Decisionmaking in Congressional Elections*, ed. Robert Biersack, Paul S. Herrnson, and Clyde Wilcox. Armonk, NY: M.E. Sharpe.
Uhlaner, Carole Jean, and Kay Lehman Schlozman. 1986. "Candidate Gender and Congressional Campaign Receipts." *Journal of Politics* 48: 30-50.
Webster v. *Reproductive Health Services*. 1989. 492 U.S. 490.
Witt, Linda, Karen Paget, and Glenna Matthews. 1994. *Running as a Woman*. New York: Macmillan.
Zellner, A. 1971. *An Introduction to Bayesian Inference in Econometrics*. New York: John Wiley and Sons.

APPENDIX A. Definition and Coding of Variables

Political experience: A dummy measure coded 1 for those who previously held an elected office and 0 otherwise.
Open seat: A dummy measure coded for 1 for a candidate in an open seat and 0 otherwise.
Incumbent vulnerability: The district vote received by the nominee of the nonincumbent's political party in the 1992 House general election.
District partisanship: For Democrats, Clinton's national mean (43%) subtracted from his district performance. For Republicans, Clinton's district performance subtracted from his national mean.
Primary opponent: A dummy measure coded 1 for those who faced a primary opponent and 0 otherwise.
Democrat: A dummy measure coded 1 if the candidate was a Democrat and 0 otherwise.
Women's PAC Seed Money: An aggregate measure of all women's PACs' contributions received by candidates during the first two filing periods of the campaign.

APPENDIX B. Women's PACs Used in This Study[8]

1) American Nurses Association
2) Emma's List
3) EMILY's List
4) Hollywood Women's Political Committee
5) Los Angeles Women's Campaign Fund
6) Minnesota Women's Campaign Fund
7) Missouri Women's Action Fund
8) National Abortion and Reproductive Rights Action League PAC
9) National Federation of Business and Professional Women's Clubs
10) National Organization for Women PAC
11) National Women's Political Caucus Campaign Support Committee
12) National Women's Political Caucus Victory Fund
13) Susan B. Anthony Fund
14) WISH List
15) Women . . . for a Change
16) Women for:
17) Women for Life
18) Women for Washington
19) Women in Energy
20) Women in Leadership
21) Women in Psychology for Legislative Action
22) Women Running
23) Women's Action for New Directions
24) Women's Action for Nuclear Disarmament
25) Women's Alliance for Israel
26) Women's Business Coalition
27) Women's Business Owner's PAC
28) Women's Campaign Fund
29) Women's Democratic Coalition
30) Women's Leadership Network
31) Women's Political Committee
32) Women's Political Fund
33) Women's Power Campaign Delegate Committee
34) Women's Pro-Israel National PAC
35) Women's Victory Campaign

Electoral Context, Issues, and Voting for Women in the 1990s

Kathleen Dolan, University of Wisconsin-Milwaukee

SUMMARY. This research hypothesizes that, because of the particular stimulation provided by the focus on candidate sex and gender-related issues in the electoral environment, there was a unique set of demographic and attitudinal variables related to voting for a woman candidate for the House of Representatives in 1992. Because the environments of the elections of 1994 and 1996 were relatively "gender-free," these variables were not related to voting behavior in these years. The analysis supports the hypothesis that the determinants of support for women congressional candidates are different in 1992 than in subsequent elections. It also suggests that the differing environments of the three elections may be a contributing factor to these differences.

Recent work on the "gender basis of electoral behavior" done by Sapiro and Conover suggests that "gender matters differently and to different degrees in different elections" because of a complex interaction of voter, candidate, party, and environmental influences (1997, 523). The authors use the "Year of the Woman" election of 1992 as a case study: women candidates were prominent, but their success was influenced by structural considerations, the gender gap was variable across several Senate races and the presidential election, and gender issues

[Haworth co-indexing entry note]: "Electoral Context, Issues, and Voting for Women in the 1990s." Dolan, Kathleen. Co-published simultaneously in *Women & Politics* (The Haworth Press, Inc.) Vol. 23, No. 1/2, 2001, pp. 21-36; and: *Women and Congress: Running, Winning, and Ruling* (ed: Karen O'Connor) The Haworth Press, Inc., 2001, pp. 21-36. Single or multiple copies of this article are available for a fee from The Haworth Document Delivery Service [1-800-HAWORTH, 9:00 a.m. - 5:00 p.m. (EST). E-mail address: getinfo@haworthpressinc.com].

played differently in certain states and certain races. This, they suggest, is evidence of the fact that gender does not operate in one consistent fashion as an electoral influence and that "context is a crucial mediator in creating gender differences in voting" (Sapiro and Conover 1997, 501).

Considering the context of a particular election, or series of elections, is an important element of understanding the gender dynamic in elections. We must recognize that each election environment is shaped by unique candidate, party, and political influences, and that these factors can have an impact on whether gender and gender-related issues will have a significant role in shaping behaviors. The research reported here attempts to examine how the environment in which elections are conducted influences gender considerations in vote choice in congressional elections in the 1990s. Specifically, it examines whether the amount of gender information in the electoral environment has an impact on the public's vote choice considerations when faced with a woman candidate in 1992, 1994, and 1996.

Much of the recent work on gender in American elections has focused on 1992 (Cook 1994; Dolan 1998; Gaddie and Bullock 1995; Paolino 1995; Plutzer and Zipp 1996; Sapiro and Conover 1997). This "Year of the Woman" was one of tremendous success for women candidates, particularly at the congressional level. A record number of women ran for Congress that year, capitalizing on an increase in open seats following the 1990 redistricting, on increased sources of campaign financing and support from political parties and women's PACs such as EMILY's List, and on significant public attention to gender issues such as abortion and sexual harassment, as well as on the under-representation of women in office (Burrell 1994; Nelson 1994; Wilcox 1994). Perhaps the most indelible image from this election is the dramatic increase in women elected to Congress–from 31 to 53 after the 1992 election (CAWP 2000). Several factors–the presence of numerous women candidates, issues, structural considerations, and electoral context among others–joined to make 1992 an election year in which gender considerations played an important role.

Congressional elections since 1992 have been different. If one focuses only on outcomes, 1992 appears to be something of an anomaly. The dramatic increase in women elected to Congress has not been repeated in subsequent elections. Indeed, women's representation has increased incrementally. This has occurred despite a steadily increasing number of women candidates (CAWP 1998). Recent work suggests that neither the number and quality of candidates nor bias on the part of parties, financial contributors, or voters can easily explain the differing outcomes of the elections of the 1990s for women candidates (Berch 1996; Burrell 1995). While the success of women candidates in 1992 can be partially explained by the number of open seat opportunities in that election, this is not the only explanation. At the same time, a decrease in open seat opportunities since 1992 is not the sole explanation for the results since. Readers will correctly recall the research that indicates that women candidates are as successful as their male counterparts in comparable electoral circumstances (Newman 1994). But Sapiro and Conover's (1997) work would caution us away from the assumption that women's success in 1992 was solely because of these structural considerations. An election with plentiful open seat opportunities took place with a particular set of candidates competing in a particular environment, which elicited a particular response from voters. To understand the gender dynamics of the 1992 election more fully, we need to examine that electoral environment more closely and to place that election in context by comparing it with subsequent elections.

Perhaps the most obvious difference between 1992 and subsequent elections was what I term the "electoral environment." The environment of the 1992 election was one with a heavy focus on gender issues: women candidates received large amounts of attention, as did so-called "women's issues" such as abortion, family leave, and sexual harassment. Many of the women candidates for Congress ran "as women" and as outsiders of a corrupt institution. An argument for the influence of the electoral environment would suggest that the presence of these women candidates and the focus on them and the gender issues they articulated created a unique dynamic that had an impact on voters. Such an argument draws on research on opinion formation that treats opinion formation as a function of the information to which people are exposed (Lazersfeld, Berelson, and Gaudet 1968; Zaller 1992). Here it is suggested that candidate sex and other gender-related issues are pieces of information in the electoral environment being communicated to voters. In the gender-rich environment of 1992, the salience of these issues is increased and the likelihood that voters will use them in making a voting decision is increased as well. In such a circumstance, voters rely on gender-related considerations precisely because of the amount of gender-based information available to them.

There is ample evidence that the focus on women candidates and gender-related issues in 1992 had an impact on voters and the public at large. For example, the presence of women candidates significantly increased political proselytizing among the public, particularly women

(Hansen 1997). The presence of women Senate candidates increased the psychological engagement of women in the election (Koch 1997). Sapiro and Conover (1997) report that living in a context in which a women candidate was running for House, Senate, or governor boosted the media attentiveness and electoral activities of women. Voters, too, were influenced by women candidates and gender issues. Dolan (1998) demonstrates that the determinants of voter support for women candidates for Congress were different from those determining support for men or Democrats. Cook (1994) indicates that the gender gap in voting for women candidates in 1992 was pronounced, with 10 of the 11 women Senate candidates receiving more votes from women than from men. Plutzer and Zipp (1996) suggest that this gender gap in voting for women was driven by a "shared gender identity," while Paolino (1995) suggests that women voters were seeking representation on gender-related issues such as abortion and sexual harassment. The cumulative impact of these studies is the conclusion that candidate sex and gender-related issues were an influential part of the electoral environment of 1992. However, several of these studies (Cook 1994; Dolan 1998; Paolino 1995; Plutzer and Zipp 1996; Sapiro and Conover 1997) focus exclusively on 1992, leaving us to question whether this gender dynamic is a new force in congressional elections or simply a unique by-product of 1992.

In contrast to the gendered environment of 1992, the electoral environments of the two subsequent congressional elections were much different. In 1994, women candidates did not receive the same media attention, nor was there a focus on gender-related issues (Fox 1997; Rubin 1994). Instead, the tone of the congressional elections was one of anger–at President Clinton, at the Democrats, at incumbents (Greenberg 1994). In 1996, the major focus of the congressional elections was the Republican party's attempt to hold on to its newly-won majority status in the face of a lackluster presidential campaign by their nominee, Bob Dole. While the 1994 and 1996 elections both saw a record number (to that time) of women candidates, neither their sex nor their issues were in the spotlight. As Susan Carroll's work on the way the media frame gender issues in elections suggests, "The Year of the Woman frame proved to be a mixed blessing. One of the major downsides was that women candidates seemed to be old news after 1992 and the media paid very little attention to women candidates in 1994 or 1996" (1999, 8).

This lack of focus on candidate sex and gender-related issues in the elections after 1992 is illustrated by the results of a search of newspaper articles about women candidates in 1992, 1994, and 1996. The articles were identified through a search of the "Major Papers" section of the

NEXIS news library, using the keywords "women candidates" and "elections." The time period examined was from June 1 to the day before the election in each year. During this time period in 1992, 180 articles on women candidates appeared. In 1994, there were 37 articles, and in 1996, there were 22. While perhaps a rough gauge of media attention to women candidates, these figures support the idea that the electoral environments of the three years under study were different with respect to the amount of gendered information that was available to voters.

If voters gained information about women candidates in the gender-rich electoral environment of 1992, it is possible that they learned less about women candidates or were less likely to think about the salience of gender issues in the different environments of 1994 and 1996. This, in turn, could have an impact on voting behavior. One possible consequence of an absence of gender information in these elections is that the influence of demographic or attitudinal variables expected to be important in contests involving a woman candidate might not be activated without the stimulation offered by the electoral setting. A "salience" argument, then, would suggest that because the electoral environment of 1992 was so distinctive, it is possible that the underlying patterns of support for women candidates that year were distinctive as well.

Since the environment of 1992 provided a great deal of information about women candidates and gender-related issues, I would expect that these considerations would be significant in structuring people's vote choice. At the same time, since 1994 and 1996 were comparatively "gender-free," I would expect that gender-related issues are less likely to be related to vote choice in those years. Of course, the gender-rich electoral environment of 1992, or any other election, is only meaningful as an influence if voters are aware of it. If candidate sex and gender-related issues are pieces of information that exist in the environment and voters use this information to inform their vote choice, then I would expect gender-related variables to be more important to those voters who were more aware of the environment. Voters who take in more of this gender information during an election campaign will obviously have more of it at their disposal when evaluating candidates and framing a vote choice, making it more likely that a gendered environment will shape their voting behavior than that of people who are relatively oblivious to the messages of the environment.[1]

METHODOLOGY

To test the hypotheses under consideration here, I examine the individual-level sources of support for women candidates for the House of Representatives in 1992, 1994, and 1996 using National Election Study (NES) data. Since the NES does not interview respondents in every state or congressional district, not every race with a woman candidate is included in the sample. However, for each of the years under analysis, the districts included in the NES sample that have women candidates for the House are representative of all districts with women candidates from the perspective of seat status. For example, in 1996, 31% of the NES districts with women candidates included a woman incumbent, 58% of the districts had a woman challenger, and 11% had women running for an open seat. For all women candidates in 1996, 34% of the women were incumbents, 54% were challengers, and 12% contested open seats. Therefore, I can say that the districts with women candidates included in the NES are not systematically different from the population of women House candidates. (See Appendix A for all districts and states with women candidates in the analysis and the seat status comparisons.)[2] Races in which both major-party candidates were women or when a woman was unopposed in the general election are excluded from the analysis.

The analysis conducted seeks to determine whether electoral environment has an impact on the considerations that shape vote choice; specifically, does the presence or absence of information about candidate sex and gender-related issues have an influence on the determinants of support for women candidates? The dependent variable is vote choice, coded to reflect whether respondents voted for the woman candidate (1) or her male opponent (0). The models estimating support for women candidates include a number of variables considered to be relevant to vote choice and variables intended to measure the influence of the electoral environment. Control variables include respondent party identification, ideology, sex, race, and age. I also include a measure of the incumbency status of the woman candidate and a variable that accounts for the degree of correspondence between the party identification of the respondent and the woman candidate ("party correspondence" in the model). This variable allows for an examination of whether Democrats are more likely to vote for women candidates than are Republicans after controlling for the expected influence of party identification, namely that people tend to vote for the candidate of their party.

The remaining variables in the model account for general and gender-related issues that are likely to shape respondent vote choice, particularly when there are women candidates in the race. Previous work has indicated that voters often hold stereotyped views of the competencies of women and men candidates and may use these in formulating their vote choice (Brown 1994; Huddy and Terkildsen 1993). Included here are measures of respondents' positions on evaluating Congress, defense spending, social welfare spending, abortion, government spending on child care, and attitudes towards feminists/the women's movement. (See Appendix B for all items used in this research.) These variables appear in the model in two ways. I enter the variables themselves and then I also employ a series of interactions to test whether the presence or absence of gender-related information in the electoral environment shapes vote choice determinants. Recall that the hypothesis is that, if candidate sex and gender-related issues are part of the electoral environment, then those respondents who are more likely to be aware of the environment (and its content) should be more likely to employ those considerations in their voting decision. Therefore, the measure of the role of the electoral environment is created by interacting the issue variables with a measure of the amount of information about government and politics respondents possess. As recent works have suggested, relying on self-reported measures of media usage as an indicator of awareness of information or an electoral environment is problematic (Price and Zaller 1993; Zaller 1992). Instead, I use the interviewer assessment of the respondent's awareness of government and political issues.[3] The expectation here is that the interaction terms will be significant in 1992, signaling that gender-related information in the environment was most significant to those voters who are most aware of the environment and its messages, but less so in subsequent elections.

ANALYSIS

Since the argument being advanced here is that the gender-related information in the environment of an election can influence the considerations voters use in formulating their vote choice, we would expect to find that voters in 1992 were more likely to employ gender issues in deciding to vote for a woman candidate than voters in 1994 or 1996.[4] Table 1 presents the models for each of the three election years. Beginning with 1992, we can see the influence of the electoral environment on voters in that year. First, while the demographic and issue variables are of greatest interest, readers should note that the control variables in each

TABLE 1. Determinants of Support for Women Candidates for the House of Representatives (Logistic Regression Analysis)

	1992	1994	1996
Constant	5.359	−7.145*	−4.679
Female Incumbent	3.865*	.700*	1.663*
Party Identification	.809*	.379*	.092
Party Correspondence	6.539*	4.241*	4.124*
Ideology	−1.106*	−.058	.493*
Sex	−1.633*	.256	.283
Age	.075*	.005	−.016
Race	4.893*	−2.482*	−.580
Evaluation of Congress	−10.861*	.773	−.220
Defense Spending	1.270	1.885	.951
Social Welfare	−6.081*	.133	−.631
Abortion	1.441	.030	−.243
Child Care	.130	.138	−1.232
Feminist FT	.205*	−.011	.056
Evaluation of Congress*Aware	−2.578*	−.395	.158
Defense Spending*Aware	.573	−.732	.564*
Social Welfare*Aware	−2.105*	.297	.232
Abortion*Aware	.149	.220	.153
Child Care*Aware	.404	.099	.462
Feminist FT*Aware	.072*	.019	.003
N	133	149	204
Chi Square	131.014	104.973	150.655
PRE	82.501	60.311	67.889

* < .05; one-tailed test

model generally perform as expected. The variable measuring the presence of an incumbent woman candidate and whether the respondent and candidate share the same party identification are both positive and significant in all three models. Clearly, important long-term influences such as incumbency and shared party affiliation provide the same benefits for women candidates as they do for men. However, party identification and political ideology do not demonstrate a consistent influence on voting for a woman across the three elections. Therefore, Democrats are not consistently more likely to vote for women than Republicans, controlling for the "same party" effect, and liberals are not necessarily more likely to do so than conservatives. Instead, incumbency and shared party affiliation are much more likely to motivate vote choice in these elections.

Beyond these controls, there are a number of variables significantly related to voting for women House candidates in 1992. Voter sex, age, and race are all significant, as women, older people, and minorities are all more likely to choose the woman candidate. Several issue concerns are also significant. Negative evaluations of Congress, positive attitudes towards feminists, and a desire to see the federal government increase spending on social welfare programs are all important to respondents choosing women candidates. Each of these findings supports an argument for the importance of the electoral environment: there were gender gaps in support for women candidates in many races; the election of 1992 was strongly anti-incumbent; several candidates, including Bill Clinton, campaigned for a renewed focus on domestic issues; and many women candidates ran "as women," focusing on their sex and their different approaches to many issues. This evidence is especially compelling because none of these variables is significantly related to vote choice in the analysis of 1994 or 1996.

This argument is further strengthened by the significant relationship between voting for women candidates and the interaction terms for these three issues in the model. Here the effect of these issues on vote choice is strongest among those with the most information. Those respondents who were most aware of the electoral environment and its heavy focus on gender-related issues are the most likely to employ these issues in choosing a woman candidate. This is evidence of the ability of information in the electoral environment to activate personal and attitudinal attributes in evaluating women candidates: the environmental connection influenced voting behavior.

If 1992 was an election with a strong presence for women candidates and gender-related issues, 1994 was the mirror opposite. Despite another record number of women candidates for the House, the electoral environment of 1994 was almost entirely without emphasis on candidate sex or gender-related issues. The second model in Table 1 indicates that there are very few significant determinants of voting for women candidates in this year. The only significant influence beyond the control variables (incumbency and party) is race, with minorities being more likely to support women candidates. But there is no gender gap in support for these women, no influence of issues thought to be important to women candidates, no evidence that the most informed people focused on these issues. The considerations relevant to voting for women in 1992 were not significant in 1994: voters relied not on gender-related information, but instead on the more traditional influences of incumbency and party. In short, this suggests that the electoral environment of 1994 did not provide a specific focus on women candidates and gender-related issues, which may have resulted in people finding it difficult to make the connection between these candidates or issues and their own political interests.

The third model in Table 1 indicates that 1996 was more like 1994 than 1992. Beyond the control variables, there is limited evidence of respondent demographics or gender-related issues being related to voting for women. However, the one significant variable, the interaction of position on defense spending and respondent awareness, does support the hypothesis about the influence of the electoral environment. Here, people who supported lower levels of defense spending were more likely to support women candidates. The impact of this attitude was strongest among those respondents with the most information. While 1996 was not an election year with a strong focus on women candidates per se, this finding might indicate that people who were more aware of the information that *was* in the environment were able to identify the greater focus on domestic issues advanced by many woman candidates. But, again, the lack of significance of most of the gender-related variables and interaction terms to voting in 1996 is an indication of the lack of prominence of these issues in the campaign. Instead, the focus in the congressional campaigns was more partisan in nature, centering on whether the Republicans could retain their majority status. This focus is borne out in the analysis: the decision to vote for a woman or not is primarily driven by traditional factors like party, incumbency, and ideology.

DISCUSSION

One of the limitations on our ability to fully understand the election of 1992 is the fact that much of the work to date has treated this election in isolation. This project attempts to analyze the unique features of 1992 by comparing it to other years. The analysis presented here demonstrates that voters approached women candidates for Congress differently in 1992 than they did in subsequent elections. Voters that year experienced a relatively unique electoral environment, one in which there was a tremendous amount of attention to, and information about, candidate sex and gender-related issues. This research suggests that voters used a unique set of personal and issue considerations as a basis for their vote choice exactly because the information that helped them make the link between these concerns and the woman candidate for whom they voted was available. In contrast, in the relatively "gender-free" settings of the 1994 and 1996 elections, personal or attitudinal attributes that might have been related to voting behavior in races involving a woman were not, because people were not stimulated by the electoral environment to make the necessary connections. Instead, people relied more heavily on traditional determinants of the vote like party identification and incumbency.

This view of 1992 as a unique electoral environment is supported by the findings of other work on women candidates in the 1990s. Koch (1997) finds that the presence of women candidates for the Senate in 1992 significantly increases the psychological engagement of women in politics, but that the women Senate candidates in 1990 do not produce the same effect. Hansen (1997) finds that the presence of women candidates for the House and Senate in 1992 increased political proselytizing, internal efficacy, and media usage among both women and men, but not in 1990 and 1994. Sapiro and Conover (1997) find the same effect; women in 1992 who lived in a district or state with a woman candidate for the House, Senate, or governor were more interested and involved in the election.

Also relevant is the fact that these authors conclude that it is not merely the presence of women candidates alone that made 1992 different, but that it was the particular context of that election. Koch concludes that women's increased attention to the Senate campaigns in 1992 is a function of the presence of women candidates in concert with "contemporary political events that underscore the descriptive underrepresentation of women in the political process" (1997, 129). In finding no effect of women candidates on political proselytizing in 1994, Hansen states that "The 1994 pattern suggests that it is not the presence of women alone, but women focusing on issues of concern to women, that mobilizes women to proselytize" (1997, 96).

The research reported here finds that gender-related vote considerations were more important to voters choosing women candidates in 1992 than in subsequent elections and that the gendered information was most important to those people who were more aware of the electoral environment. This work, along with the work cited above, indirectly supports the assumption that electoral context is an important part of the relationship between women candidates and the public.[5] A focus on gender and gender-related issues may make it easier for some voters to identify correspondence between their interests and particular women candidates. Without this focus, it may be that women candidates are simply candidates in the minds of many voters. For women candidates and those who support their election, such a conclusion is a double-edged sword. On the one hand, it may signal a true diminishing of voter bias against women candidates. On the other, it may indicate that, barring particularly advantageous electoral environments in the future, women's increased presence in Congress may be incremental. But understanding the impact that electoral environment and context can have on the fortunes of women candidates helps us draw a more complete picture of recent congressional elections. The Year of the Woman was a unique election, not just in the sense that more women were elected, but in the sense that the gendered context of the election stimulated a different pattern of voting behavior than has occurred in later years. In short, the context of the election of 1992 influenced the behavior of the electorate.

AUTHOR NOTE

The author would like to thank Tom Holbrook, Eric Plutzer, Janet Boles, Gina Sapiro, and several anonymous reviewers for their comments and suggestions on earlier versions of this manuscript. The author would also like to acknowledge the support of the Carrie Chapman Catt Center for Women and Politics.

NOTES

1. Readers might suggest that the degree to which women campaigned "as women" or the degree to which they campaigned on domestic issues could have an impact on voter's perceptions and vote choice. While this may be true, there is no way to know whether and to what degree any of the 145 women candidates included in these three NES surveys emphasized their sex or women's issues or domestic issues in their campaigns. To do so would require a survey of these women or a content analysis of their campaign literature, speeches, appearances, etc. This question, while interesting, is beyond the scope of this study.
2. The 1992 sample includes respondents from 38 House districts in which one of the major-party candidates was a woman and the other a man. In 1994, respondents from 43 House districts with a woman candidate were surveyed and in 1996, there were respondents from 64 House districts.
3. Alternative measures of awareness of the electoral environment are difficult given the NES data. Many scholars today advocate the use of the open-ended candidate likes and dislikes, either alone or in combination with some of the factual information questions (Smith 1989; Zaller 1992). This is not possible when analyzing both presidential and midterm elections since the NES does not ask the candidate affect questions in the midterm years. Employing the factual information questions alone is also problematic since the questions are different in every NES survey, offering no consistent basis for a judgement of awareness. Also, the possibility exists that some facts are "easier to know" in some years than others. For example, the answer to the NES question about

which party holds the majority in the House of Representatives may have been easier for people after the dramatic election of 1994 than it was either before or since. Because I am including both presidential and midterm elections in this analysis, the only question that is the same in all three years is the one used here.

4. It should be noted that comparing presidential and mid-term electorates requires acknowledging the lower voter turnout in mid-term elections and the potential differences in the composition of these electorates. For example, the smaller electorates in mid-term elections may be more partisan or have more skewed demographic characteristics than the presidential electorate. These differences could, in turn, stimulate the parties and/or candidates to make different sorts of appeals. However, for the purposes of this research, I do not believe that these differences would have a substantive impact on the findings here. Readers might suggest that the often-cited drop-off of voter turnout among women from 1992 to 1994 could be relevant here. But, since this project is not focused exclusively on whether women support women candidates, this change in electoral composition should not be a factor. Further, while women experienced this drop-off, men did as well and to a similar degree. Turnout among both men and women was higher in 1996 than 1994, but neither year exceeded the levels of 1992. In all three years, more women turned out than men (CAWP 1997).

5. There is currently little data available that allow for a direct test of a hypothesis that women benefitted in terms of the electoral support they received from the gendered environment of 1992. We lack a way to make the link between the presence of women candidates, voter's consumption and use of information about them, and the vote choices they eventually make. For example, we might categorize people by their media consumption or information about the candidates or about politics in general and then compare the significant determinants of the vote for each group. However, attempts to conduct such an analysis using available NES data are stymied by the high degree of correlation between low information consumption (measured in a number of ways) and nonvoting, frequently resulting in extremely small subsamples.

REFERENCES

Berch, Neil. 1996. "The Year of the Woman in Context: A Test of Six Explanations." *American Politics Quarterly* 24: 169-193.

Brown, Clyde. 1994. "Judgements about the Capabilities of City Councilors and Support for Female Representation on City Council." *Social Science Journal* 31: 355-73.

Burrell, Barbara. 1994. *A Woman's Place Is in the House: Campaigning for Congress in the Feminist Era*. Ann Arbor: University of Michigan Press.

Burrell, Barbara. 1995. "Did We Get More Than One 'Year of the Woman'?: Defending and Expanding the Victories of 1992 in U.S. House of Representative's Elections in 1994." Presented at the annual meeting of the Midwest Political Science Association.

Carroll, Susan. 1999. "The Disempowerment of the Gender Gap: Soccer Moms and the 1996 Elections." *PS: Political Science & Politics* 32: 7-12.

Center for the American Woman and Politics (CAWP). 2000. *Fact Sheet*. "Women in the U.S. Congress." New Brunswick, NJ: Center for the American Woman and Politics. http://www.rci.rutgers.edu/~cawp/pdf/cong.pdf

Center for the American Woman and Politics (CAWP). 1998. *Fact Sheet.* "Women Candidates for Congress: 1974-1998." New Brunswick, NJ: Center for the American Woman and Politics. http://www.rci.rutgers.edu/~cawp/pdf/CongCand.pdf

Center for the American Woman and Politics (CAWP). 1997. *Fact Sheet.* "Sex Differences in Voter Turnout." New Brunswick, NJ: Center for the American Woman and Politics. http://www.rci.rutgers.edu/~cawp/pdf/sexdiff.pdf

Cook, Elizabeth Adell. 1994. "Voter Responses to Women Senate Candidates." In *The Year of the Woman: Myths and Realities,* ed. Elizabeth Adell Cook, Sue Thomas, and Clyde Wilcox. Boulder: Westview.

Dolan, Kathleen. 1998. "Voting for Women in the Year of the Woman." *American Journal of Political Science* 42: 272-293.

Fox, Richard. 1997. *Gender Dynamics in Congressional Elections.* Thousand Oaks, CA: Sage.

Gaddie, Keith, and Charles Bullock. 1995. "Congressional Elections and the Year of the Woman: Structural and Elite Influences on Female Candidates." *Social Science Quarterly* 76: 749-762.

Greenberg, Stanley. 1994. *The Revolt Against Politics.* Washington, DC: Democratic Leadership Council.

Hansen, Susan. 1997. "Talking About Politics: Gender and Contextual Effects on Political Proselytizing." *Journal of Politics* 59: 73-103.

Huddy, Leonie, and Nayda Terkildsen. 1993. "Gender Stereotypes and the Perception of Male and Female Candidates." *American Journal of Political Science* 37: 119-147.

Koch, Jeffrey. 1997. "Candidate Gender and Women's Psychological Engagement in Politics." *American Politics Quarterly* 25: 118-133.

Lazarsfeld, Paul, Bernard Berelson, and Hazel Gaudet. 1968. *The People's Choice: How the Voter Makes Up His Mind in a Presidential Campaign.* 3rd ed. New York: Columbia University Press.

Nelson, Candice. 1994. "Women's PACs in the Year of the Woman." In *The Year of the Woman: Myths and Realities,* ed. Elizabeth Adell Cook, Sue Thomas, and Clyde Wilcox. Boulder: Westview.

Newman, Jody. 1994. *Perception and Reality: A Study Comparing the Success of Men and Women Candidates.* Washington, DC: National Women's Political Caucus.

Paolino, Philip. 1995. "Group-Salient Issues and Group Representation: Support for Women Candidates in the 1992 Senate Elections." *American Journal of Political Science* 39: 294-313.

Plutzer, Eric, and John Zipp. 1996. "Identity Politics, Partisanship, and Voting for Women Candidates." *Public Opinion Quarterly* 60: 30-57.

Price, Vincent, and John Zaller. 1993. "Who Gets the News? Alternative Measures of News Reception and Their Implications For Research." *Public Opinion Quarterly* 57: 133-164.

Rubin, Alissa. 1994. "1994 Elections Are Looking Like the 'Off-Year' of the Woman." *CQ Weekly*, October 15.

Sapiro, Virginia, and Pamela Johnston Conover. 1997. "The Variable Gender Basis of Electoral Politics: Gender and Context in the 1992 US Election." *British Journal of Political Science* 27: 497-523.

Smith, Eric R.A.N. 1989. *The Unchanging American Voter*. Berkeley: University of California Press.
Wilcox, Clyde. 1994. "Why Was 1992 the 'Year of the Woman'? Explaining Women's Gains in 1992." In *The Year of the Woman: Myths and Realities*, ed. Elizabeth Adell Cook, Sue Thomas, and Clyde Wilcox. Boulder: Westview Press.
Zaller, John. 1992. *The Nature and Origins of Mass Opinion*. New York: Cambridge University Press.

APPENDIX A

The following are the House districts with women candidates included in the NES samples for 1992, 1994, and 1996 and the seat status comparisons.

1992–38 districts with women candidates included

AZ-06, AR-01, CA-04, CA-08, CA-35, CA-39, CA-44, CA-45, CO-01, CT-03, FL-03, FL-04, FL-20, FL-22, GA-01, GA-04, IL-07, IN-04, IA-03, KS-03, MD-02, MD-04, MD-08, MI-03, MI-04, MI-9, MI-15, MO-02, NJ-05, NJ-11, NY-14, PA-13, TN-03, TX-25, WA-01, WA-08, WI-05, WI-09

1994–43 districts with women candidates included

AZ-04, AZ-06, CA-04, CA-06, CA-09, CA-10, CA-12, CA-35, CA-50, CO-01, CO-02, CO-04, FL-02, FL-03, FL-15, IA-03, IL-12, IN-04, IN-06, MD-04, MD-08, MI-03, MI-09, MI-15, MN-05, MO-05, MO-6, NC-01, NC-09, NJ-07, NY-03, NY-10, NY-14, NY-18, NY-19, PA-13, TX-18, TX-26, VA-01, WA-02, WA-08, WV-01, WY-01

1996–64 districts with women candidates included

AL-06, AZ-04, CA-04, CA-06, CA-08, CA-09, CA-10, CA-25, CA-33, CA-35, CA-42, CA-44, CA-45, CA-46, CA-47, CA-51, CO-01, CO-02, CO-06, CT-03, FL-03, FL-17, GA-01, GA-04, HA-02, IN-06, IN-09, IA-04, KS-03, MD-02, MD-08, MA-01, MI-03, MI-04, MI-10, MI-15, MN-01, MO-02, MO-03, MO-05, MO-06, MO-07, NH-02, NJ-02, NJ-09, NJ-10, NY-01, NY-04, NY-07, NY-10, NY-11, NY-12, NY-13, NY-14, NY-18, NY-19, PA-05, TX-6, TX-12, TX-18, VA-03, WA-08, WV-03, WY-01

Seat Status Comparison

1992	*NES*	*All women candidates*
Woman Incumbent	34%	25%
Woman Challenger	32%	38%
Women Running in Open Seat	34%	37%
1994	*NES*	*All women candidates*
Woman Incumbent	35%	39%
Woman Challenger	49%	47%
Women Running in Open Seat	16%	14%
1996	*NES*	*All women candidates*
Woman Incumbent	31%	34%
Woman Challenger	58%	54%
Women Running in Open Seat	11%	12%

APPENDIX B

The following are the NES questions used to create the variables in this analysis:

Party Identification: Strength of party identification based on 7-point scale. (1992: v3634, 1994: v655, 1996: v960420)

Ideology: Self-rated 7-point liberal/conservative scale. (1992: v3509, 1994: v839, 1996: v960365)

Sex: Respondent sex. (1992: v4201, 1994: v1434, 1996: v960066)

Age: Respondent recoded age. (1992: v3903, 1994: v1203, 1996: v960605)

Race: Respondent race. (1992: 4202, 1994: v1435, 1996: v960067)

Defense: 1992: v3603–Some people say the U.S. should maintain its position as the world's strongest military power even if it means continuing high defense spending. Would you say that you 1 = agree strongly, 2 = agree somewhat, 3 = neither agree nor disagree, 4 = disagree somewhat, or 5 = disagree strongly? 1994: v827, 1996: v960463–Should federal spending on defense spending be increased, decreased, or kept about the same?

Social Welfare: 1992: v3817, 1996: v960565–Should federal spending on solving the problems of poor people be 1 = increased, 2 = kept about the same, or 3 = decreased? 1994: v820 substituted "welfare" for "poor people."

Evaluation of Congress: In general, do you 1 = disapprove, or 2 = approve of the way the U.S. Congress had been handling its job? (1992: v5949, 1994: v320, 1996: v960270)

Abortion: There has been some discussion about abortion during recent years. Which one of the opinions on this page best agrees with your view? The result is a five-point scale where 1 = by law, abortion should never be permitted, 2 = the law should permit abortion only in the case of rape, incest or when the woman's life is in danger, 3 = the law should permit abortions for reasons other than rape, incest, or danger to the woman's life, but only after the need for the abortion has been clearly established, 4 = by law, a woman should always be able to obtain an abortion as a matter of personal choice, 5 = rejects the concept that abortion should be regulated by law; law has nothing to do with it. (1992: v3732, 1994: v1014, 1996: v960503)

Child Care: 1992: v3745–Do you think that 1 = the government should provide child care assistance to low and middle income working parents, or 2 = it isn't the government's responsibility? 1994: v824, 1996: v960564–Should federal spending on childcare be increased, decreased, or kept about the same?

Attitudes Toward Feminist/the Women's Movement: 1992: v5317–Feeling thermometer for "feminists." 1994: v308, 1996: v961039–feeling thermometer for "the women's movement."

Candidate Sex and Congressional Elections: Open Seats Before, During, and After the Year of the Woman

Kim U. Hoffman, University of Central Arkansas
Carrie Palmer, University of Oklahoma
Ronald Keith Gaddie, University of Oklahoma

SUMMARY. In 1992, an unprecedented number of women were elected to Congress. This election seemed to debunk the notion of female disadvantage as female candidates ran better than males. Since 1992, however, female candidates have failed to compete as effectively as men in congressional elections, again raising the specter of a sex bias. In this paper, we examine 365 open seat congressional elections held since 1982 in order to ascertain whether the indicators of female success in the 1980s and early 1990s structured female candidate success and/or failure after 1992. For this study, these indicators include candidate attributes such as financial quality and candidate experience. Our examination indicates that candidate attributes have significantly weakened as predictors of open seat election outcomes, especially in female versus male races. Instead, a strong increase in the correlation of the presidential normal vote and the congressional vote in open seats since 1992 indicates the emergence of elections where candidate attributes are secondary to the partisanship of the district. Female versus male races demonstrate much higher partisan coherence than all-male open seat contests, and Democratic women run about six points behind Republican women when district partisanship is controlled. These factors, combined with the increasingly

[Haworth co-indexing entry note]: "Candidate Sex and Congressional Elections: Open Seats Before, During, and After the Year of the Woman." Hoffman, Kim U., Carrie Palmer, and Ronald Keith Gaddie. Co-published simultaneously in *Women & Politics* (The Haworth Press, Inc.) Vol. 23, No. 1/2, 2001, pp. 37-58; and: *Women and Congress: Running, Winning, and Ruling* (ed: Karen O'Connor) The Haworth Press, Inc., 2001, pp. 37-58. Single or multiple copies of this article are available for a fee from The Haworth Document Delivery Service [1-800-HAWORTH, 9:00 a.m. - 5:00 p.m. (EST). E-mail address: getinfo@haworthpressinc.com].

Democratic distribution of female nominations, mitigate against female gains through open seats after 1992.

INTRODUCTION

The combined effects of redistricting and incumbent retirement created a record number of open seats in 1992, thereby allowing for a change in the composition of Congress and affording opportunities for female advancement (Burrell 1994). The remarkable addition of 19 women in the House in 1992 (referred to as the "Year of the Woman") prompted an exploration of the role of open seats in creating opportunities for women to advance to Congress (Green 1998). Among the questions raised in studies of female advancement to Congress is whether women utilized the same stepping stones used by men–political experience and ample campaign funds. Subsequent to the Year of the Woman, a second shift occurred in the representative composition of Congress, as the GOP captured majority status in the House for the first time since 1955. Some have described this shift as realignment, representing a fundamental change in the nature of American electoral politics (Ladd 1995).

The paucity of descriptive female representation has been a continuing concern for American political science (Bullock and Heys 1972; Burrell 1994; Darcy, Welch, and Clark 1994; Gertzog 1979; Thomas and Wilcox 1998). Since the election of Jeanette Rankin of Montana in 1916 as the first female member of Congress, the gains by women in the House have been slow, to just nineteen women out of 435 total representatives in 1980. A net of nine additional women were elected to the House between 1982-1990, with twelve open seat gains and five women defeating incumbents. These gains were offset by one incumbent female loss and the death, retirement, or pursuit of other office by seven other women. Women continued to increase their numbers in the 1990s, as women first shattered the mathematic ceiling described by Darcy and Choike (1986) in 1992, and then continued incremental gains throughout the 1990s.

Most of these came via open seats. In 1992, women won 21 of 34 open seats they contested (61.8%), while from 1982-1990 women prevailed in only 11 of 27 open seats they contested (40.7%). Between

1994 to 1998, 19 of the 44 women running in open seats succeeded (43%), down from the 52% success rate from 1982 to 1992 (32 of 61). Female success in open seats has returned to a level observed in the 1980s, an era characterized as one of female disadvantage (Green 1998). There is also a partisan dimension to the success rates of females in open seat elections. Since 1994, Republican women have a 50% success rate in female versus male open seat contests (6 of 12), while Democratic women have a success rate of 38% (10 of 26). In contrast to Gaddie and Bullock's (1995) expectation that female success would be tied to the general performance of the Democrats in congressional elections, Democratic female success was actually worse in 1996 than in 1994. In 1998, the success rate of female Democrats was lower than 50% in open seats, despite an election year that featured overall Democratic gains in open seat contests.

We are interested in whether the findings of prior research still apply post-Year of the Woman, namely whether financial quality, candidate experience, and district partisanship condition the election of women. These are the factors that others have found useful in explaining congressional election outcomes (Jacobson 1997) and which have been observed to be explicitly significant in advancing women in open seats. If the perceived change in American politics is accurate, other factors, such as the general partisanship of the district, should be more important in explaining female political advancement.

WOMEN AND LEGISLATIVE ELECTIONS

In an analysis of open seat congressional elections, Gaddie and Bullock observed that, before the 1970s, women in Congress often "followed a funeral procession" into the chamber (2000, 129). Their interpretation was based on earlier research which examined the careers of 66 women elected to the House of Representatives between 1917 and 1970. This research found that almost half of those women (47%) succeeded to their late husband's seats (Bullock and Heys 1972). Widows were over twice as likely as regularly-elected women to serve one term and then quickly opt out of electoral politics. Although women subsequently entered Congress largely in their own right, their numbers remained small (Gertzog 1979). As Rosenthal (1998) has indicated in her research on state legislatures, there is a critical mass that women must achieve to move past a role of "tokenism" in a legislative body. For women to be effectively represented in the House, there must be a substantial increase in descriptive female representation.

Why was the number of women in the House so small? Anderson and Thorson (1984) claim female representation is disadvantaged by the presence of incumbents with institutional advantages and by the scarcity of female nominees. Data compiled by the Center for American Women and Politics reinforce this view. As indicated in Figure 1, the number of female challengers to incumbents traditionally far outnumbered the number of women nominated in open seats, meaning that women generally ran in districts where they had little hope of winning. This interpretation is reinforced by the data graphed in Figure 1, which show that with one exception (1980) the success rate of female nominees has been greater in the open seats (43.75% of female open seat nominees win) than in the challenger races (4.2% of challenging women prevail) since 1974.

An argument for institutional disadvantage is supported by Volgy, Schwartz, and Gottleib (1986), who argue that women are outsiders in American politics. As outsiders, they should confront greater difficulty raising money and garnering organizational political support for their elective efforts. Anita Pritchard (1992) reinforces this view by observing that female gains in the Florida state legislature in the early 1980s were precipitated by a redistricting that radically altered constituency boundaries, displaced incumbents, and generally created an environ-

FIGURE 1. Success Rate of Woman Open Seat Nominees and Woman Challengers

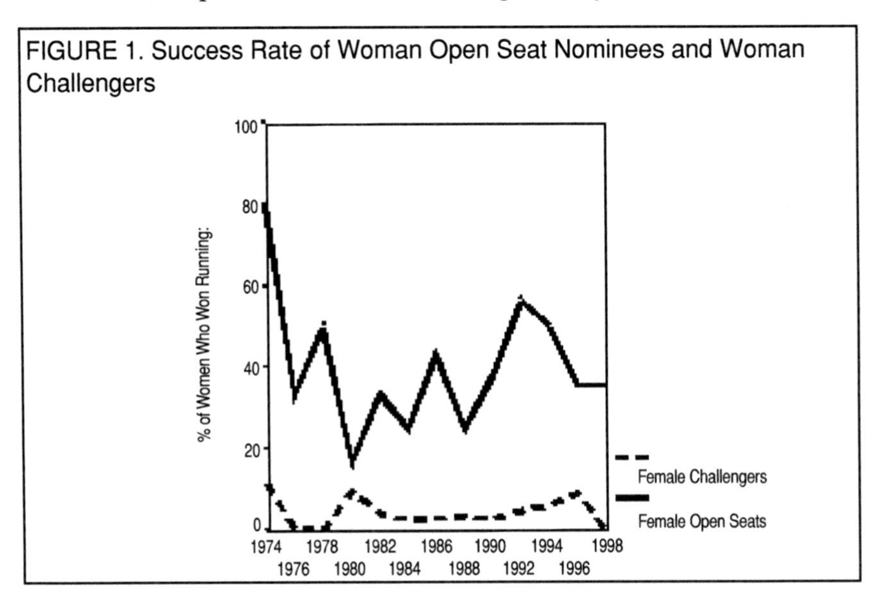

ment where elite barriers to female election were removed.[1] The recurrent theme of incumbency as a deterrent to the advancement of women was articulated most effectively in a formal analysis by Darcy and Choike (1986). Their examination of the impact of legislative turnover on female representation concluded that the rate of incumbent turnover and the presence of women candidates are the two driving forces behind female representation. Assuming constant rates of incumbent success and female candidate emergence, they predicted that women in Congress would increase slowly before stabilizing at 43 (10%). The size of the female gains in 1992, when 47 women were elected to Congress, overshot the earlier expectations of political scientists. The results also comported with the expectations of the literature. Women gained entry into Congress through the advantages of incumbency (retaining 23 of 26 seats where incumbent women ran) and by performing especially well in open seat elections.[2]

Gaddie and Bullock's (1995) look at the impact of various candidate factors on the advancement of women through the venue of open seats, found that candidate attributes such as financial quality and prior political experience explained female political success, thus providing evidence that female congressional elections were not distinctive. This finding also reinforced the prior assertions of Burrell (1994) and Darcy, Welch, and Clark (1994). Gaddie and Bullock also speculated on the future of female advancement to Congress through open seats, observing that:

> When the great success of women in 1992 is compared with the modest gains of 1982 and 1994, we see that open seats are necessary but by no means sufficient for increasing the ranks of congresswomen. Once final campaign spending data are available for 1994, we expect to see that women were not disadvantaged in funding or experience. We expect that the relatively small percentage of female nominees among Republicans explains the insubstantial gains. (1995, 761)

In other words, the preponderance of female nominations in the Democratic Party mitigated female gains if partisan tides worked against Democrats.

In this paper we contrast trends in female candidate performance in open seats since the Year of the Woman against a reanalysis of open seat contests since 1982. We focus on the factors that are traditionally examined in the study of congressional elections, such as candidate experience and financial quality. Further, we consider whether district partisanship is a significant factor in determining female electoral success.

DATA

We examined 365 open seat general elections between 1982 and 1998. By analyzing the open seats, we will be able to assess how candidate sex and a variety of other candidate and constituency attributes impact the results of congressional elections without having to deal with the stifling effects of incumbency. District-level data were gathered on candidate expenditures,[3] prior political experience,[4] district partisanship,[5] and the sex of the candidates.

This data set allows us to consider the impact of the sex of a candidate absent certain structural biases from two perspectives. First, we are curious whether the sex of a candidate has a significant and separate influence on the vote for the candidate. By analyzing all open seats, we can compare female and male candidates in terms of experience and campaign expenditures and also assess the independent influence of candidate sex as an exogenous effect on the district vote outcome. Second, we narrow the analysis to only those contests where women and men opposed each other. By selecting these contests and coding all variables relative to the female candidate,[6] we will be able to assess differences in female candidate performance against male candidates, based on spending, experience, and party. We also perform these analyses across three distinct periods: the 1980s (1982-1990), the Year of the Woman (1992), and the period of the new GOP majority (1994-1998). This division will allow us to assess the effect of candidate sex in elections before the watershed 1992 election, in that election, and subsequent to that election. We begin by briefly discussing candidate financial quality and experience before moving to a set of multivariate analyses of open seat elections.

FINANCIAL QUALITY AND CANDIDATE EXPERIENCE

The demonstrated significance of money as a factor in the success of candidates in elections has led to many studies examining the ability of female candidates to raise campaign funds. Uhlaner and Schlozman (1986) found that females were not well-funded in the 1980 elections, but they attributed these discrepancies to political characteristics such as incumbency rather than sex. They concluded that "any reluctance to encourage women to run for Congress on the grounds of inability to raise funds has no basis in fact" (46). Gaddie and Bullock (1995) found that between 1982 and 1992, female candidates were able to raise as much money as male candidates. Furthermore, in contrast with the argument that women must rely on exogenous, nontraditional sources of funding when seeking political office (Volgy, Schwarz, and Gottleib 1986), subsequent research finds women are no less able to attract money than men when incumbency is controlled (Herrick 1996; Theilmann and Wilhite 1991).

When examining the financial quality of female candidates versus their opponents, Gaddie and Bullock (1995) and Green (1998) both found that successful female candidates generally outspent their opponents from 1982 to 1992. Similar to these initial findings, successful female candidates in the 1994-1998 open seat elections outspent their male opponents by an average of $350,000. While successful male candidates also outspent their female opponents in these elections, they did so at a lower rate of $250,000. This result can lend itself to two interpretations. On the one hand, it could be argued that female candidates were capable of raising large amounts of money in the absence of incumbents and dramatically outspending their male opponents. On the other hand, it has also been argued that women had to spend more to win, implying a disadvantage by having to spend more than a male candidate to achieve the same result (Green 1998).

The difference between the prior elective experience of men and women from 1982-1992 is not statistically significant (Gaddie and Bullock 2000). Among female candidates in open seats between 1994 and 1998, 26 of 44 had prior elective experience (59%). In contrast, fewer male than female candidates held prior elective office in this period, only 110 of 226 (49%). The experienced female candidates were very successful with 16 of 26 winning the open seat (62%). Experienced male candidates were also successful with 73 of 110 winning the election (66%). If we consider the flip-side of this analysis, the performance of candidates who lack elective office experience, we see a startling contrast. Of the 116 novice men, 36 won (31.3%). Among the 18 women who lacked elective experience, none were elected to Congress, indicating that men with no elective office experience had far greater electoral success than similarly situated women. These results are similar to those prior to 1994 and in those observed in special elections, which show that experienced women typically win, and that the women who run are usually more experienced than the pool of male nominees (Gaddie and Bullock 1997).

MULTIVARIATE ANALYSIS

The descriptive analysis above indicates that financial quality and candidate experience are indicators of female success. The data also indicate that female candidates have not been as successful in the mid-1990s as they were in 1992. In order to determine why female candidates have not maintained the level of success evident in the 1992 election, we specified two sets of regression equations that examined the exogenous effect of candidate sex on the outcome of open seat elections and the impact of endogenous candidate attributes on the performance of female candidates in female versus male contests.

The first regression equation, applied to all open seats from 1982-1998, is similar to a model used by Gaddie and Mott (1998) in their analysis of open seat elections in 1996. This model includes measures of Democratic and Republican candidate political experience, Democratic and Republican candidate spending, the GOP normal vote in the district, the sex of the Democratic and Republican candidates,[7] and, for the analyses that include more than one election year, a set of year-shift dummy variables to control for the independent effects that might be observed in respective election years.[8] The results of this multivariate analysis appear in Table 1.

For 1982-1990, the equation explains 64% of the variance in the Republican vote share. Individual candidate attributes exhibit strong, statistically significant influences on open seat congressional elections. The candidate sex coefficients are not statistically significant, indicating that sex has little direct impact on the electoral success of candidates in open seats. The regression equation produces an even closer fit for the 1992 open seat elections, explaining 76% of the variance in the Republican vote share. The district partisanship, experience measures, and Republican spending are statistically significant, while the candidate sex coefficients are not. Furthermore, the Democratic campaign expenditure variable is not statistically significant in this model. For 1994-1998, the candidate attribute model explains 80% of the variance in the Republican vote share. Neither candidate sex nor Democratic candidate political experience had a significant effect on the dependent variable, while candidate spending, district partisanship, and GOP candidate experience affected the GOP district vote in the expected direction.

We observe that while the influences of candidate spending and experience are at some variance in terms of the magnitude and significance of their impact, candidate spending and experience are consistently in the same direction across the three sets of elections, with the

TABLE 1. Sex and Open Seat Elections, 1982-1998

Variable	1982-1990	1992	1994-1998
Constant	17.68	10.62	4.00
Female Democratic Candidate (1 = female, 0 = male)	3.33 (1.99)	0.46 (1.59)	1.09 (1.15)
Female Republican Candidate (1 = female, 0 = male)	0.83 (2.74)	−0.07 (2.07)	−0.38 (1.49)
Democratic Candidate Experience (1 = held prior office, 0 otherwise)	−3.48 (1.30)*	−4.49 (1.74)*	−1.59 (1.00)
Republican Candidate Experience (1 = held prior office, 0 otherwise)	4.40 (1.30)*	6.47 (1.70)*	2.18 (1.00)*
Democratic Spending (in $100,000)	−0.69 (0.18)*	0.03 (0.24)	−0.23 (0.13)*
Republican Spending (in $100,000)	1.22 (0.22)*	0.64 (0.36)*	0.21 (0.10)*
Year 1984 (1 = 1984, 0 otherwise)	4.74 (1.91)*	-	-
Year 1986 (1 = 1986, 0 otherwise)	−2.28 (1.78)	-	-
Year 1988 (1 = 1988, 0 otherwise)	−2.64 (2.12)	-	-
Year 1990 (1 = 1990, 0 otherwise)	−1.54 (1.89)	-	-
Year 1994 (1 = 1994, 0 otherwise)	-	-	4.77 (1.23)*
Year 1996 (1 = 1996, 0 otherwise)	-	-	−3.09 (1.28)*
Normal Vote (Republican presidential vote, averaged across previous two elections)	0.51 (0.70)*	0.60 (0.08)*	0.94 (0.06)*
Adjusted-R^2	0.64	0.76	0.80
	N = 158	N = 72	N = 135

* significant .05 level, one-tailed test
N.B.: Unstandardized regression coefficients are reported (standard error in parentheses).

exception of 1992 when the slope of the Democratic spending variable is essentially zero. Further, the sex of either party's candidate is not a significant predictor of the election outcome in any of the analyses. The normal vote does start to emerge as a more powerful predictor of the congressional vote in the open seats after 1992, a development which we will demonstrate is of significance in understanding the success and failure of female congressional candidates.[9]

The second set of regression equations, which examine the performance of women in female versus male open seat contests, appears in Table 2. Since 1982, there have been 90 female versus male open seat contests. Between 1982-1990, there were 27 such contests. In 1992, there were 35 female candidates who ran for open seats, but five of these contests were female versus female and were omitted from the analysis, leaving 25 contests. From 1994-1998, there were 44 female open seat candidates with three female versus female contests. These contests were omitted, leaving 38 female versus male open seat contests.[10]

For 1982-1990, the model explains 66% of the female candidates' vote share. The only candidate attributes that achieved significance in this model were the party of the female candidate and the spending by the female candidate. The normal vote for the female candidate was also a significant and positive predictor. Republican women ran over 11 points behind Democratic women. This not only indicated a decided advantage for women running as Democrats, but it also reinforces a long-held suspicion that while the GOP fielded women as often as Democrats in the 1970s and 1980s, those women were often sacrificial candidates who did not perform especially well in general elections. For the 1992 cases, the model explains 75% of the female candidates' vote share. Again, district partisanship and the female candidate's party are significant and act in the same manner as in the 1982-1990 analysis. Male candidate experience is also statistically significant, with experienced male candidates knocking over 10 points off the performance of a female candidate in the Year of the Woman.

When applied to elections from 1994-1998, the model explains 86% of the female candidates' vote share. Male candidate spending and male candidate experience are significantly and negatively related to the vote share of the female candidate, while none of the female candidate attributes, except party, are statistically significant. Further, candidate party performs an abrupt shift, from an 11 point disadvantage for Republican women in 1982-1990 to a six point advantage for Republican women over Democratic women in 1994-1998. This represents a net change in the slope coefficient of over 16 points to the disadvantage of Democratic women. Subsequent to the Year of the Woman, we observe open seat elections that are more partisan in general and which in particular disadvantage women who run as Democrats.[11]

The regression equation explains increasing amounts of the variation in the female vote from the 1980s to 1992 to the late 1990s, even though female candidate attributes (other than party) decline in significance. Why? This finding can be explained by the fact that the normal vote is responsible for explaining most of the variance in the recent elections.[12] Prior research has shown that female electoral success was a product of the quality of female candidates, indicating that experienced and well-funded women were elected to Congress. We have observed a de-

TABLE 2. Female versus Male Open Seat Elections, 1982-1998

Variable	1982-1990	1992	1994-1998
Constant	7.46	22.97	1.98
Female Candidate Experience (1 = held prior office, 0 otherwise)	5.94 (3.10)	4.72 (3.56)	0.59 (1.97)
Male Candidate Experience (1 = held prior office, 0 otherwise)	6.09 (4.10)	−10.28 (4.01)*	−3.48 (1.96)*
Female Spending (in $100,000)	0.74 (0.41)*	0.62 (0.66)	−0.06 (0.28)
Male Spending (in $100,000)	−0.01 (0.37)	0.46 (0.76)	−0.38 (0.19)*
Female's Party (1 = Republican, 0 = Democrat)	−11.04 (4.05)*	−9.77 (3.75)*	6.29 (1.96)*
Female Normal Vote (Presidential vote, averaged across previous two elections, for the female's party)	0.71 (0.13)*	0.59 (0.17)*	0.97 (0.10)*
Adjusted-R^2	0.66	0.75	0.86
	N = 27	N = 25	N = 38

* significant at .05 level, one-tailed test
N.B.: Unstandardized regression coefficients are reported (standard error in parentheses).

cline in the significance of candidate attributes when explaining the outcomes of open seat contests, especially female versus male contests.

One reason for the decline of the candidate attribute model is the increased coherence between open seat election results and the presidential normal vote. In the previous section, we observed the powerful influence of a partisanship measure on the results of open seat contests. In the analyses of all open seat elections and female versus male open seat contests, we see an increase in the slope of the normal vote toward +1, a shift by the intercept of the regression toward 0 in the 1994-1998 period, and an increase in explained variance by the model. We also see that the normal vote has a steeper slope across all election periods for the female versus male contests than in the analysis of all open seats. Is it possible that underlying influences–reflected in the normal vote–have been traditionally more powerful in districts featuring female versus male contests in the 1980s and that those influences are even more powerful in open seat contests involving women in the mid-1990s?

We graph the relationship between the two-party normal GOP vote and the GOP vote for Congress in the open seats since 1982 (Figure 2 [A-F]). In Figure 2A the relationship is presented for female versus male contests from 1982-1990. In Figure 2B, the relationship is presented for the all-male contests during the same time period. The fit between the normal vote and the congressional vote is much tighter in the female versus male contests ($R^2 = .60$) than it is in the all-male contests ($R^2 = .46$). In 1992 (Figures 2C and 2D), open seat congressional elections generally aligned themselves more closely with the normal vote. As indicated in Figure 2C, the relationship between female versus male contests and the normal vote was virtually unchanged from the prior decade ($R^2 = .59$), while the all-male contests (Figure 2D) correlated much more closely with the normal vote ($R^2 = .73$).

After 1992, all open seat congressional elections aligned more closely with the normal vote than in the 1980s (Gaddie and Bullock 2000; Gaddie and Mott 1998). Most of this strong partisan coherence is occurring in the female versus male contests (Figure 2E), where the normal vote explains a phenomenal 87% of the variance in the two-party vote. The relationship between the normal vote and all-male contests is greater from 1994-1998 (Figure 2F) than in the 1980s, but the relationship is weaker than what we observed in 1992. Open seat congressional elections become more partisan during the 1990s, a trend previously observed by Gaddie and Bullock (2000, 20-24, 175). A last look at these

FIGURE 2A. The Normal Vote and Candidate Sex, 1982-1998: Female-Male Contests, 1982-1990

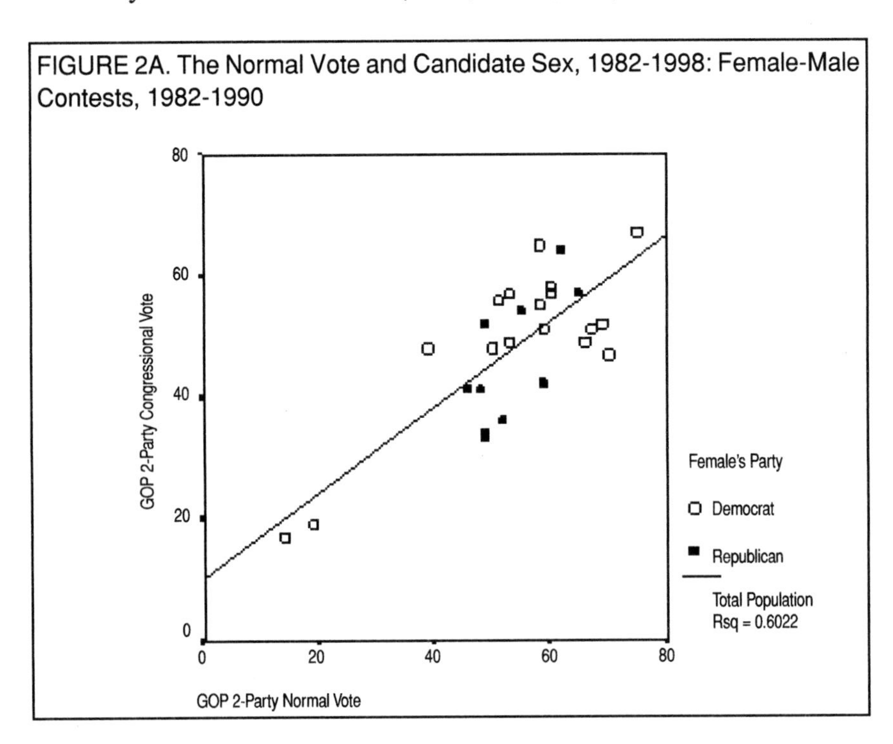

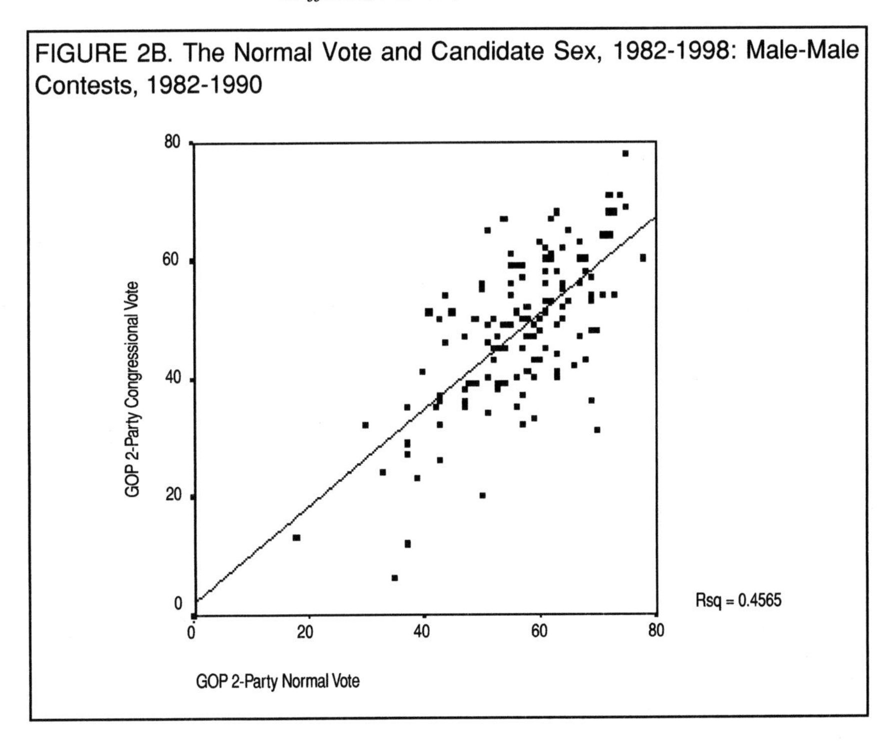

FIGURE 2B. The Normal Vote and Candidate Sex, 1982-1998: Male-Male Contests, 1982-1990

plots indicates that while congressional elections became generally more partisan, this relationship is especially pronounced in contests involving women.

These results provide evidence that experience and financial quality are not sufficient to secure the electoral success of women. As Green (1998) observed in an earlier analysis of female campaign finance in open seats through 1994, women raise more money to achieve the same electoral result. In a more close examination of female versus male races, it appears that even substantial spending, out of proportion to that of male candidates, is not sufficient to elect female candidates. In addition to these other factors, U.S. House elections are also becoming more partisan. Based on this evidence, we can initially conclude that the limited female advancement in the 1990s is partly structural. An examination of these scatterplots reveals that a disproportionate number of districts where female candidates ran leaned toward the opposite party at the presidential level. In those races, the presidential and congressional vote were more closely correlated, both in comparison to female

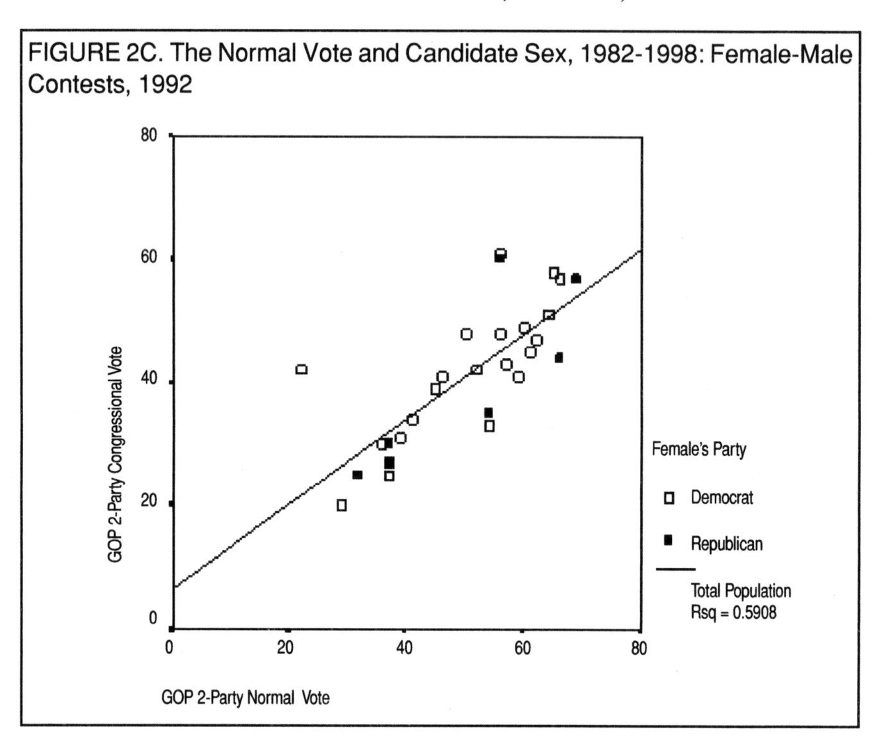

FIGURE 2C. The Normal Vote and Candidate Sex, 1982-1998: Female-Male Contests, 1992

versus male contests in prior years and in comparison to all-male contests held in the same time frame.

These results are also interesting because they comport relatively well with experimental research on voter choices and candidate sex. King and Matland (1997), taking advantage of a rare experimental study of likely voter reactions to the sex of candidates, modeled the preference and reactions of Republican, Democratic, and independent voters to a pair of Republican candidates. The only factor that varied across the candidates was the candidate sex. The female Republican candidate was more likely to attract Democratic support than the male candidate, while the converse was true among Republican voters. King and Matland conclude that the nature of congressional voters is such that women will have greater difficulty winning GOP nominations but an easier time winning general elections as Republicans; women will have an easier time winning nominations as Democrats but greater difficulty attracting independent and GOP crossover votes as Democrats. This data, gathered in late 1993, foreshadowed the actual events of the open seats after the Year of the Woman. Republican women did run

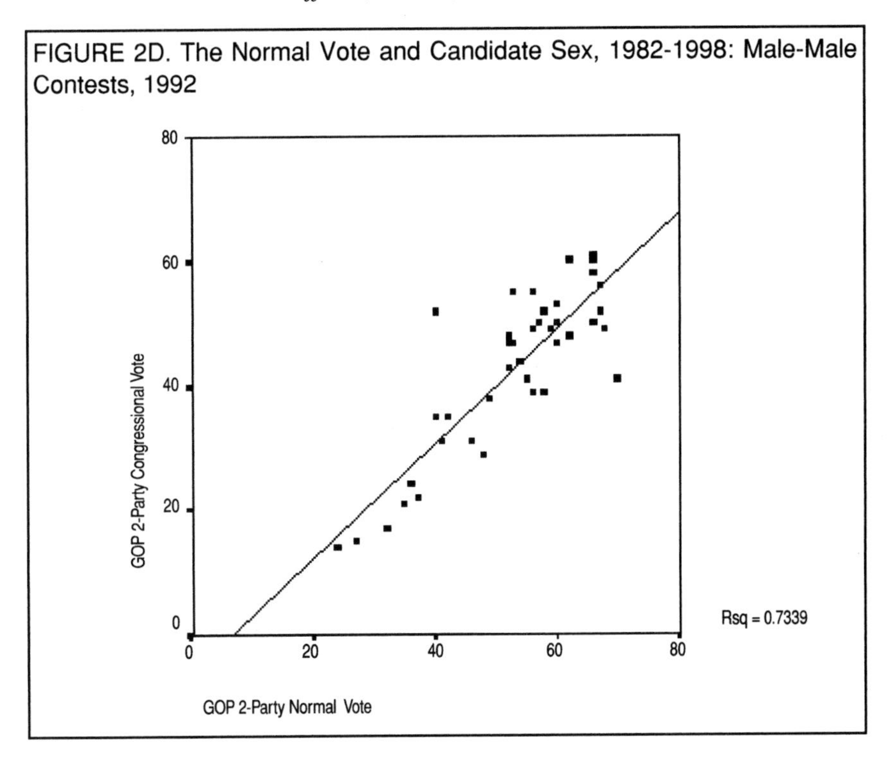

FIGURE 2D. The Normal Vote and Candidate Sex, 1982-1998: Male-Male Contests, 1992

better than Democratic women, but more Democratic than Republican women were nominated.

When taking account of the experimental evidence offered by King and Matland, the implications of our evidence for the advancement of women to Congress are substantial. In Figure 3, we present a time-series of female nominations in open seats since 1974. Until 1986, the few women nominated in open seats came equally from both major parties. In 1988 and 1990, the few women nominated in open seats were all Democrats. The number of female open seat candidates increased substantially in 1992, and in 1994, 1996, and 1998 the numbers of women who were nominated in open seats continued at numbers far greater than in the decades preceding the Year of the Woman. Compared to the previous decades, however, the nomination of women is disproportionately a Democratic phenomenon. Women are more often running in and winning Democratic Party open seat primaries. The prospect for descriptive female advancement–electing more women, regardless of ideology or party–is increasingly staked on Democratic Party success and

FIGURE 2E. The Normal Vote and Candidate Sex, 1982-1998: Female-Male Contests, 1994-1998

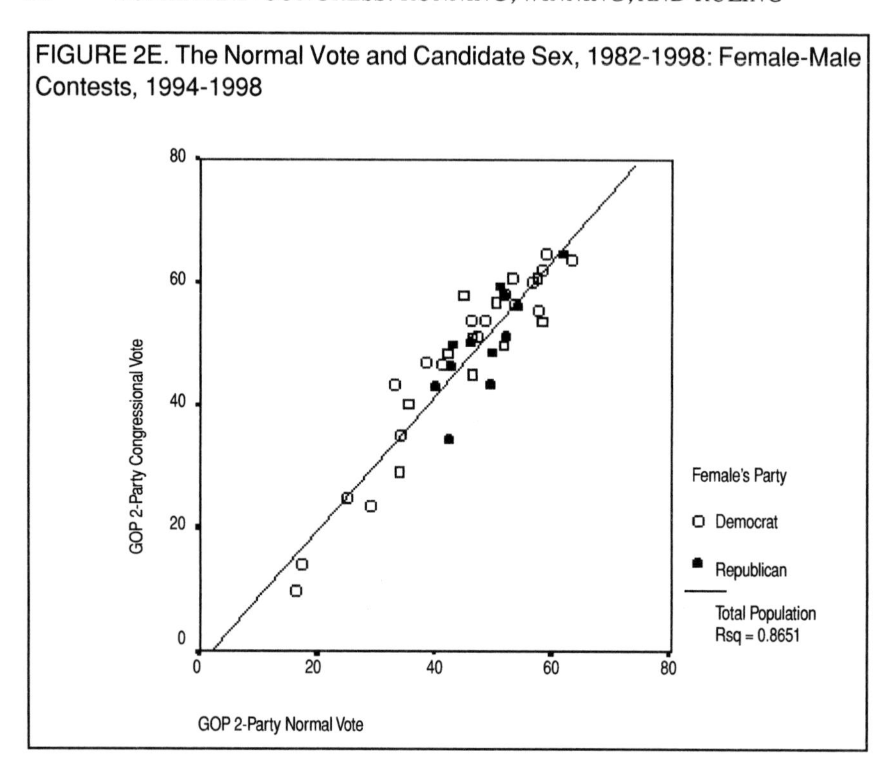

failure. When this phenomenon is paired with congressional voting that is increasingly related to top-of-the-ticket indicators like the normal vote, prospects for political advancement become more vulnerable to partisan tides and less dependent on particular candidate performance. This is not necessarily news for observers of women in politics, and we are not advancing the argument that female political opportunities be spread evenly across both parties. To do so ignores the basic reasons why more women than men vote Democratic and why politically active women are more likely to choose the Democratic Party as an avenue for advancement. The conclusion reached here is that the calculus of American politics in the congressional districts indicates two costs to descriptive advancement as female opportunities become tied to one party. The first cost is that female advancement becomes directly linked to partisan tides. The second, hidden cost is that female Democrats run behind female Republicans who seek office under similar circumstances, and this lag in support, if we accept the results of experimental research, is a product of candidate sex.

FIGURE 2F. The Normal Vote and Candidate Sex, 1982-1998: Male-Male Contests, 1994-1998

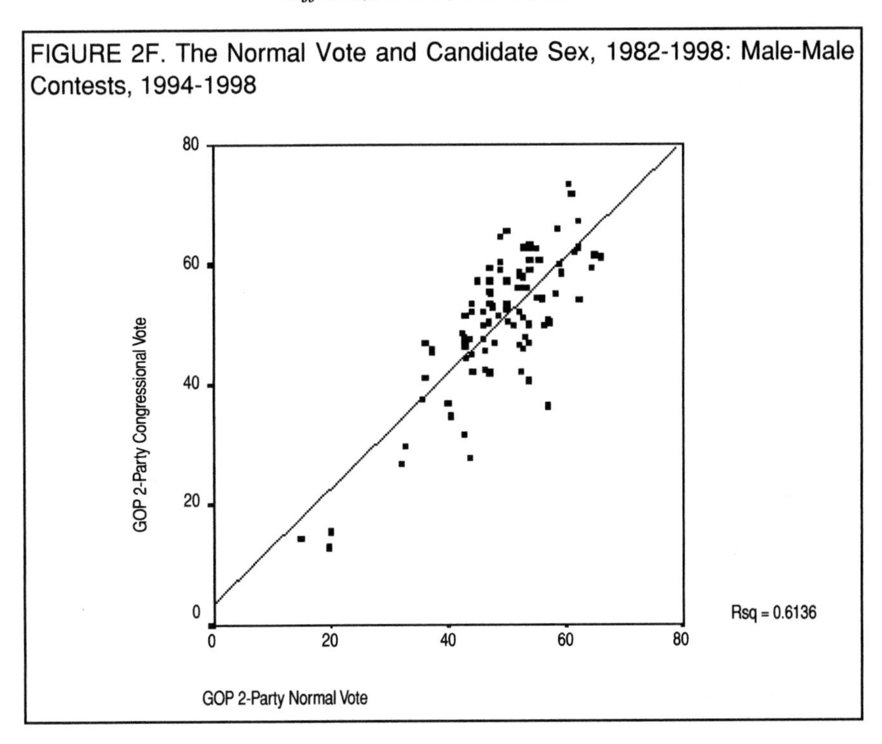

These results also confirm previous studies of the behavior of Americans toward female candidates. In low information elections, like U.S. House races, female Democrats fare better than males among liberals and worse among conservatives, while Republican female candidates have no clear effect on voter choice (McDermott 1997). So, while there are partisan stereotypes in congressional elections (Rahn 1993), there are also sex stereotypes. Our analysis indicates that the impact of candidate sex in the 1990s is against Democrats, and then only relative to other female candidates. If American congressional elections are growing in partisan coherence relative to the normal vote, and if this effect is especially pronounced in female versus male races, it may be because sex as a cue pulls voter perceptions toward ideological extremes (Koch 2000).

CONCLUSION

Some research shows that women are as likely as men to win elections for the House once candidate quality is controlled (Darcy, Welch,

FIGURE 3. Party of Women Nominated in Open Seats, 1974-1998

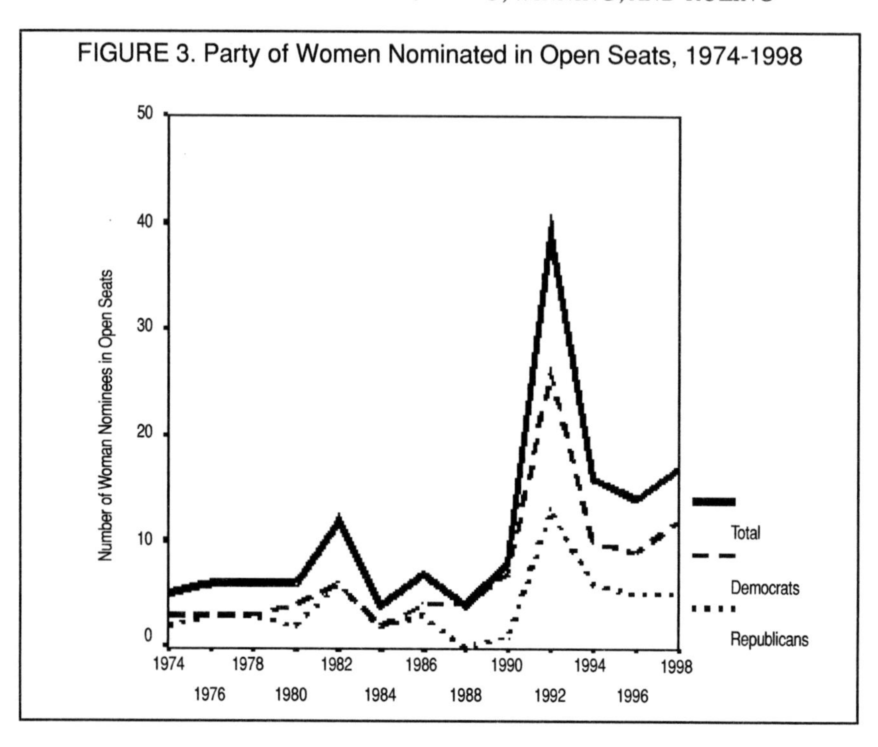

and Clark 1994). Despite female gains in 1992, the disadvantages evidenced in the 1980s appear to be back. As in previous research, our analysis indicates that candidate sex has no direct impact on election outcomes when we control for candidate quality and district partisanship. Women have nonetheless failed to maintain the same level of success in congressional open seats that was evident in 1992, and the factors that explained both female electoral success and open seat elections in general before the 1990s became less significant after 1992. There appears to be a notable change in the nature of open seat elections. This change holds consequences for female political advancement.

We must ask why female candidates have not maintained the level of success evident in 1992, despite the presence of experienced and well-funded female candidates. In addition, we must ask whether the reason that women performed less well in open seats after 1992 is because they ran in districts that have a stronger partisan orientation. It is evident that there is greater partisan congruence in open seats in the 1990s and that Republicans have performed better during this period. This could help explain why female candidates did not fare as well in the mid-1990s. If female candidates chose to run in districts where the partisan tide ran counter to them, this would explain their lack of electoral success.

The fact that women typically run against men under conditions of greater partisanship compared to the all-male contests raises a third question. Are these races more partisan because of the presence of female candidates, or are these more partisan districts? In the former case, campaigns become potentially more important in terms of how voters differentiate or tie female and male candidates to their presidential parties. If female versus male contests reinforce partisan differences, there are two possibilities. There is either a perception about female candidates that causes voters to fall back on candidate cues which would diminish candidate attributes in the eyes of voters, or the rhetoric and issues of female candidates and their opponents have a polarizing effect that is absent from all-male contests. If the latter is the case, then female advancement is tied to district partisanship because those districts produce female nominees. A certain deterministic quality emerges in congressional elections, which holds that the advancement of women depends on developing female candidates and securing nominations in the party of favor in the district.

AUTHOR NOTE

An earlier version of this paper was presented at the annual meeting of the Southwestern Political Science Association, Galveston, TX, March 15-18, 2000. The authors wish to thank the anonymous reviewers (especially the initial reviewer #1 and reviewer #2 from the second review round), Cindy Simon Rosenthal, Glenn Peterson, Chuck Bullock, and *Women & Politics* editor Karen O'Connor for their comments and constructive criticisms of previous versions of the manuscript. Data for Figures 1 and 3 were collected from the Center for American Women and Politics (CAWP). This data can be accessed from the CAWP Website at http://www.rci.rutgers.edu/~cawp. Errors of fact or interpretation reside with the authors.

NOTES

1. Gaddie and Bullock noted the prominent role of this redistricting in creating a pool of female quality candidates who propelled themselves into the U.S. House from Florida via open seats in 1992 (2000, 131-134).

2. Only 2 of 41 female challengers defeated incumbents in 1992, a rate comparable to the general rate of incumbent defeats in the 1980s and 1990s (Fowler 1993).

3. Legislative elections research consistently finds a relationship between the expenditures of non-incumbent candidates and district-level election outcomes in single-member districts. Campaign finance data were obtained from the Federal Election Commission and standardized to constant 1994 dollars.

4. The prior political experience of congressional candidates is considered to be a key indicator of their political success against incumbents (Jacobson 1997). Gaddie (1995) also found substantial experience effects in open seats. While a variety of political experience measures have been advanced (c.f. Green and Krasno 1988; Bond, Covington, and Fleisher 1983), the most widely accepted is Jacobson's measure, which simply indicates whether or not a candidate holds or has held prior elective office (Bond, Fleisher, and Talbert 1997). The Jacobson measure is used in this study. Candidate experience was gathered from issues of *Congressional Quarterly Weekly Report, The Almanac of American Politics,* and other candidate biographies and Websites.

5. A normal vote measure is used to estimate district partisanship. Gaddie and Mott (1998) found that this measure was a powerful predictor of open seat election outcomes in 1996 and Gaddie and Bullock (2000) observe that it also is a strong predictor in open seat outcomes in 1998. This measure averages the Republican two-party vote for president across the two elections prior to the election analyzed. Measures that incorporated additional elections have been advanced, but Bond, Fleisher, and Talbert (1997) find that the presidential normal vote measure correlates highly with the other measures, so we opt to use the most simple measure. District-level presidential vote data were obtained from issues of *The Almanac of American Politics* and, when necessary, compiled from data obtained from various state boards of election.

6. The dependent variable will be the female candidate's vote share. The spending, experience, and normal vote variables will be coded relative to the sex of the candidate (male experience, female experience, male spending, female spending, female party's normal vote, and the party of the female candidate).

7. Coded 1 if the respective candidate is a woman, 0 otherwise.

8. The years 1984, 1986, 1988, and 1990 are controlled in the 1982-1990 analysis. The years 1994 and 1996 are controlled in the 1994-1998 analysis. One year is always left out in such an analysis because to include dummy-variable controls for all election years would create a singular matrix and collapse the regression equation under perfect collinearity of the independent variables (see Stimson 1985).

9. A model was specified for each time period regressing the normal vote and the GOP candidate's share of the two-party vote. For each subsequent time period, the normal vote explained an increasing amount of the variance of the Republican vote share.

10. An examination of variance inflation factors revealed no VIFs greater than 3, indicating an absence of any problemmatic multicollinearity among the independent variables.

11. One reviewer, arguing that vote margin was unimportant compared to success or failure, asked why we did not specify our model with a dichotomous dependent variable to indicate a win or loss by a female candidate. Based on our reading of the legislative politics literature, we must disagree. Vote margins matter, both to first time winners and incumbents. Collie (1981) demonstrated that the size of reelection margins of members of Congress is related to the initial election margin of the member. Mayhew (1974) argues that declining competition in incumbent races was a product of member efforts to run up election margins and insulate themselves from future challenge. And Parker (1994) argued convincingly that members seek to build up reservoirs of votes that allow

them discretion to act as they see fit. Considered in sum, these works indicate that legislators have incentives to expand vote margins, and that the ability to expand vote margins is derived in part from the margin in the initial election. On a more fundamental level, we should not sacrifice a term which has greater precision and which captures greater variation in political performance (the vote share) than simple win-loss.

12. A model was specified for each time period regressing the normal vote and the female candidate's share of the two-party vote. For each subsequent time period, district partisanship explained an increasing amount of the variance of the female candidate's vote share.

REFERENCES

Anderson, Kristi, and Stuart J. Thorson. 1984. "Congressional Turnover and the Election of Women." *Western Political Quarterly* 37: 143-156.

Bond, Jon R., Cary Covington, and Richard Fleisher. 1983. "Explaining Challenger Quality in Congressional Elections." *Journal of Politics* 47: 510-529.

Bond, Jon R., Richard Fleisher, and Jeffrey C. Talbert. 1997. "The Experience Factor in Open Seat Congressional Elections, 1976-1994." *Political Research Quarterly* 50: 281-299.

Bullock, Charles S., III, and Patricia Lee Findley Hays. 1972. "Recruitment of Women for Congress." *Western Political Quarterly* 25: 416-423.

Burrell, Barbara C. 1994. *A Woman's Place Is in the House: Campaigning for Congress in the Feminist Era.* Ann Arbor: University of Michigan Press.

Collie, Melissa P. 1981. "Incumbency, Electoral Safety, and Turnover in the House of Representatives, 1952-76." *American Political Science Review* 75: 119-131.

Darcy, R., and James R. Choike. 1986. "A Formal Analysis of Legislative Turnover: Women Candidates and Legislative Representation." *American Journal of Political Science* 30: 237-255.

Darcy, R., Susan Welch, and Janet Clark. 1994. *Women, Elections, and Representation.* 2nd ed. Lincoln: University of Nebraska Press.

Gaddie, Ronald Keith. 1995. "Is There an Inherent Democratic Party Advantage in U.S. House Elections? Evidence from the Open Seats." *Social Science Quarterly* 76: 203-212.

Gaddie, Ronald Keith, and Charles S. Bullock III. 1995. "Congressional Elections and the Year of the Woman: Structural and Elite Influence on Female Candidacies." *Social Science Quarterly* 76: 749-762.

Gaddie, Ronald Keith, and Charles S. Bullock III. 1997. "Structural and Elite Features in Open Seat and Special Elections: Is There a Sexual Bias?" *Political Research Quarterly* 50: 457-466.

Gaddie, Ronald Keith, and Charles S. Bullock III. 2000. *Elections to Open Seats in the U.S. House: Where the Action Is.* Lanham, MD: Rowman and Littlefield.

Gaddie, Ronald Keith, and Jonathan D. Mott. 1998. "The 1996 Open-Seat Congressional Elections." *Social Science Quarterly* 79: 444-454.

Gertzog, Irwin. 1979. "Changing Patterns of Female Recruitment to the U.S. House of Representatives." *Legislative Studies Quarterly* 4: 429-446.

Green, Donald Philip, and Jonathan S. Krasno. 1988. "Salvation for the Spendthrift Incumbent: Reestimating the Effects of Campaign Spending in House Elections." *American Journal of Political Science* 32: 884-907.

Green, Joanne Connor. 1998. "The Role of Gender in Open-Seat Elections for the U.S. House of Representatives: A District Level Test for a Differential Value for Campaign Resources." *Women & Politics* 19(3): 33-55.

Herrick, Rebekah. 1996. "Is There a Gender Gap in the Value of Campaign Resources?" *American Politics Quarterly* 24: 68-80.

Jacobson, Gary C. 1997. *The Politics of Congressional Elections*. 4th ed. New York: HarperCollins.

King, David C., and Richard E. Matland. 1997. "Experimental Evidence on the Viability of Women Candidates for Congress." Presented at the annual meeting of the Southwest Social Science Association.

Koch, Jeffrey W. 2000. "Do Citizens Apply Gender Stereotypes to Infer Candidate's Ideological Orientations?" *Journal of Politics* 62: 414-429.

Ladd, Everett Carll. 1995. "The 1994 Congressional Elections: The Postindustrial Realignment Continues." *Political Science Quarterly* 110: 1-23.

Mayhew, David R. 1974. "Congressional Elections: The Case of the Vanishing Marginals." *Polity* 6: 295-317.

McDermott, Monika L. 1997. "Voting Cues in Low-Information Elections: Candidate Gender as a Social Information Variable in Contemporary United States Elections." *American Journal of Political Science* 41: 270-283.

Parker, Glenn R. 1994. *Institutional Discretion and the Creation of Modern Congress*. Ann Arbor: University of Michigan Press.

Pritchard, Anita. 1992. "Changes in Electoral Structure and the Success of Women Candidates: The Case of Florida." *Social Science Quarterly* 73: 62-70.

Rahn, Wendy M. 1993. "The Role of Partisan Stereotypes in Information Processing about Political Candidates." *American Journal of Political Science* 37: 472-496.

Rosenthal, Cindy Simon. 1998. *When Women Lead: Integrative Leadership in State Legislatures*. New York: Oxford University Press.

Stimson, James T. 1985. "Regression in Space and Time: A Statistical Essay." *American Journal of Political Science* 29: 914-947.

Theilmann, John, and Al Wilhite. 1991. *Discrimination and Congressional Campaign Contributions*. New York: Praeger.

Thomas, Sue, and Clyde Wilcox. 1998. *Women and Elective Office: Past, Present, and Future*. New York: Oxford University Press.

Uhlaner, Carole Jean, and Kay Lehman Schlozman. 1986. "Candidate Gender and Congressional Campaign Receipts." *Journal of Politics* 48: 30-50.

Volgy, Thomas J., John E. Schwarz, and Hildy Gottleib. 1986. "Female Representation and the Quest for Resources: Feminist Activism and Electoral Success." *Social Science Quarterly* 67: 156-168.

The Political Glass Ceiling: Gender, Strategy, and Incumbency in U.S. House Elections, 1978-1998

Barbara Palmer, American University
Dennis Simon, Southern Methodist University

SUMMARY. Why has the integration of women into elective office, particularly Congress, been so slow? We argue that incumbency and the general lack of competition in American elections serve as a "political glass ceiling," having a dampening effect on the number of women running in both primary and general U.S. House elections. With data from House elections from 1978-1998, we find that although there have been general upward trends in the number of women running in primaries, winning primaries, and winning election to Congress, there is a distinct gender gap between the parties. The growth in the presence of women since 1988 is largely a Democratic phenomenon. In addition, women are strategic in their decisions regarding whether or not they will run; the likelihood of success influences the decision to become a candidate. Women are far more likely to run in districts with an open seat than they are in districts where they would face a safe incumbent. This implies that the number of women entering the House depends upon the political cycle of redistricting or unanticipated events and "crises" that create large numbers of open seats.

[Haworth co-indexing entry note]: "The Political Glass Ceiling: Gender, Strategy, and Incumbency in U.S. House Elections, 1978-1998." Palmer, Barbara, and Dennis Simon. Co-published simultaneously in *Women & Politics* (The Haworth Press, Inc.) Vol. 23, No. 1/2, 2001, pp. 59-78; and: *Women and Congress: Running, Winning, and Ruling* (ed: Karen O'Connor) The Haworth Press, Inc., 2001, pp. 59-78. Single or multiple copies of this article are available for a fee from The Haworth Document Delivery Service [1-800-HAWORTH, 9:00 a.m. - 5:00 p.m. (EST). E-mail address: getinfo@haworthpressinc.com].

At the dawn of the 21st century, only 22.4% of state legislators were female, only four states and Puerto Rico had women governors, and only 13% of Senators and 13.6% of the Members of the House of Representatives were female (CAWP 2001). This raises an important question: why has the integration of women into elective office, particularly Congress, been so slow? Building on the work of Burrell (1994), Carroll (1994), and Darcy, Welch, and Clark (1994), we address the gaps in the literature on women congressional candidates regarding our understanding of the role of incumbency. With data collected from all primary and general House elections from 1978-1998, we argue that incumbency fosters a general lack of competitiveness in both primary and general elections in the United States, serving as a political glass ceiling.

Within this framework, we attempt to provide a more complete analysis of several overlooked trends concerning the participation of women in congressional elections. More specifically, we find that the general trend of slow but steady growth in the participation of women in primary and general elections masks measurable differences between the parties. Beginning in 1988, the increase in the presence of women candidates is disproportionately a Democratic phenomenon. In other words, most of the gains that women made in the congressional electoral arena through 1998 were primarily attributable to one party. In addition, we are able to show that women act strategically with regard to when they will run. In districts with safe seats where they would face an entrenched incumbent, women are much less likely to run. In open seats, seats with the highest chance of victory, women are substantially more likely to run. Thus, we are able to show that the entry of women into the electoral arena is based, at least in part, on the probability of success.

WHY ARE THERE SO FEW WOMEN IN CONGRESS?

During the 1980s, research specifically directed at women candidates began to emerge, and scholars of congressional elections began paying more attention to the role of gender in campaigns (Fowler and McClure 1989; Gertzog 1984; Mandel 1981). The dramatic increase of women in the early 1990s, particularly 1992, prompted another wave of research, suggesting myriad explanations for the slow integration of women into Congress, and recognizing the structural and social barriers that confront female candidates.

One of the structural barriers that women face in running for Congress is the "pipeline." In the American electoral arena, there is a hierarchy of political offices that serves as a career ladder for elected officials (Schlesinger 1966). In other words, politicians begin their careers serving in local and state offices before running for Congress. Thus, once women begin serving in these lower political offices in greater numbers, only then will we see serious increases in the number of women serving in the House, and eventually the Senate (Carroll 1994; Carroll and Strimling 1983; Darcy, Welch, and Clark 1994; Herrick 1995; Norrander and Wilcox 1998). Sex-role socialization, however, creates numerous barriers that discourage women from even entering the pipeline (Duerst-Lahti 1998). Women have been traditionally steered away, or even barred, from professions that typically lead to political office. Traditionally female-dominated jobs, such as nursing and teaching, are generally seen as "less compatible" with politics than male-dominated jobs in law and business (McGlen and O'Connor 1998; C. Williams 1990). Recently, many women have been successful precisely because they come from fields other than law, such as health and education. At any rate, the pipeline theory suggests that as women become integrated into traditionally male-dominated fields, they will run increasingly for local and state offices, which will eventually lead to more women running for Congress.

Another line of research emphasizes that gender and sex-role stereotyping can impede the progress of those women who do enter the pipeline. Voters, for example, have expectations regarding appropriate gender roles and traits, which can affect their evaluations of women candidates. There is, however, a great deal of disagreement over just how expectations regarding gender roles affect voters' assessments of male and female candidates. Some research shows that women still face discrimination and are hurt by traditional gender stereotypes (Fox and Smith 1998; Huddy and Terkildsen 1993), while other work suggests that women candidates actually have an advantage over men (Cook 1998; Kahn 1994). Still more research has found that the gender of a candidate is irrelevant to voters (Cook 1998; Seltzer, Newman, and Leighton 1997; Thompson and Steckenrider 1997).

Although this research generally suggests that attitudes among voters no longer appear to be a major hurdle for women candidates, gender does seem to play a role in determining the effectiveness of women's campaigns (Fox 1997; Whillock 1991; Witt, Paget, and Matthews 1995). Women do face unique challenges in fundraising, with regard to how they raise money and their ability to compete financially with male candidates (Burrell 1998; Fox 1997; Green 1998; Herrick 1996). In addition, women candidates must learn how to use the media and sex-role stereotypes to their advantage, or face serious repercussions at the polls (Iyengar et al. 1997; Kahn 1994, 1996; Kahn and Gordon 1997; L. Williams 1998).

The power of incumbency has also been acknowledged as another barrier that women face (Burrell 1994; Carroll 1994; Darcy, Welch, and Clark 1994). Once candidates win an election, obtain office, and become members of Congress, they have substantial advantages when they run for reelection, such as name recognition and the use of the franking privilege (Herrnson 1998; Jacobson 1997). In addition, incumbents have the added advantage of having a substantial "money machine" at their disposal, typically outspending their challengers at a rate of three to one (Ornstein, Mann, and Malbin 1998). For both genders, this makes crossing the threshold from challenger to office holder most difficult. It is a barrier created by an electoral context in which the power of incumbency is substantial. Thus, women have had a hard time winning seats in the U.S. House not because they are women, but because of incumbency. And most incumbents are men.

Building on the foundation set by Burrell (1994), Carroll (1994), and Darcy, Welch, and Clark (1994), we add that the general lack of competitiveness in both primary and general elections in the United States contributes to the low numbers of women in Congress. As suggested earlier, incumbency is a large hurdle for challengers. The vast majority of members of Congress are renominated by their parties in their primary election and win the general election with tremendously high success rates. Thus, incumbency serves as the primary barrier for women candidates, a barrier that is not accounted for by either changes in socialization or the pipeline theory.

We hope to provide a much more complete understanding of the role of incumbency and its effect on the number of women congressional candidates. For example, we argue that the power of incumbency actually discourages candidates from running in the first place; a substantial proportion of congressional elections are simply uncontested. When they do run for reelection, incumbents typically face no competition in their primary election. In addition, they may have no competition in their general election as well. While the power of incumbency has been recognized in general elections, much less work has been done on its impact on primary elections (but see Bernstein 1997; Burrell 1992, 1994; Gertzog and Simard 1991), thus ignoring a vital step in the process of running for congressional office.

HYPOTHESES

Our intent is to combine the insights provided by the pipeline theory with our understanding of congressional incumbency to develop a richer explanation for the slow integration of women into Congress. Gaining a seat in Congress involves three distinct steps: (1) seeking the nomination of a party, which in the vast majority of instances means running in a primary; (2) winning the primary; and, (3) winning the general election. All incumbents and challengers must go through these steps in every election cycle, and each of these steps must be examined to present a more complete picture of the barriers faced by women congressional candidates.

To date, most research on the pipeline theory focuses exclusively on step 3, winning the general election. Steps 1 and 2, however, are necessary preludes to winning the office. In other words, if the pipeline theory is accurate, we should observe a parallel growth in the number of women for each step in the path to a House seat. Thus, we offer:

> *Hypothesis 1*: Along with the number of women winning a House seat, the number of women running in primary elections and the number of women winning the nomination should exhibit a pattern of slow growth over time.

The work of Schlesinger (1966) emphasizes that movement within the hierarchy of offices is based, in part, upon the strategic decisions made by those with progressive ambition. In fact, other research has shown that there is a calculus underlying the decision to run for office (Carroll 1994; Jacobson and Kernell 1981; Rohde 1979). The gist of this research is that not all opportunities to run are equivalent with respect to the probability of success. Clearly, whether the would-be candidate must challenge a sitting incumbent in a primary or general election is a major factor in assessing this probability. More specifically, we argue that the presence of an incumbent in the race and the electoral security of that incumbent will influence both the decision of women to seek the nomination and how they fare once they enter the electoral arena. This leads to:

> *Hypothesis 2*: The proportion of women seeking the nomination, as well as the proportion of women winning the nomination and general election, will vary with the "incumbency status" of the dis-

trict. The proportions will be highest in open districts and will be lowest in districts held by safe incumbents.

Our discussion also implies that the power of incumbency is "gender neutral." That is, the advantages of incumbency do not provide disproportionate benefits to men because they are men. Rather, men benefit because they are the vast majority of incumbents. Defeating an incumbent is an arduous task and the probability will be low, regardless of the challenger's gender. Accordingly, we offer:

> *Hypothesis 3*: There are no gender effects in the probability of defeating an incumbent. There will be no significant differences in the proportions of male and female challengers who defeat sitting incumbents.

Our discussion also implies that when women do become incumbents, they too will enjoy the electoral benefits and advantages of holding office (see Seltzer, Newman, and Leighton 1997, but see Deber 1982). This leads to the following hypothesis:

> *Hypothesis 4*: There are no gender effects in defending a House seat. There will be no differences in the reelection rates of male and female incumbents.

DATA ON WOMEN CONGRESSIONAL CANDIDATES

To test these hypotheses, we have developed an original data set that includes the number of women who entered the electoral arena in races for the U.S. House from 1978 to 1998. The unit of analysis in this study is the congressional district. For each district in each election year, we gathered and compiled the following information: the number of female candidates running for the Democratic and Republican nominations respectively, the total number of candidates seeking each party's nomination, whether a woman won the Democratic or Republican nomination, and the outcome of the general election.[1] For each district, we also recorded the party and gender of the incumbent, whether the incumbent was seeking reelection, and the incumbent's share of the two-party vote in the prior election.

This information was collected from the series, *America Votes*. Identifying the gender of candidates was done by first assessing the names listed for each district in each election. The gender of most names is easy to identify. In the case of questionable names (e.g., Pat Lear), the following procedure was employed. First, we consulted relevant editions of *The Almanac of American Politics* and *Congressional Quarterly Weekly Report*. Quite often, the coverage in these sources provides information about the gender of the party nominees. Second, for those questionable names that remained, we conducted a NEXIS search of newspaper coverage. In almost every case, we were able to find media coverage that indicated the gender of these candidates. Finally, if the NEXIS search provided no information, the name was excluded from our count of candidates. Using these procedures, out of the 15,266 candidates examined, only 32 names were excluded.

SETTING THE CONTEXT: THE POWER OF INCUMBENCY

Throughout this discussion, we have argued that the small number of women elected to the House is due, in part, to the power of incumbency. As a prelude to testing our hypotheses, Table 1 is designed to illustrate this electoral power, underscoring the formidable task of challenging an incumbent.

Not surprisingly, Table 1 shows that House incumbents are among the most secure of all elective officeholders. The rate of reelection ranges from 98.5% (1986 and 1998) to a "low" of 90.9% in 1994. The 1994 figure is noteworthy in and of itself; even in this year of the "Republican Revolution," over nine of ten incumbents were returned to office. But not only do incumbents win, they win by substantial margins. The second column of Table 1 presents the proportion of House incumbents who garnered 60% or more of the vote in their contests. The proportion of "blowouts" is substantial, ranging from 59.9% in 1996 to 87.3% in 1988. Moreover, column three of Table 1 shows there was a considerable number of elections in which the incumbent faced no major party opposition.

Table 1 also illustrates that primary elections are even less competitive than general elections. Only once did the renomination rate for incumbents dip below 97.5%. This occurred in 1992 when eight incumbents, each of whom wrote 100 or more overdrafts at the House bank, were challenged and defeated in their primaries. Aside from scandals like the banking debacle, the renomination of an incumbent is virtually routine. In fact, as Table 1 illustrates, incumbents frequently face no opposition in the primary arena. The proportion of uncontested nom-

TABLE 1. The Electoral Context: Incumbency and Elections to the U.S. House of Representatives, 1978-1998

Year	Percent of Incumbents Reelected	Reelected with 60% or more of 2-party vote[a]	Uncontested: Incumbent Faces No Major Party Opponent	Percent of Incumbents Renominated	Percent Facing No Primary Challenge	Open Districts[b]
1978	95.0	76.6	17.2 (65)	98.7	69.8	13.3 (58)
1980	90.7	72.9	13.8 (54)	98.5	71.0	9.9 (43)
1982	92.4	68.9	14.9 (56)	97.5	68.9	13.3 (58)
1984	96.1	78.9	16.4 (67)	99.3	64.6	6.2 (27)
1986	98.5	84.5	18.4 (72)	99.2	66.8	10.1 (44)
1988	98.3	87.3	19.6 (80)	99.8	78.9	6.0 (26)
1990	96.3	79.5	20.7 (84)	99.8	74.9	6.7 (29)
1992	93.1	65.0	7.9 (27)	94.8	59.2	21.4 (93)
1994	90.9	63.0	13.3 (51)	99.0	67.4	11.7 (51)
1996	94.5	59.9	6.0 (23)	99.5	73.1	12.2 (53)
1998	98.5	77.3	23.7 (95)	99.8	80.2	7.8 (34)

[a]The percentages were recorded from Stanley and Niemi (1998), Table 1-17, pp. 49-50.
[b]The count of open districts includes the new districts awarded to states as a result of the reapportionment in 1982 (n = 22) and 1992 (n = 19).

inations ranges from a low of 59.2% in 1992 to a high of 78.9% in 1988. Between 1978 and 1998, the overall proportion of incumbents facing no primary opponent was 70.6%.

The lesson of Table 1 is that the defeat of an incumbent in a primary or general election is a rare event. The noncompetitive nature of House elections thus creates a "political glass ceiling" based not upon conscious discrimination, but on the difficulty of defeating an incumbent. It is no surprise, then, that most who gain entry to the House arrive by winning an election for a seat that comes open when an incumbent dies, retires, or resigns to seek another office. Yet, as the last column of Table 1 reveals, in only one instance (1992) has the proportion of open seats topped 20%.[2] Save for the year of 1992, the number of open seats varied from 6.0% (1988) to 13.3% (1978 and 1982), suggesting that at least since 1978, open seats are relatively rare in American House elections.

Our data show, however, that open seats are, in fact, an "avenue of opportunity" that stimulate strategically minded politicians to enter the electoral arena. Excluding the incumbent, the average number of candidates running in primaries in districts with a sitting incumbent was 1.8. This average increased to 6.4 in contests for open seats. The bivariate correlation between the number of open seats in an election year and the total number of candidates competing in primaries is .89. Thus, trends regarding the entry of women into the arena of House elections are likely to be influenced, at least in part, by the availability of open seats. It is to these trends that we now turn.

TESTING THE HYPOTHESES: WOMEN AS CANDIDATES FOR THE HOUSE OF REPRESENTATIVES

As suggested earlier, gaining entry into the House of Representatives involves more than just winning the general election. Candidates must seek nomination by a party and enter the primary, they must obtain the nomination by winning the primary, and then they must win the general election. Figure 1 tracks the number of women who sought the nomination, won the nomination, and won a seat in the House in the election cycles from 1978 to 1998.[3]

As hypothesized, the general trends for each step in the process are similar. There is some upward progress, albeit minimal, between 1978 and 1990. There were 80 women who ran in primary elections in 1978. This number peaks in 1986 and then drops to 107 in 1990. During this period, the number of women winning a primary increases from 44 to 67, and the number of women elected to the House increases from 16 to 28. Then in 1992, there is a substantial jump, when 211 women seek the nomination, 104 women are nominated, and 48 are elected to the House. Thereafter, the numbers do not drop back to their pre-1992 levels. By 1998, 118 women won their party's nomination and 56 were elected to the House.

Figure 1 clearly reveals a "step function" associated with the House elections of 1992. Women as candidates, successful or not, rose to a new level in 1992 and now fluctuate around that new level. Labeled the "Year of the Woman," the substantial increase in the number of women running and winning in 1992 has been attributed to a number of reasons (Cook, Thomas, and Wilcox 1994), but two factors from our data are noteworthy. First, there were an inordinate number of open seats due to the House banking scandal, and as we indicated earlier, open seats tend to stimulate more primary candidacies. Second, the election of 1992 marked the first election after reapportionment based on the 1990 census. This redistricting created strategic opportunities. There were new open seats available. In addition, in some instances incumbents had to run in districts with substantially redrawn lines. As a result, those in-

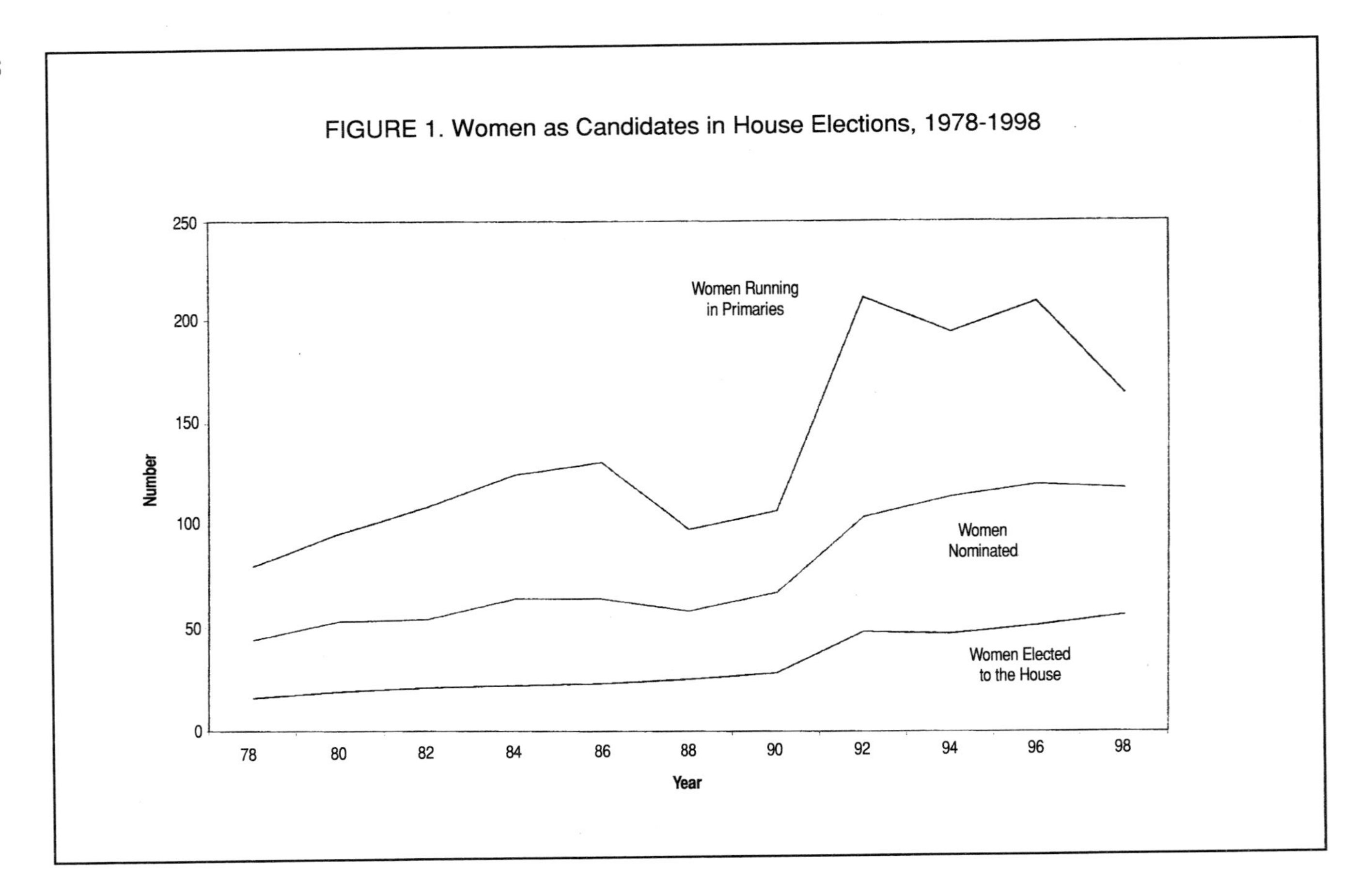

FIGURE 1. Women as Candidates in House Elections, 1978-1998

cumbents were perceived as more vulnerable than usual, which induced more candidates to enter the race.

While the trends depicted in Figure 1 represent general trends regarding the emergence of women candidates, differences between the parties can also be explored to determine whether the apparent "pipeline effect" is a general phenomenon or is partisan-based. Figure 2 presents the number of Democratic and Republican women who won their party's nomination for the elections from 1978 to 1998. Prior to 1988, there were negligible differences between the parties in the number of women winning their primaries and the Democratic and Republican nominations. During this time period, the greatest difference between the parties occurred in 1984 when 36 women won the Republican nomination and 28 women secured the Democratic nomination.

A disparity develops, however, in 1988, with 34 female nominees among the Democrats and 26 female nominees among the Republicans. This disparity systematically widens over time, reaching a peak in 1996 when 73 women won the Democratic nomination as opposed to 45 women in the Republican ranks. The implication is that, from the perspective of nomination politics, the Year of the Woman in 1992 was clearly a Democratic phenomenon. More generally, while the number of women winning the nomination for a House seat increased through 1988, this increase was primarily attributable to the Democratic Party.

A similar pattern is apparent when we back up a step in the process, and consider the number of women running in primaries. Figure 3 presents the *proportions* of Democrat and Republican women running for their respective party's nomination.[4] As with the data on nominations, there are negligible differences in the early part of the series. From 1978 to 1986, the proportions of women seeking the nomination for the House are nearly identical. A gender gap develops, however, in 1988 and persists through the 1990s. Both proportions display an upward trend, but this trend is more pronounced among the Democrats, peaking in 1996 when women aspirants comprised 17.3% (131 of 755) of Democratic Party primary candidates, compared to only 9.9% (78 of 790) within the Republican Party. In 1996, the Democrats attracted almost 40% more women candidates than the Republicans.

This partisan-based gender gap is particularly evident when examining open seat primaries. While the numbers of Democratic and Republican women running in primaries generally trend together until 1986, the disparity between the two parties is substantial in the elections of 1988, 1990, and 1992, with Democratic women candidates outnumbering Republicans almost three to one. In 1994, however, the proportion of

FIGURE 2. Women as Nominees for the House of Representatives, Democrat vs. Republican, 1978-1998

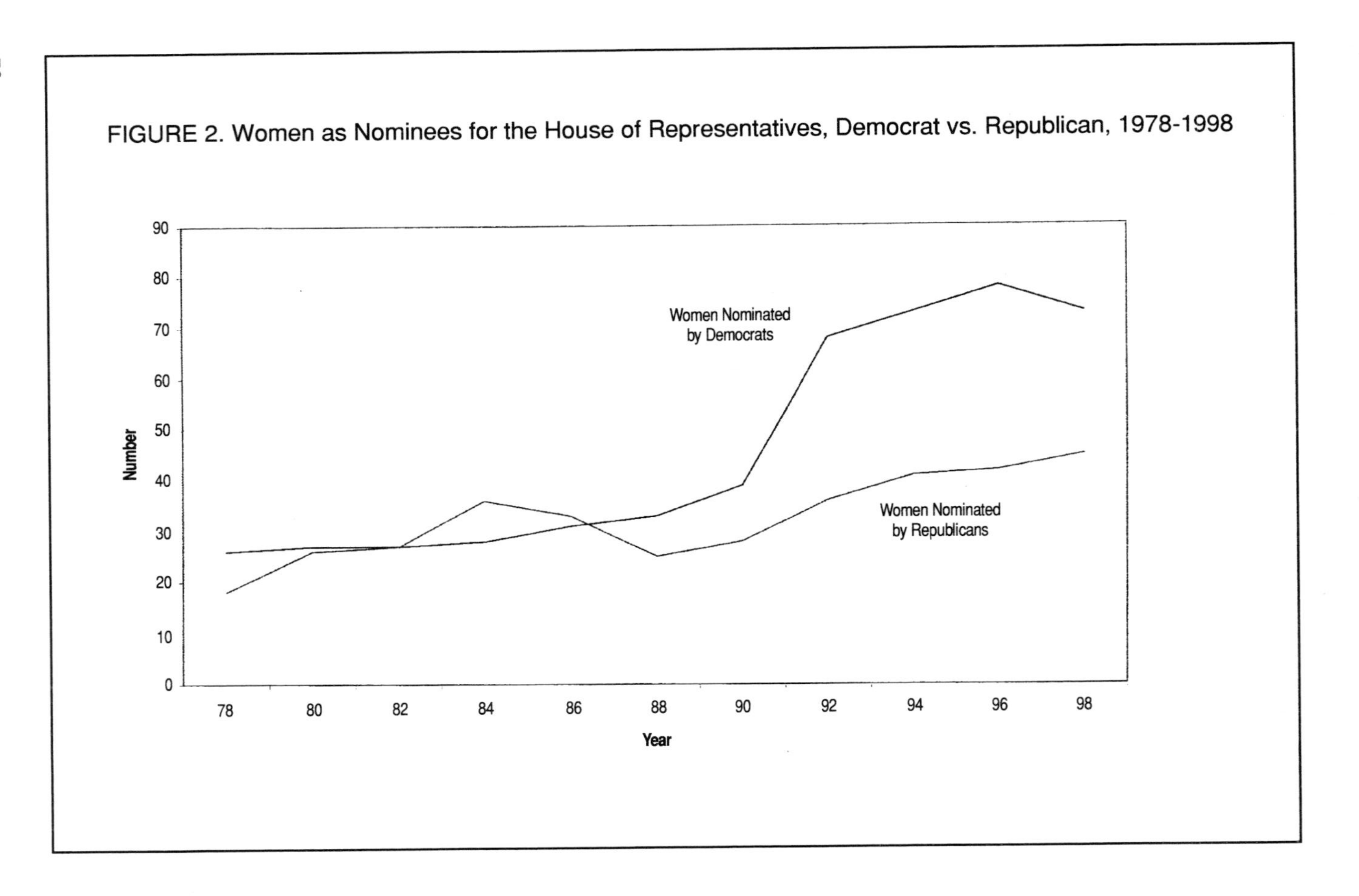

FIGURE 3. Women as a Proportion of All Candidates Running for Nomination to the U.S. House of Representatives, Democrat vs. Republican, 1978-1998

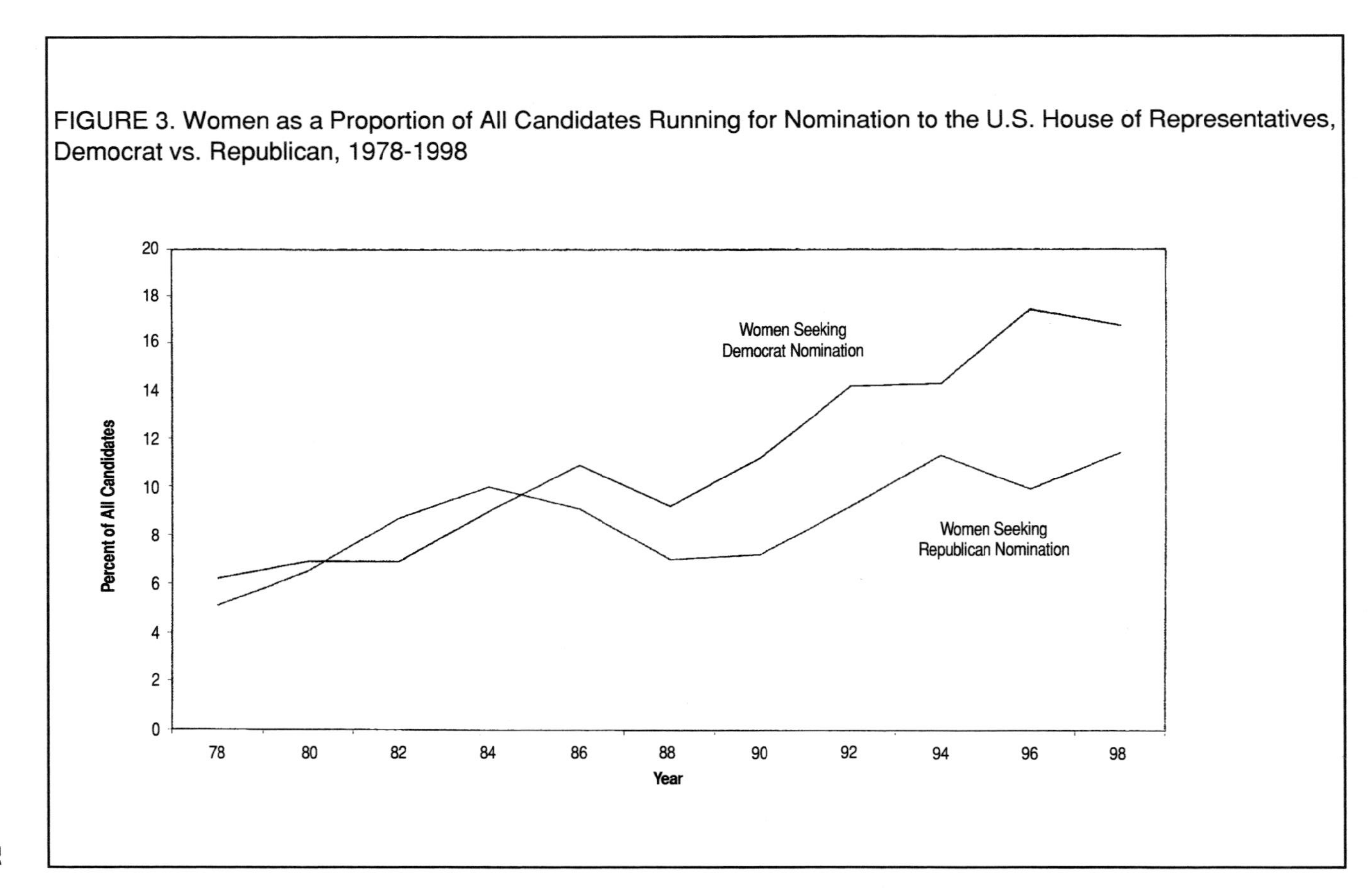

women seeking the Democratic nomination in open districts dropped from 20.2% to 14.8%, temporarily closing the gap between the parties during this election cycle. However, the disparity between the parties reappeared in the primary elections of 1996 and 1998.

The patterns displayed in Figures 2 and 3 are strikingly similar. Beginning in 1988, the growing number of women entering the electoral arena was disproportionately a Democratic phenomenon. Thus, we conclude that the data support Hypothesis 1, but add the proviso that there is a party-based difference in the size of those increases.[5]

Our second hypothesis is grounded upon the expectation that the pattern of entry for women challengers will vary according to the incumbency status of the district. To test this hypothesis, we isolated those elections in which women faced either a male incumbent or a male opponent in an open district.[6] These elections were then divided into three categories: safe male incumbents, marginal male incumbents, and open districts.[7] For each category, we calculated the proportion of women who sought the nomination, won the nomination, and won the general election. The results are displayed in Table 2.

The results support Hypothesis 2. In each row of the table, there is a pattern of growth across the categories of incumbency.[8] The proportion of women running in a primary increases from 6.7% in safe districts to 12.1% in open districts, while the proportion of women winning the nomination increases from 9.6% in safe districts to 23.3% in open districts. The results pertaining to the female "victory rate" are most dramatic. The proportion of women winning the general election increases from 2.2% in safe districts to 14.3% in marginal districts and then to 43.1% in open districts.[9] The results demonstrate that there is a strategic element in the emergence of women as candidates for the House of Representatives. The entry of women into the electoral arena is based, at least in part, on the probability of success.

Our remaining propositions, Hypotheses 3 and 4, pertain to the relationship between incumbency and gender. Essentially, given the advantages of holding a House seat, we offered the twin propositions that women will do very well once they become incumbents, but they will do poorly as challengers. Table 3 is constructed to evaluate these expectations and displays the incumbent "victory rates" for four combinations of gender and incumbency: male incumbents facing male challengers (cell A), male incumbents facing female challengers (cell B), female incumbents facing male challengers (cell C), and female incumbents facing female challengers (cell D). In each case, the challenger victory rate is simply the result of subtracting the incumbent victory rate from 100.

TABLE 2. Gender, Incumbency, and Strategic Behavior. Women as Challengers in Elections for the House of Representatives, 1978-1998

Category	Districts with Safe Male Incumbents Seeking Reelection	Districts with Marginal Male Incumbents Seeking Reelection	Open Districts in Which One Party Nominates a Male
Women as a Proportion of All Candidates Seeking the Nomination	6.7% (613/9071)	7.6% (143/1872)	12.1% (397/3291)
Women as a Proportion of Those Winning the Nomination	9.5% (321/3378)	12.4% (71/574)	21.7% (110/508)
Women as a Proportion of Those Winning the General Election	2.2% (7/321)	14.1% (10/71)	43.6% (48/110)

Each row of the table is based upon a 2 x 3 cross-tabulation. The chi-square statistic associated with the cross-tabulations are: 91.9 for women as a proportion of all candidates seeking the nomination, 66.1 for women as a proportion of all nominees, and 125.0 for the female victory rate in general elections. All are statistically significant [$p < .01$].

Table 3 clearly supports our expectations. In fact, the victory rates presented in Table 3 are indistinguishable from one another.[10] Female challengers fare quite poorly. They lose to male incumbents 95.6% of the time. They also lose to female incumbents 93.2% of the time (compare cells B and D). In addition, the rates for female challengers do not statistically differ from the track record of male challengers (compare cells A and B as well as cells C and D). Male challengers lose to male incumbents in 94.4% of these elections, and they lose to female incumbents in 94.6% of these elections.

As incumbents, women win reelection at rates that are indistinguishable from their male counterparts (compare cells A and C as well as cells B and D). Female incumbents won 94.6% of their contests facing a male challenger and 93.2% of their contests facing a female challenger. Overall, then, the results presented in Table 3 are clear. Male and female incumbents are equally successful in winning reelection; male and female challengers are equally unsuccessful in unseating an incumbent. As such, in general elections for the U.S. House, incumbency clearly trumps gender.

CONCLUSION

The remarkably slow integration of women into Congress has been well noted by scholars, women's activists, and the media. While there

TABLE 3. Incumbent Victory Rates, by Gender, in Elections for the U.S. House of Representatives, 1978-1998

Gender and Incumbency	Challenger Is Male	Challenger Is Female
	A	B
Incumbent Is Male	94.4% (2755/2917)	95.6% (376/393)
	C	D
Incumbent Is Female	94.6% (209/221)	93.2% (41/44)

The cells present the proportion of victories won by incumbents.

are numerous explanations, our understanding of this slow pace was limited by a lack of complete longitudinal data on the three-step process of winning a seat in the House of Representatives. Our initial examination of these data leads to several conclusions regarding incumbency. First, although there are general upward trends in the number of women seeking the nomination for a congressional seat, winning the nomination, and winning election to Congress, these trends are neither uniform nor general. There is a distinct gender gap between the Democratic and Republican parties. The growth of the presence of women in the electoral arena is disproportionately a Democratic phenomenon, at least since 1988, when women have made the most significant advances. Second, women are strategic in their decisions regarding whether or not they will run. In other words, the likelihood of success influences the decision to become a candidate. Women are far more likely to run in districts with an open seat than they are in districts where they would face a safe incumbent. This implies that the number of women entering the House depends upon the political cycle of redistricting or unanticipated events and "crises" (e.g., the House banking scandal) which induce incumbents to retire. Thus, the power of incumbency serves as a dampening effect, creating a political glass ceiling in the American electoral arena.

AUTHOR NOTE

We would like to thank our research assistants, Lindsay Abbate, Kristi Katsanis, Emily Katt, Elizabeth Myers, Steve Schulte, Jennifer Sumrall, and Brenda Tutt.

NOTES

1. In gathering these data, there are several special cases. The states of Connecticut, Utah, and Virginia employ a mixed system of conventions and primaries to nominate their congressional candidates. The nominating conventions are held first, with primaries scheduled only if there is a significant challenge to the designated convention nominee. In instances where there is no primary, we coded the gender of the nominees only because the number of candidates seeking the nomination at the convention is unknown.

Louisiana is yet another special case. The state employs an open primary system in which candidates, regardless of party, run in a single primary. If a candidate wins an absolute majority of the primary vote, the candidate is elected to the House and there is no general election. For Louisiana, we coded the number of Democrats and Republicans (women and total) running in the initial primary. In instances where there was a general election, we followed the same conventions used with other states, noting, of course, instances in which the general election involved two candidates from the same party.

Finally, there are states that have a primary run-off system. In these states, a candidate must win an absolute majority of the primary vote to obtain the party nomination. If no candidate wins a majority, there is a run-off primary between the top two finishers. The winner of the primary then becomes the party nominee. Our coding records the number of candidates (women and total) in the initial primary and the gender of the ultimate nominees.

2. The inordinately large number of retirements in 1992 can be attributed, in part, to the House banking scandal. Of the incumbents who wrote 100 or more overdrafts, 12 retired prior to the 1992 election. See the *1992 Congressional Quarterly Almanac,* "Wave of Diversity Spared Many Incumbents," p. 17-A.

3. The data on women running in party primaries excludes those congressional districts where nominees are chosen at a party convention.

4. Proportions are used in this instance because, unlike the total number of nominations (870) or House seats (435), the total number of candidates varies from election to election. As noted earlier, this number varies quite strongly with the number of open seats. Failure to "control" for the total number of candidates could be misleading (e.g., the case where the number of men and women both decline from one election to the next).

5. To confirm whether these differences between the parties are statistically meaningful, we performed the following test. First, we divided the elections into two periods, 1978-1986 and 1988-1998. Second, for each time period, we calculated the Democratic and Republican proportions of women who won their party's nomination, ran in the primary, and ran in primaries in open districts. Third, for each Democratic-Republican comparison in each period, we performed a difference of proportions test. The results were straightforward and unambiguous. Between 1978 and 1986, there are no statistically significant differences between the parties. The proportions of women running and winning the party nominations are indistinguishable. However, when the proportions for the 1988-1998 period are examined, party differences appear. There is a disparity of 5.6 points in the proportion of women winning the nomination, a 4.4 difference in the proportion of women entering primaries, and a 9-point gap in the special case of open districts, all of which are statistically significant. Although the

proportion of women in each category increases for both parties, the increases for the Democrats are more sizable and produce a measurable gender gap.

6. The case of a female incumbent facing a female challenger is not considered in testing Hypotheses 3 and 4. In our data, there are only eight elections in which a woman faced another woman in an open district.

7. In this analysis, we rely upon the conventional definition of safe and marginal districts (see, for example, Fiorina 1989). A marginal district is one in which the incumbent wins less than 55% of the two-party vote.

8. We also examined whether there were party-based differences in the proportion of women running, winning the nomination, or winning the general election. These differences were small, and none was statistically significant.

9. Each row of Table 2 is condensed from an individual 2×3 crosstabulation. For example, row 3 of the table is based on a crosstabulation of the election outcome (win or lose) by the incumbency status of the district. Thus, for each row of Table 2, we can calculate a statistic, chi-square, that provides a test of whether the pattern across the incumbency categories differs significantly from what is expected by chance. In each instance, the chi-square value is statistically significant and allows us to conclude that the relationship specified in the hypothesis is supported by the data.

10. This discussion is based upon the following statistical tests. Given the four cells, there are six paired comparisons (cell A vs. cell B), (cell C vs. cell D), (cell A vs. cell C), (cell B vs. cell D), (cell A vs. cell D), and (cell B vs. cell C). For each of the comparisons, we tested whether the *difference* in the victory rates was significantly different from zero. In every instance, the difference in victory rates was indistinguishable from zero.

REFERENCES

Bernstein, Robert. 1997. "Might Women Now Have the Edge? Open-Seat House Primaries." *Women & Politics* 17(2): 1-26.

Burrell, Barbara. 1992. "Women Candidates in Open-Seat Primaries for the U.S. House, 1968-1990." *Legislative Studies Quarterly* 17: 493-508.

Burrell, Barbara. 1994. *A Woman's Place Is in the House: Campaigning for Congress in the Feminist Era*. Ann Arbor: University of Michigan Press.

Burrell, Barbara. 1998. "Campaign Finance: Women's Experience in the Modern Era." In *Women and Elective Office*, ed. Sue Thomas and Clyde Wilcox. New York: Oxford University Press.

Carroll, Susan. 1994. *Women as Candidates in American Politics*. Bloomington: Indiana University Press.

Carroll, Susan, and Wendy S. Strimling. 1983. *Women's Routes to Elective Office: A Comparison with Men*. New Brunswick, NJ: Center for the American Woman and Politics.

Center for American Women and Politics (CAWP). 2001. *Fact Sheet Summaries*. "Women in Elected Office 2001" New Brunswick, NJ: Center for the American Woman and Politics. http:// www.rci.rutgers.edu/~cawp/facts/cawpfs.html.

Cook, Elizabeth Adell. 1998. "Voter Reactions to Women Candidates." In *Women and Elective Office*, eds. Sue Thomas and Clyde Wilcox. New York: Oxford University Press.

Cook, Elizabeth Adell, Sue Thomas, and Clyde Wilcox. 1994. *The Year of the Woman: Myths and Reality*. Boulder: Westview Press.

Darcy, Robert, Susan Welch, and Janet Clark. 1994. *Women, Elections, and Representation*. 2nd ed. Lincoln: University of Nebraska Press.

Deber, Raisa. 1982. " 'The Fault, Dear Brutus': Women as Congressional Candidates in Pennsylvania." *Journal of Politics* 44 (2): 463-479.

Duerst-Lahti, Georgia. 1998. "The Bottleneck: Women Becoming Candidates." In *Women and Elective Office*, eds. Sue Thomas and Clyde Wilcox. New York: Oxford University Press.

Fiorina, Morris. 1989. *Congress: Keystone of the Washington Establishment*, 2nd ed. New Haven: Yale University Press.

Fowler, Linda, and Robert McClure. 1989. *Political Ambition*. New Haven: Yale University Press.

Fox, Richard, and Eric R.A.N. Smith. 1998. "The Role of Candidate Sex in Voter Decision-Making." *Political Psychology* 19: 405-419.

Fox, Richard. 1997. *Gender Dynamics in Congressional Elections*. Thousand Oaks, CA: Sage.

Gertzog, Irwin. 1984. *Congressional Women*. New York: Praeger Press.

Gertzog, Irwin, and Michele Simard. 1991. "Women and 'Hopeless' Congressional Candidacies: Nomination Frequency, 1916-1978." *American Politics Quarterly* 9: 449-66.

Green, Joanne Connor. 1998. "The Role of Gender in Open-Seat Elections for the U.S. House of Representatives: A District Level Test for a Differential Value for Campaign Resources." *Women & Politics* 19(3): 33-55.

Herrick, Rebekah. 1995. "A Reappraisal of the Quality of Women Candidates." *Women & Politics* 15: 25-38.

Herrick, Rebekah. 1996. "Is There a Gender Gap in the Value of Campaign Resources?" *American Politics Quarterly* 24(1): 68-80.

Herrnson, Paul S. 1998. *Congressional Elections: Campaigning at Home and in Washington*. Washington, DC: Congressional Quarterly Press.

Huddy, Leonie, and Nayda Terkildsen. 1993. "Gender Stereotypes and the Perception of Male and Female Candidates." *American Journal of Political Science* 37: 119-147.

Iyengar, Shanto et al. 1997. "Running as a Woman: Gender Stereotyping in Political Campaigns." In *Women, Media and Politics*, ed. Pippa Norris. New York: Oxford University Press.

Jacobson, Gary C. 1997. *The Politics of Congressional Elections*. 4th ed. New York: HarperCollins.

Jacobson, Gary C., and Samuel Kernell. 1981. *Strategy and Choice in Congressional Elections*. New Haven: Yale University Press.

Kahn, Kim Fridkin. 1994. "Does Gender Make a Difference? An Experimental Examination of Sex Stereotypes and Press Patterns in Statewide Campaigns." *American Journal of Political Science* 38: 162-195.

Kahn, Kim Fridkin. 1996. *The Political Consequences of Being a Woman*. New York: Columbia University Press.

Kahn, Kim Fridkin, and Ann Gordon. 1997. "How Women Campaign for the U.S. Senate." In *Women, Media and Politics*, ed. Pippa Norris. New York: Oxford University Press.

Mandel, Ruth. 1981. *In the Running: The New Woman Candidate*. New York: Ticknor and Fields.
McGlen, Nancy, and Karen O'Connor. 1998. *Women, Politics, and American Society*. 2nd ed. Upper Saddle River, NJ: Prentice Hall.
Norrander, Barbara, and Clyde Wilcox. 1998. "The Geography of Gender Power: Women in State Legislatures." In *Women and Elective Office,* eds. Sue Thomas and Clyde Wilcox. New York: Oxford University Press.
Ornstein, Norman, J., Thomas E. Mann, and Michael J. Malbin, eds. 1998. *Vital Statistics on Congress*. Washington, DC: Congressional Quarterly.
Rohde, David W. 1979. "Risk-Bearing and Progressive Ambition: The Case of the United States House of Representatives." *American Journal of Political Science* 23: 1-26.
Schlesinger, Joseph. 1966. *Ambition and Politics: Political Careers in the United States*. Chicago: Rand McNally.
Seltzer, Richard, Jody Newman, and Melissa Voorhees Leighton. 1997. *Sex as a Political Variable*. Boulder: Lynne Rienner.
Thompson, Seth, and Janie Steckenrider. 1997. "The Relative Irrelevance of Candidate Sex." *Women & Politics* 17: 71-92.
"Wave of Diversity Spared Many Incumbents." 1992. *Congressional Quarterly Almanac*. Washington, DC: Congressional Quarterly.
Whillock, Rita Kirk. 1991. *Political Empiricism: Communication Strategies in State and Regional Elections*. New York: Praeger Press.
Williams, Christine. 1990. "Women, Law and Politics: Recruitment Patterns in the Fifty States." *Women & Politics* 10(3): 103-23.
Williams, Leonard. 1998. "Gender, Political Advertising, and the 'Air Wars.' " In *Women and Elective Office,* eds. Sue Thomas and Clyde Wilcox. New York: Oxford University Press.
Witt, Linda, Karen Paget, and Glenna Matthews. 1995. *Running as a Woman: Gender and Power in American Politics*. New York: Free Press.

The Electoral Glass Ceiling? Gender, Viability, and the News in U.S. Senate Campaigns

Martha E. Kropf, University of Missouri-Kansas City
John A. Boiney, San Gabriel Valley Council of Governments

SUMMARY. Scholars such as Kahn and others have shown that the print news media have covered women candidates in ways likely to diminish their electoral viability. Those effects have yet to be verified in a non-experimentalsetting or extended to television. We offer non-experimental evidence of news-based effects for print news and television. We examine the effects of media coverage patterns by analyzing Senate races using the 1988-92 ANES Senate Election Study. Our results provide consistent support for the contention that news media coverage has disadvantaged women candidates in the eyes of voters. This work suggests a need for greater attention to research on broadcast news coverage of women candidates. *[Article copies available for a fee from The Haworth Document Delivery Service: 1-800-HAWORTH. E-mail address: <getinfo@haworthpressinc.com> Website: <http://www.HaworthPress.com>*

Since the Year of the Woman in 1992, several viable women candidates have run for national elective office. During the 2000 election cycle, Elizabeth Dole was initially viewed by many as a strong possible nominee for the Republican candidacy for President. Dole, however, pulled out of the race before the primary season even began.

[Haworth co-indexing entry note]: "The Electoral Glass Ceiling? Gender, Viability, and the News in U.S. Senate Campaigns." Kropf, Martha E., and John A. Boiney. Co-published simultaneously in *Women & Politics* (The Haworth Press, Inc.) Vol. 23, No. 1/2, 2001, pp. 79-103; and: *Women and Congress: Running, Winning, and Ruling* (ed: Karen O'Connor) The Haworth Press, Inc., 2001, pp. 79-103. Single or multiple copies of this article are available for a fee from The Haworth Document Delivery Service [1-800-HAWORTH, 9:00 a.m. - 5:00 p.m. (EST). E-mail address: getinfo@haworthpressinc.com].

While some scholars argue that women have been winning as frequently as men in races for higher office such as Congress (see Broder 1994), historically, women have enjoyed little success as candidates for the U.S. Senate. Of the 49 women who ran for the U.S. Senate between 1988-1998, only 14 were successful (CAWP 1998). One, Barbara Mikulski, defeated another woman. The advantages of incumbency for men may not solely account for this poor record, because many times women are quality challengers. In 1990, only one of the eight women who ran for the Senate won, despite the existence of challengers such as Pat Saiki of Hawaii, Claudine Schneider of Rhode Island, and Lynn Martin of Illinois. All were prominent Republicans who had served in the U.S. House.[1] Literature on Senate campaigns often tries to explain why Senate incumbents are more likely to lose than House incumbents. This paper asks why it is that women Senate candidates, who have not necessarily been incumbents but who are often quality challengers, cannot often win.

Puzzled by the poor electoral performance of women Senate candidates, scholars have proposed and tested a variety of explanations. Evidence demonstrates that the most obvious explanation, incumbency, cannot *completely* explain women's poor success in vying for office (Krasno 1994; Westlye 1991). Other factors that might help fill the explanatory gaps have generated thoroughly mixed evidence. Some scholars have argued that women may lack the necessary political resources to mount a viable campaign (Epstein 1981; Gertzog 1979), or that those resources may have a more powerful effect for men than for women (Herrick 1996). Others have shown that women do have the money to mount a campaign. In recent elections, women have surpassed male candidates in amounts of money raised, disbursed, and in early money raised (Burrell 1994; see also Darcy, Welch, and Clark 1994; Uhlaner and Schlozman 1986). Other evidence has indicated that money has helped women more than men (Burrell 1985). Furthermore, women's groups have mounted campaigns to target more and earlier money toward the campaigns of women (Burrell 1994; Nelson 1994).

Another explanation for the poor electoral showing of women in the Senate may be that women are victims of voter sex stereotyping; that women do not possess the "traits" or "characteristics" necessary to hold political office (Anderson and Alexander 1993; Bowman 1984; Huddy and Terkildsen 1993a, 1993b; Sapiro 1981-82). The weight of evidence suggests that voters do employ stereotypes, especially when they lack adequate information about a candidate (Alexander and Anderson 1993; Conover 1981; Kahn 1996; Leeper 1991). However, stereotypes can benefit women, because many of the stereotyped qualities are ones which people tend to value in candidates, such as an outsider status and honesty (Burrell 1994; Kahn 1996). This was especially true in the elections from 1988-92, the ones considered in this analysis.

One of the more promising areas of research is how news media coverage affects electoral performance. Kahn (1996, 1994a, 1994b, 1993, 1992) and Kahn and Goldenberg (1991) have shown that women candidates receive less and poorer quality coverage in the print media. In an experimental setting, Kahn demonstrated that women are disadvantaged by this coverage. Kahn and Goldenberg (1991) contend the results of their study indicate that patterns of press coverage are an obstacle for women running for the Senate. They hypothesize that if their results are correct, voters will be less likely to be able to recognize and rate women Senate candidates and that voters will use perceived viability when rating women Senate candidates.

At the root of each of these explanations for women's poorer performance is the amount and quality of information that voters have about women running for office. On the campaign side, the money women spend and the media attention given to them will affect this level of information. On the voter side, the amount of time the voter spends watching and reading news, as well as the stereotypes he or she may already hold about women, will affect the level and type of information voters ultimately have about a woman candidate. This paper connects the two to show that even those who watch the most television news and read the paper the most are less likely to be able to recognize and rate a woman than a man candidate. As we show, a woman's electoral viability depends critically on a voter's ability to recognize her name, as well as a voter's ability to identify things he or she likes about the candidate.

This paper, which tests Kahn and Goldenberg's hypothesis–in a nonexperimental setting–can help determine whether the media significantly disadvantages female candidates relative to their male counterparts. Furthermore, there is as yet no evidence regarding the television news coverage of women candidates. We look for evidence of sex-specific effects from news media exposure–both print and broadcast–using individual-level data from the 1988-92 American National Election Study (ANES) Senate Election Study. As the United States moves into another electoral cycle, it is important to analyze and understand whether voters are exposed to television and newspaper coverage about women candidates, and whether this exposure helps or hinders women candidates for higher office.

FACTORS AFFECTING ELECTORAL PERFORMANCE

We are interested in the electoral viability of women candidates. A minimum precondition to viability is simple name recognition. Voters are unlikely to pull the lever for someone whose name they do not recognize (Abramowitz 1980, 1975; Goldenberg and Traugott, 1987b; Hinckley 1980; Mann and Wolfinger 1980; Westlye 1991). At higher electoral levels such as the U.S. Senate, name recognition may be achieved readily by many candidates (Krasno 1994; Westlye 1991). Remaining viable thus demands that voters not only know a candidate's name, but that they also possess a reasonably well-developed set of favorable cognitions about him or her. A candidate unable to become known or to foster favorable impressions among voters is unlikely to attract significant support.

Women candidates are very likely to begin at a disadvantage in terms of name recognition and impression formation simply because they are rarely incumbents. Thus, they will be unable to obtain attention for the positions they take on issues or legislation, advertise themselves with the resources accorded to office holders, or claim credit for the kinds of particularized benefits that grateful constituents will remember (Cain, Ferejohn, and Fiorina 1987; Fiorina 1989; Mayhew 1974).

However, Senate races may well turn on factors other than incumbency, because Senate challengers tend to be high quality candidates, i.e., with experience, money and visibility (Abramowitz 1980; Abramowitz and Segal 1992; Goldenberg and Traugott 1987a; Westlye 1991). In analyzing all Senate challengers in 1988, Squire (1992) found that higher quality challengers–those who had held higher political office–were more likely to get votes than lower quality challengers. Women candidates for Senate, though likely to be challengers, nonetheless may well have the resources and background to make the race intense and match the incumbent's level of recognition.

Of course, being a quality challenger may be insufficient, and the experiences of Saiki, Schneider, and Martin in 1990 suggest this may be especially true for women. Though possessing the backgrounds that should have made them viable, each quickly fell far behind the incumbent and, by fall, both their party and the media had written them off, suggesting their experiences may have been different than other–male–challengers.

Given the importance of mass media to political campaigns, an explanation for women's electoral viability may be sought in the patterns of news media coverage of women candidates. The news media have repeatedly been shown to influence (a) citizen's beliefs about the relative importance of political issues (Cohen 1963; Iyengar and Kinder 1987); (b) citizen's definitions of political events (Gamson 1992; Iyengar 1991; Neuman, Just, and Crigler 1992); and (c) citizen's standards for evaluating political leaders (Iyengar and Kinder 1987; Krosnick and Kinder 1990). Iyengar and Kinder (1987) conducted experiments on the informing and priming effects of news coverage regarding candidates in the context of an ongoing congressional race. They found that subjects exposed to local news coverage were better able to identify the candidate's party affiliation, and had more to say about both candidates, than those with no news exposure.

Senate elections are an especially appropriate context for examining news media effects because earned media is such an integral part of any Senate campaign. Unlike most House contests, Senate campaigns attract a good deal of news attention. They are more likely to be competitive–due to quality of challengers, the amount of money spent, and the extent of paid media–and therefore more likely to be newsworthy (Hinckley 1980; Jacobson 1992; Westlye 1991). Journalists also regard the Senate as being more prestigious, and therefore worthy of more coverage (Fenno 1982; Goldenberg and Traugott 1987a). Thus, it is not surprising that Abramowitz (1980) and Abramowitz and Segal (1992) reported that voters had more "contact" (either visual or physical) with Senate candidates than with House candidates, in large part because of the influence of the news media.

Senate campaigners, recognizing both their need for mass mediated exposure (a grassroots campaign across an entire state is usually impractical) and the news organizations' inherent interest in them, will tailor their strategy to attract coverage. Such strategy can pay dividends. Goldenberg and Traugott (1987b) found that voters who watched or read more news were significantly more familiar with candidates. One should not expect this relationship to be different between men and women candidates, unless the quantity of news media coverage of the candidate is less. If the coverage of women candidates differs either quantitatively or qualitatively from that of men candidates, that difference is likely to have consequences for the electoral viability of those women candidates.

There is evidence that such differences in news media coverage do exist. In particular, scholars have shown that newspaper campaign coverage varies in sex-specific ways. Kahn and Goldenberg (1991) and Kahn (1996, 1994a, 1994b, 1993, 1992) consistently observe lower rates of coverage for women than men Senate candidates, even controlling for incumbency. Furthermore, Kahn and Goldenberg's content analytic study indicated that women Senate candidates between 1982 and 1986 not only received less news coverage, but (1) their coverage focused on viability rather than issues, and (2) the viability coverage was more negative for women than men. There is, as yet, no evidence that television news covers men and women candidates differently.

That this disparity in news coverage disadvantages women candidates has yet to be verified in a nonexperimental setting.[2] Further, the sex-specific effects of television coverage have not been analyzed at all in this context. We expect to observe that media do adversely affect the viability of women candidates relative to men candidates. Specifically, increased exposure to news should better enable respondents to recognize and form favorable impressions of any candidate (Goldenberg and Traugott 1987b). However, a voter who watches the news seven days a week should be able to recognize a candidate, to name something they like about the candidate, or to name several things they like about the candidate, as much for women as for men, unless there is some difference in news coverage, controlling for other relevant correlates of recognition.[3] Using data from the ANES Pooled Senate Election Study (1988-1992), we test the following hypotheses:

> H_1: Exposure to news will contribute less to a respondent's probability of recognizing a female candidate than to the probability of recognizing a male candidate.
>
> H_2: Exposure to news will contribute less to a respondent's probability of naming at least one thing liked about a female candidate than to the probability of naming at least one thing liked about a male candidate.
>
> H_3: Exposure to news will contribute less to overall favorability for a female candidate than to favorability for a male candidate.

METHODOLOGY

We test these hypotheses using the ANES pooled Senate Election Study (SES), 1988, 1990, 1992 (Miller et al. 1993). The sample is stratified to obtain responses from every state.[4] Pooling the data over three election cycles yields a sample size with enough statistical power to provide a sophisticated assessment of how candidate sex interacts with respondent news exposure and thus familiarity with the candidate. We analyze all the Senate races[5] involving a woman candidate during the

1988-1992 period (21 races).[6] The unit of analysis is the respondent: the total number surveyed in the states examined is 1,275–95 in 1988, 618 in 1990, and 562 in 1992. In this study, we analyze race-, candidate- and respondent-level variables and their effects on the ability of a respondent to recognize or form cognitions about a candidate. We estimate a series of regression models (both logistic and ordinary least squares [OLS], depending on the dependent variable) using the ANES pooled Senate data.[7]

Dependent Variables

The dependent variables in each hypothesis examine the factors that make a candidate a viable one. The first hypothesis examines the correlates of simple name recognition. A voter is unlikely to vote for someone whose name they do not recognize (Mann and Wolfinger 1980). Simple name recognition is assessed simply by asking respondents if they recognize the Senate candidate's name. However, it is imperative for candidates to make sure voters learn more about them than just their name. The voter must like the candidate. Therefore, in the second hypothesis, we assess the relationship between news exposure and simple ability to name at least one thing liked about a candidate, a slightly more stringent test of the information environment.

The final test is provided in the third hypothesis where we examine the correlates of the type of information the respondent possesses about a candidate. We weigh both the things the respondent offers they like and dislike about the candidates in creating an "overall favorability" scale. Here, we measure "overall favorability" by subtracting the total number of "dislikes" from the number of "likes" each respondent offered, creating an eleven-point favorability scale.[8] This variable does not so much measure the level of information an individual possesses about a candidate as the type (negative or positive).[9]

Controlling for relevant factors such as partisanship (and candidate spending and quality), one should not expect there to be differences between male and female candidates in these three dependent variables unless media coverage is different.

Independent Variables

Individual (Respondent) Level Variables

Media Exposure. Our theoretical interest rests with the possible impact of the media habits of the respondent, both print and television.

Thus, we utilize self-reported measures of television news viewing and newspaper reading per week.[10] This measure of news exposure has received criticism on the grounds that it does not differentiate among individual differences in the likelihood of news reception (Price and Zaller 1993). Price and Zaller argue that background political knowledge is the single best predictor of who will receive the news. Thus, along with level of education and interest in the campaign, we include a measure of political knowledge. This measure is an additive index of knowledge about the senator not up for reelection and the ideological stance of the two major political parties. We also control for partisanship–it is well-documented that individuals expose themselves selectively to information with which they agree (Backstrom and Hursh-Cesar 1981). Education, interest in political campaigns, political knowledge,[11] and partisanship must all be considered in a model that examines the effects of television and newspaper exposure, and indirectly the effects of television and newspaper coverage.

Race Specific Variables

Market Congruence/Fragmentation. We also employ a measure of the relative congruence of the television markets in a given state, which is a determinant of the amount of coverage the Senate race in each state receives. Stewart and Reynolds (1990) show that citizens are less likely to see candidates on television in states with more highly fragmented television markets. This, in turn, affects whether the respondent sees the female or male candidate (see also Campbell, Alford, and Henry 1984; Goldenberg and Traugott 1984). We adopt one of the two measures of market structure used by Stewart and Reynolds: news mix.[12] Based upon the overlap of television markets and state boundaries, this measure expresses for each respondent the proportion of television news that will be about the state. Respondents from states with a high news mix value (approaching 1.0) are assumed, all else equal, to have greater exposure to television news about their Senate race than respondents from states with a low news mix value. This measure is an important variable to consider when looking at respondent ability to recognize candidates across several different Senate races.

Year. Given that 1992 was reputed to be the Year of the Woman, we account for the possibility that women candidates running in 1992 might be better recognized or liked because they were a part of that presumed phenomenon. Women may have also received more news coverage during 1992. This is especially important if one is comparing the candidates across the years. A dummy variable is coded zero for 1988 and 1990, one for 1992.

Candidate Specific Variables

Campaign Spending. The impact of media exposure is placed in context by controlling for a number of factors likely to relate to respondents' abilities to recognize or evaluate candidates. Certain candidate variables are obviously important, such as campaign spending and candidate quality. The effects of candidate spending on the vote share is a subject open to debate (see Abramowitz and Segal 1992; Green and Krasno 1990; Herrnson 1995; Jacobson 1990, 1992; Krasno 1994). It seems reasonable to assume that the more a candidate spends on the campaign, the more likely the respondents are at least to recognize that candidate. This is buttressed by the finding of Abramowitz and Segal, who indicate that challenger spending was the most important factor affecting the outcomes of Senate elections (1992: 113).

Candidate spending also provides an important control variable, in that it proxies the amount of paid advertising the candidate used. Given our interest in news media impact, we need to separate the effects of paid media from that of earned media on viability. We include in the model the spending for both a candidate and his/her opponent, standardized by voting age population, and use the log of spending per voting age person to account for the diminishing marginal returns to spending.

Opponent Spending. Because of the fact that challenger spending is so important, we also include a measure of opponent spending. Furthermore, we cannot disregard the fact that much political advertising is comparative, and therefore the opponent's name may be mentioned several times, potentially having an effect on the ability of the candidate to become recognized.

Candidate Quality. It has been well-documented that incumbency is not as important to Senate races as it is to House races (Krasno 1994; Squire 1992; Squire and Smith 1996; Westlye 1991). Squire (1992) and Squire and Smith (1996) find that challenger quality has a significant effect on a respondent's personal and media contact with the candidate, whether a respondent could recognize or recall the candidate's name, number of "likes" a respondent could mention about a candidate, and the thermometer rating of the candidate. Modeling the measure employed by Squire, we include an index of candidate quality ranging from six (incumbent) to zero (no elective or appointive office, or no campaign management position).[13] While the women candidates in campaigns we studied conformed to the historically disadvantaged pattern, they did represent the full spectrum of quality: two of 21 were incumbents, 13 had some significant political experience, six had essentially no significant political resumé.

RESULTS

Tables 1, 2, and 3 present the relevant results for each aspect of viability. Each table presents the same model, estimated first for men candidates, then women candidates. We repeatedly observe evidence consistent with sex-specific news coverage working to the advantage of male candidates. Our evidence encompasses not only print news, consistent with the work of Kahn and others, but also television news.

Recognition

The models generate coefficients for each of our media exposure variables that are higher for men than for women candidates. One's level of exposure to a newspaper relates significantly to the likelihood of recognizing both women and men candidates. The self-report measure of television news exposure is not significantly related to likelihood of recognition for men or women candidates. Ironically, the more congruent a state's television markets, the less likely the respondent is to recognize the woman candidate. The news mix variable has no effect on the ability to recognize a man.[14] (See Table 1.) It is surprising that news mix is negatively related to recognition for women candidates. Interestingly, the states with the lowest values appear to affect this relationship; when one removes the state with the lowest value for news mix (Delaware), the coefficient for news mix is no longer statistically significant for women.[15]

The gap between men and women candidates regarding newspaper exposure can be interpreted as follows. As respondents move from the extreme of zero newspaper exposure to that of daily exposure, their probability of recognizing a male candidate increases by a factor of 3.15. For women candidates, the increase is by a factor of 1.83.[16]

While news media exposure works consistently to the disadvantage of women candidates relative to men, the interest in the campaign seems to go in the other direction. Interest in the campaign relates positively to likelihood of recognition for women candidates only. Zaller (1992) suggests that interest may play a mediating function between news impact

TABLE 1. Results of Logistic Regression for Recognition Likelihood–Female versus Male Senate Candidates

	Female Candidate		Male Candidate	
	Parameter	Odds Ratio	Parameter	Odds Ratio
Intercept	−1.83 (1.20)		−8.36 (1.06)	
Television	−.01 (.04)	.99	.02 (.06)	1.03
Newspaper	0.09* (0.04)	1.09	.16*** (.05)	1.18
News Mix	−1.40* (.54)	.25	−.86 (.87)	.42
Candidate Spending (log)	1.14*** (.12)	3.14	.42*** (.09)	1.52
Opponent Spending (log)	−.56*** (.15)	.57	.80*** (.19)	2.23
Candidate Quality	−.04 (.10)	.96	.48*** (.10)	1.61
Year	−.14 (.22)	.87	−.26 (.30)	.77
Same Party	.28 (.20)	1.32	−.20 (.25)	.82
Respondent Interest	0.26** (.08)	1.29	.12 (.10)	1.13
Respondent Education	.08 (.05)	1.13	.17** (.06)	1.18
Respondent Political Knowledge	.34*** (.09)	1.40	.20 (.11)	1.23
Model Fit	294.84		266.98	
Correct classifications	86.1%		89.9%	
n	1,123		1,103	

Coefficients are unstandardized. Standard errors given in parentheses. All probabilities reported for a 2-tailed test.
*** $p < .001$
** $p < .01$
* $p < .05$

and public opinion. Analysis reveals, however, that there is no interactive relationship between interest and either of the two news media measures. These findings for interest seem to indicate that a voter must simply have more interest in order to recognize a female candidate's name, but not a male. Respondent political knowledge and education are either significant or marginally significant for both male and female candidates.

Beyond the news media measures, we observe several interesting relationships. First, better candidate quality provides recognition benefits

TABLE 2. Results of Logistic Regression for Probability of "Likes" Mention–Female versus Male Senate Candidates

	Female Candidate		Male Candidate	
	Parameter	Odds Ratio	Parameter	Odds Ratio
Intercept	−4.93 (.62)		−6.63 (.69)	
Television	.02 (.03)	1.02	.13*** (.03)	1.14
Newspaper	.04 (.03)	1.04	.03 (.03)	1.04
News Mix	.31 (.35)	1.36	−.01 (.34)	.99
Candidate Spending (log)	.50*** (.09)	1.65	.42*** (.08)	1.52
Opponent Spending (log)	−.18* (.07)	.84	0.15* (.07)	1.17
Candidate Quality	.13* (.05)	1.13	.18** (.05)	1.20
Year	−.39* (.15)	.68	−.55** (.15)	.58
Same Party	.90*** (.14)	2.45	.53*** (.14)	1.70
Respondent Interest	.26*** (.06)	1.30	.18** (.06)	1.20
Respondent Education	.07* (.03)	1.07	.02 (.03)	1.02
Respondent Political Knowledge	.22** (.06)	1.25	.15* (.06)	1.17
Model Fit	259.70		232.04	
Correct classifications	76.6%		74.3%	
n	1,126		1,107	

Coefficients are unstandardized. Standard errors given in parentheses. All probabilities reported for a 2-tailed test.
***p < .001
**p < .01
*p < .05

for men, but not women. Women appear to enjoy some advantage in terms of their own spending; they seem to derive a bit more marginal benefit from their dollars than men do. However, their ability to become recognized is undermined, significantly, by their opponent's spending, while men are helped by opponent spending.[17] This finding may be partially due to the fact that women have not often been incumbents. An incumbent may be more likely to talk about his or her record than about the opponent. A challenger may be more likely to discuss and challenge

TABLE 3. Results of OLS Regression for Overall Favorability–Female versus Male Senate Candidates

	Female Candidate	**Male Candidate**
	Parameter	Parameter
Intercept	−.05 (.34)	−.70 (.37)
Television	.02 (.02)	.06** (.02)
Newspaper	.006 (.02)	−.007 (.02)
News Mix	.04 (.20)	−.02 (.24)
Candidate Spending (log)	.06 (.04)	.07 (.04)
Opponent Spending (log)	−.08 (.04)	.009 (.05)
Candidate Quality	.12*** (.03)	.08* (.03)
Year	−.22* (.09)	−.14 (.10)
Same Party	.55*** (.08)	.60*** (.09)
Respondent Interest	−.006 (.03)	.004 (.04)
Respondent Education	.02 (.02)	−.02 (.02)
Respondent Political Knowledge	−.02 .03	−.005 .04
Model Fit	0.11 (adj.)	.06 (adj.)
n	1,127	1,108

Coefficients are unstandardized. Standard errors given in parentheses. All probabilities reported for a 2-tailed test.
***p < .001
**p < .01
*p < .05

the record of the incumbent. This may afford the incumbent further name recognition. Further, perhaps females, believing their "outside" status is beneficial, spend more time comparing themselves to males, where males may not even mention their opponent. Finally, according to our evidence, the so-called Year of the Woman did not confer any benefits on women candidates.

"Likes" Mention

Most candidates, male or female, are recognized. But the step from recognizing a candidate's name to associating that name with some essentially positive cognition is a vital one if support for her or him is to follow. As with recognition, the separately estimated models indicate that women candidates tend to be disadvantaged relative to men candidates, but here, the difference is in broadcast news exposure (see Table 2). Newspaper reading does not play a role for men or women.[18]

The coefficient for respondent television news exposure is higher and statistically significant for men. Television news exposure does not enhance the ability of a respondent to name something they like about the female candidate. Thus, in the shift from zero to daily self-reported television news exposure, the likelihood of being able to mention at least one favorable comment about a male candidate more than doubles, increasing by a factor of 2.45. Market congruence has no significant relationship to the ability to name something liked about a candidate for either men or women candidates. Since there are so many people who recognize candidates, it is not necessarily surprising that there are differences between the model of recognition and the ability to name something liked about a candidate. A visual impression of the candidate could help cement an individual's cognitions about a candidate.

Other patterns observed with respect to recognition hold again for naming something liked about a candidate. Spending contributes significantly for both male and female candidates, but females are the only ones hurt significantly by opponent's spending, whereas males are helped. Respondent interest and political knowledge matter for both, but an edge is enjoyed by women candidates.[19] Respondent education matters for women but not for men.[20] Unlike the patterns for recognition, the probability of being able to name at least one positive thing about either candidate was affected by election year. However, the surprise here is that the sign of this parameter is negative, indicating that females and males both were significantly more likely to elicit at least one favorable mention in 1988 or 1990 than in 1992.

Overall Favorability

As "overall favorability" measures whether respondents possess positive or negative information about a candidate, and not the amount of information, the parameters are slightly different from the previous models. Interestingly, television exposure relates significantly to overall favorability for men candidates, but not at all for women candidates. Newspaper exposure bears no significant relationship to favorability for any candidate.

Women, again, are more disadvantaged by opponents' spending; a relationship is marginally significant (p = .0557 for a two-tailed test).[21]

This result is not surprising given the fact that much money has been spent on negative advertising, which has an effect on the number of negative things people may be able to say about a candidate. Not surprisingly, since this is not a test of the amount of information, education, or interest in the campaign,[22] and political knowledge had no effect on favorability, partisanship did for both men and women. Women had significantly higher favorability ratings in 1988 and 1990 than in 1992, the Year of the Woman, a finding which is consistent with both the recognition and the "likes" models. However, one change from the previous measures of viability is that candidate quality contributes significantly to favorability for both men and women candidates, and somewhat more substantially for women.

What Does It Mean? The Effect on the Vote

In order to assess the substantive meaning of our results, we regressed respondent vote on each of the measures of viability along with a series of controls: the log of candidate per capita spending, candidate quality, and partisanship. Those results, given in Table 4, support our expectations. Being of the same party as a given candidate, not surprisingly, seems the single most important correlate. However, each measure of viability also relates positively to vote. Recognition of the candidate is marginally significant ($p = 0.086$ for a two-tailed test). The ability to offer at least one favorable comment about a candidate appears to exert a substantial impact on voting. That parameter's odds ratio is second only to partisanship. Overall favorability also had a positive and significant effect on the probability of voting for a certain candidate. These findings indicate quite clearly that the ability of a candidate to become known to voters and inculcate in them a reasonably positive set of cognitions significantly enhances his or her chances of winning office.[23] Understanding the role of media exposure in developing these cognitions is vital.

CONCLUSION

When scholars observe a quality candidate such as Elizabeth Dole pull out of the presidential race, a natural question to ask is "What happened?" This paper suggests that the media play a role in the viability of women candidates. Questions concerning the electoral viability of women candidates are significant because of representation that women offer. Pitkin (1967) argues that when a group is excluded from the policy

TABLE 4. Results of Logistic Regression–Probability of Vote for Candidate

	Vote	
	parameter	odds ratio
Intercept	−3.49 (.40)	
Recognition	.52 (.24)	1.68
"Likes" Mention	.89* (.17)	2.44
Overall Favorability	.52* (.06)	1.68
Candidate Spending (log)	.11 (.06)	1.12
Candidate Quality	.23* (.04)	1.26
Same Party	1.91* (.14)	6.76
Model Fit	645.20	
Correct classifications	87.7%	
N	1,534	

Coefficients are unstandardized. Standard errors given in parentheses. All probabilities reported for a 2-tailed test.
*p < .001

making process, decisions may be skewed toward the ruling group–in this case, men. "Women's" issues may be marginalized. Studies show that women do "act for" and "stand for" other women. While there have been mixed results concerning whether women vote differently than men in the U.S. Congress (see Burrell 1994; Dolan 1997; Frankovic 1977; Leader 1977; Thomas 1994; Welch 1985), as the numbers of women grow, at least they may be more likely to stand up and speak about their experiences (Mezey 1994).

Our results, based upon data from campaigns between 1988 and 1992, which analyze the Senate races of 21 women candidates of varying partisanship and electoral quality, provide considerable support for the contention that news media coverage disadvantages women candidates. While we cannot discount the importance of incumbency, we have observed that the viability of the candidate often depends upon the candidate's gender. A respondent's media exposure, controlling for partisanship, education, political knowledge, and interest in the campaign, is related to ability to recognize a candidate, name something liked, or say positive things about that candidate. Our findings are consistent with Kahn's evidence of sex-specific print coverage that had electorally consequential effects. Here, increased respondent exposure to print coverage of campaigns helps voters to recognize and then to name something liked about candidates, but less so for female candidates. Moreover, extending beyond Kahn's evidence, we observe support for the expectation that television news exposure affects the viability of men and women candidates unequally. In particular, television news exposure increases the likelihood of mentioning something favorable about a male candidate. The same holds true for mentioning more positives than negatives. While the result for ability to name something liked about a candidate is mitigated somewhat by the respondent's interest in the campaign, the evidence does seem to indicate that female candidates may not receive the same benefit from news coverage as male candidates do.

We were inspired to pursue these questions by the work of Kahn and others who have tended to find evidence of sex-specific news coverage and its negative consequences for women candidates. Our findings are generally consistent with the research. Our additional evidence, regarding television news, tells much the same story. This is important because, up to this point, there has been no careful content analytic study of television news coverage of female candidates, in part because television coverage of Senate campaigns is relatively sparse compared to gubernatorial or certainly presidential races. Our work suggests that while less plentiful, television news treatment of Senate campaigns has consequences for female candidates at least as substantial as treatment by the press, and probably more substantial. This work suggests that a careful content analytic study of television coverage of women candidates is in order.

AUTHOR NOTE

The authors have been listed reverse alphabetically to reflect the fact that each bears full and equal responsibility for the manuscript. The authors wish to thank Dale Neuman (University of Missouri-Kansas City) for his insights. We also wish to thank Karen O'Connor (American University) and an anonymous reviewer for especially helpful comments.

NOTES

1. Lynn Martin (who ran for Senate in 1988) gained enough prominence in Republican circles to later serve as Secretary of Labor in the Bush Administration (1991-93).

2. In her series of articles and in her book, Kahn employs experimental evidence to demonstrate that candidates who received the coverage that female candidates received were viewed as less viable.

3. In their survey-based analysis, Darcy, Welch, and Clark (1994) observed no statistically significant difference between recognition of male and female candidates. However, they studied only House campaigns, where news media coverage is less consequential. Their data were limited to 1982 and they controlled only for type of race.

4. While it would have been interesting to extend this analysis to 1994 when nine women ran for the Senate (as well as 1996 and 1998), the ANES studies from these years were not stratified to obtain a sufficient sample size from every state. Therefore, some states had many more respondents than others, making a meaningful analysis of Senate elections difficult. See Westlye (1983, 1991) for a discussion of the importance of using stratified samples to understand the unique properties of Senate elections.

5. In addition to these Senate races, it also would have been interesting to analyze the effects of the media on gubernatorial races. However, Kahn (1995) notes that gubernatorial and Senate election coverage differs systematically. Our focus in this article is on Senate candidates primarily. A separate article could be written about women gubernatorial candidates.

6. Adding a sample of respondents from the male/male races (to increase the number of male challengers for comparison purposes) in the states in which female/male races took place does not significantly change the results of the study. Where there are differences, we note them.

7. The questions used to construct each measure are detailed in Appendix A.

8. We chose not to use thermometer measures because responses to such measures tend to cluster at one of several points on the 100-point scale, so that the instrumentation essentially collapses from something like an interval to an ordinal scale.

9. For example, if a respondent had one positive and one negative thing to say about a candidate, they would still have the same score as someone who had five positives and five negatives to say about the candidate.

10. We are aware of work (Brians and Wattenberg 1996; Hetherington 1996) that has captured news media exposure by combining self-report measures of news viewing/reading with self-reported interest in campaigns. While it is important to account for campaign interest, for our purposes it is even more important to separate interest from news exposure, because we are interested in isolating the effects of sex-specific news treatment, should it exist. To blend interest and exposure would blunt our ability to note the effects of news style and substance on female candidates. However, an interactive variable is tested of news media exposure and attention to the campaign in each of the models. It is statistically significant only in the model, which predicts the ability to name something liked about a candidate.

11. Several of the questions differ over the three years of the SES study, making valid (and reliable) measures of political knowledge for all three years difficult. Correctly identifying the political parties by ideology appears in all three years of the study, as well as ability to name the sitting Senator. These questions are not expected to measure significantly different concepts over the three years in which they are asked. See Appendix A for the building of this knowledge scale.

12. We used slightly different numbers than Stewart and Reynolds for our news mix measure, because we calculated them based on Nielsen's "Designated Market Areas" rather than Arbitron's "Areas of Dominant Influence." While these two measures of television markets are only slightly different (see *Spot Television Rates and Data* 1993), one major difference is that Hawaii is included in the listing of DMAs, but not in the listing of ADIs. This is key because two of the races including women during the time period 1988-92 took place in Hawaii.

13. Squire found that this measure of candidate quality produced essentially the same results in his analysis as one that also factored in the percentage of the state population which an office covered. For example, a representative in a state with one House district campaigns to the same population as a Senator in that state (see Squire 1992, 249). In order to confirm that our candidate quality results were valid, we ran a separate analysis where non-incumbents were separated out (challengers and open seat candidates). The results are largely the same.

14. In a model including a selection of men/men races, news mix is positive and significant for men. This suggests that men have even more of an advantage than women, for many of these races included challenger males.

15. In two of the three states with the lowest news mix values, Delaware and Wyoming, the state has some overlap from a media market located in another state that also had a Senate race involving a woman (here Philadelphia, PA, and Denver, CO). In fact, two of the three counties in Delaware are covered by the Philadelphia market. The races in Pennsylvania and Colorado appeared to be much more competitive than those in Delaware and Wyoming (looking only at the results of the race). We theorize the anomalous finding on the news mix variable may have occurred because people may have known there was a woman running for Senate, but not known who it was. They may have thought they recognized the name of the candidate (slightly inflating the recognition variable). This would have caused a negative finding in the news mix variable. The respondents would not really know any detail about the candidate when asked to name something they liked or disliked because they were thinking about the wrong candidate (accounting for the differing results on those models). More research needs to be conducted for a fuller understanding of this phenomenon.

16. Difference in probability for continuous variables is determined by multiplying the difference between values at the extremes (7.0-0.0) by the logit coefficient (0.15 or 0.09) and taking the anti-logarithm of the product. The extreme values are used for illustrative purposes.

17. Ironically, when one includes male/male races in the sample, opponent spending no longer has an effect on the recognition of male candidates.

18. In a model including a selection of male/male races, the newspaper coefficient is positive and significant for men.

19. A test for the interaction between interest and television viewing reveals the interaction is negative and significant in predicting ability to name something liked about a candidate. This suggests that the more attention one pays to the campaign, the less important television is in developing the ability to name something liked about a candidate (male or female). Interestingly, when one controls for this interactive variable (TV*Interest), the coefficient for television becomes positive and significant for women, but the television coefficient is still less than that of men ($\beta m = .28$, $\beta w = .18$). This is consistent with Zaller's (1992) hypothesis that interest plays a mediating role between news impact and public opinion. It is not surprising that this result differs from the recognition result, since recognition requires much less information than ability to name something liked about a candidate.

20. In a model which includes a selection of male/male races, education does matter for men, with a significance level of $p = 0.0001$.

21. In a model including a selection of male/male races (fewer incumbents), opponent spending is negative and significant for men.

22. There was no significant interaction effect between television exposure and interest or newspaper reading and interest.

23. These results are not different for men and women candidates. We created two separate models for men and women, and found that with the exception of candidate recognition that is insignificant for men, and spending, which is insignificant for women, the models are largely the same. Information about the candidates is important no matter what the gender of the candidate.

REFERENCES

Abramowitz, Alan I. 1975. "Name Familiarity, Reputation and the Incumbency Effect in a Congressional Election." *Western Political Quarterly* 28: 668-684.

Abramowitz, Alan I. 1980. "A Comparison of Voting for U.S. Senators and Representatives in 1978." *American Political Science Review* 74: 633-640.

Abramowitz, Alan I., and Jeffrey A. Segal. 1992. *Senate Elections*. Ann Arbor: University of Michigan Press.

Alexander, Deborah, and Kristi Anderson. 1993. "Gender as a Factor in the Attribution of Leadership Traits." *Political Research Quarterly* 46: 527-545.

Backstrom, Charles H., and Gerald Hursh-Cesar. 1981. *Survey Research*. 2nd ed. New York: Macmillan.

Bowman, Ann O'M. 1984. "Physical Attractiveness and Electability: Looks and Votes." *Women & Politics* 4: 55-65.

Brians, Craig L., and Martin P. Wattenberg. 1996. "Campaign Issue Knowledge and Salience: Comparing Reception from TV Commercials, TV News, and Newspapers." *American Journal of Political Science* 40: 172-193.

Broder, David.1994. "Key to Women's Political Parity: Running." *Washington Post* 8 September.

Burrell, Barbara C. 1985. "Women's and Men's Campaigns for the U.S. House of Representatives, 1972-1982: A Financial Gap?" *American Politics Quarterly* 13: 251-272.

Burrell, Barbara C. 1994. *A Woman's Place Is in the House: Campaigning for Congress in the Feminist Era*. Ann Arbor: University of Michigan Press.

Cain, Bruce E., John A. Ferejohn, and Morris P. Fiorina. 1987. *The Personal Vote: Constituency Service and Electoral Independence*. Cambridge: Harvard University Press.

Campbell, James E., John R. Alford, and Keith Henry. 1984. "Television Markets and Congressional Elections." *Legislative Studies Quarterly* 9: 665-678.

Center for American Women and Politics (CAWP). 1998. "Women Candidates for Congress 1974-1998: Party and Seat Summaries for Major Party Nominees." CAWP Fact Sheet available at www.rci.rutgers.edu/~cawp/Facts.html.

Cohen, Bernard. 1963. *The Press and Foreign Policy*. Princeton: Princeton University Press.

Conover, Pamela Johnston. 1981. "Political Cues and the Perception of Candidates." *American Politics Quarterly* 9: 427-448.

Darcy, Robert, Susan Welch, and Janet Clark. 1994. *Women, Elections and Representation*. 2nd ed. Lincoln: University of Nebraska Press.

Dolan, Julie. 1997. "Support for Women's Interests in the 103rd Congress: The Distinct Impact of Congressional Women." *Women & Politics* 18: 81-94.

Epstein, C.F. 1981. "Women and Power: The Role of Women in Politics in the United States." In *Access to Power: Cross-national Studies of Women and Elites*, eds. C.F. Epstein and R.L. Closer. Boston: Allen and Unwin.

Fenno, Richard. 1982. *The United States Senate: A Bicameral Perspective*. Washington, DC: American Enterprise Institute.

Fiorina, Morris P. 1989. *Congress: Keystone of the Washington Establishment*. 2nd ed. New Haven: Yale University Press.

Frankovic, Kathleen A. 1977. "Sex and Voting in the U.S. House of Representatives, 1961-1975." *American Politics Quarterly* 5: 315-352.

Gamson, William A. 1992. *Talking Politics*. New York: Cambridge University Press.

Gertzog, I. 1979. "Changing Patterns of Female Recruitment to the U.S. House of Representatives." *Legislative Studies Quarterly* 4: 429-445.

Goldenberg, Edie N., and Michael W. Traugott. 1987a. "Mass Media in U.S. Congressional Elections." *Legislative Studies Quarterly* 12: 317-339.

Goldenberg, Edie N., and Michael W. Traugott. 1987b. "Mass Media Effects on Recognizing and Rating Candidates in U.S. Senate Elections." In *Campaigns in the News: Mass Media and Congressional Elections*, ed. Jans P. Vermeer. Westport: Greenwood Press.

Green, Donald P., and Jonathan S. Krasno. 1990. "Rebuttal to Jacobson's 'New Evidence for Old Arguments.'" *American Journal of Political Science* 34: 363-372.

Herrick, Rebekah. 1996. "Is There a Gender Gap in the Value of Campaign Resources?" *American Politics Quarterly* 24: 68-80.

Herrnson, Paul. 1995. *Congressional Elections: Campaigning at Home and in Washington*. Washington, DC: Congressional Quarterly.

Hetherington, Marc J. 1996. "The Media's Role in Forming Voters' National Economic Evaluations in 1992." *American Journal of Political Science* 40: 372-395.

Hinckley, Barbara. 1980. "The American Voter in Congressional Elections." *American Political Science Review* 74: 641-650.

Huddy, Leonie, and Nayda Terkildsen. 1993a. "The Consequences of Gender Stereotypes for Women Candidates at Different Levels and Types of Office." *Political Research Quarterly* 46: 503-525.

Huddy, Leonie, and Nayda Terkildsen. 1993b. "Gender Stereotypes and the Perception of Male and Female Candidates." *American Journal of Political Science* 37: 119-147.

Iyengar, Shanto. 1991. *Is Anyone Responsible? How Television Frames Political Issues*. Chicago: University of Chicago Press.

Iyengar, Shanto, and Donald R. Kinder. 1987. *News That Matters: Television and American Public Opinion*. Chicago: University of Chicago Press.

Jacobson, Gary C. 1990. "The Effects of Candidate Spending in House Elections: New Evidence for Old Arguments." *American Journal of Political Science* 34: 334-362.

Jacobson, Gary C. 1992. *The Politics of Congressional Elections*. 3rd ed. New York: HarperCollins.

Kahn, Kim Fridkin. 1992. "Does Being Male Help? An Investigation of the Effects of Candidate Gender and Campaign Coverage on the Evaluation of U.S. Senate Candidates." *Journal of Politics* 54: 497-517.

Kahn, Kim Fridkin. 1993. "Gender Differences in Campaign Messages: The Political Advertisements of Men and Women Candidates for U.S. Senate." *Political Research Quarterly* 46: 481-502.

Kahn, Kim Fridkin. 1994a. "The Distorted Mirror: Press Coverage of Women Candidates for Statewide Office." *Journal of Politics* 56: 154-173.

Kahn, Kim Fridkin. 1994b. "Does Gender Make a Difference? An Experimental Examination of Sex Stereotypes and Press Patterns in Statewide Campaigns." *American Journal of Political Science* 38: 162-195.

Kahn, Kim Fridkin. 1995. "Characteristics of Press Coverage in Senate and Gubernatorial Elections: Information Available to Voters." *Legislative Studies Quarterly* 20: 23-35.

Kahn, Kim Fridkin. 1996. *The Political Consequences of Being a Woman: How Stereotypes Influence the Conduct and Consequences of Political Campaigns*. New York: Columbia University Press.

Kahn, Kim Fridkin, and Edie Goldenberg. 1991. "Women Candidates in the News: An Examination of Gender Differences in U.S. Senate Campaign Coverage." *Public Opinion Quarterly* 55: 180-199.

Krasno, Jonathan S. 1994. *Challengers, Competition and Reelection: Comparing Senate and House Elections*. New Haven: Yale University Press.

Krosnick, Jon, and Donald R. Kinder. 1990. "Altering the Foundations of Support for the President through Priming." *American Political Science Review* 84: 497-512.

Leader, Shelah G. 1977. "The Policy Impact of Elected Women Officials." In *The Impact of the Electoral Process*, eds. Louis Maisel and Joseph Cooper. Beverly Hills: Sage.

Leeper, Mark S. 1991. "The Impact of Prejudice on Female Candidates: An Experimental Look at Voter Inference." *American Politics Quarterly* 19: 248-261.

Mann, Thomas E., and Raymond E. Wolfinger. 1980. "Candidates and Parties in Congressional Elections." *American Political Science Review* 71: 617-632.

Mayhew, David R. 1974. *Congress: The Electoral Connection*. New Haven: Yale University Press.

Mezey, Susan G. 1994. "Increasing the Number of Women in Office: Does It Matter?" In *The Year of the Woman: Myths Realities*, eds. Elizabeth Adell Cook, Sue Thomas, and Clyde Wilcox. Boulder: Westview.

Miller, Warren E., Donald R. Kinder, Steven J. Rosenstone, and the National Election Studies. 1993. *American National Election Study: Pooled Senate Election Study, 1988, 1990, 1992*. 2nd Release. Ann Arbor: Inter-University Consortium for Pokitical and Social Research.

Nelson, Candice J. 1994. "Women's PACs in the Year of the Woman." In *The Year of the Woman: Myths and Realities*, eds. Elizabeth Adell Cook, Sue Thomas, and Clyde Wilcox. Boulder: Westview Press.

Neuman, W. Russell, Marion R. Just, and Ann Crigler. 1992. *Common Knowledge*. Chicago: University of Chicago Press.

Pitkin, Hanna. 1967. *The Concept of Representation*. Berkeley: University of California Press.

Price, Vincent, and John Zaller. 1993. "Who Gets the News? Alternative Measures of News Reception and the Implications for Research." *Public Opinion Quarterly* 57: 133-164.

Sapiro, Virginia. 1981-1982. "If U.S. Senator Baker Were a Woman: An Experimental Study of Candidate Image." *Political Psychology* 3: 61-83.

Spot Television Rates and Data. 1993. Wilmette, IL: Standard Rate & Data Service.
Squire, Peverill. 1992. "Challenger Quality and Voting Behavior in U.S. Senate Elections." *Legislative Studies Quarterly* 17: 247-263.
Squire, Peverill, and Eric R.A.N. Smith. 1996. "A Further Examination of Challenger Quality in Senate Elections." *Legislative Studies Quarterly* 21: 235-248.
Stewart, Charles, III, and Mark Reynolds. 1990. "Television Markets and U.S. Senate Elections." *Legislative Studies Quarterly* 15: 495-523.
Thomas, Sue. 1994. *How Women Legislate*. New York: Oxford University Press.
Uhlaner, Carole Jean, and Kay Lehman Schlozman. 1986. "Candidate Gender and Congressional Campaign Receipts." *Journal of Politics* 48: 30-50.
Welch, Susan. 1985. "Are Women More Liberal than Men in the U.S. Congress?" *Legislative Studies Quarterly* 10: 125-134.
Westlye, Mark C. 1983. "Competitiveness of Senate Seats and Voting Behavior in Senate Elections." *American Journal of Political Science* 27: 253-283.
Westlye, Mark C. 1991. *Senate Elections and Campaign Intensity*. Baltimore: The Johns Hopkins University Press.
Zaller, John R. 1992. *The Nature and Origins of Mass Opinion*. Cambridge: Cambridge University Press.

APPENDIX A. Questions Used to Build the Variables Employed in Analysis/Coding of Questions

Dependent Variables:

Recognition of candidates: "I'm going to read a list with names of people in politics. Many people tell us they have not heard about some of the people on this list. As I read each name, please tell me whether or not you have ever heard of this person."

CODED 1 = RECOGNIZE; 0 = OTHERWISE

Likability: "Was there anything in particular that you liked about ..."

CODED 1 = IF THE PERSON SAID YES, 0 = OTHERWISE

Favorability: "Was there anything in particular that you liked/disliked about..." "What was that?" Favorability = (Number likes) − (Number dislikes)

Independent Variables:

TV: "How many days in the past week did you watch news programs on TV?"

Paper: "How many days in the past week did you read a daily newspaper?"

News Mix: Television market structure is measured by news mix, an index borrowed from Stewart and Reynolds (1990). A state's news mix value expresses the proportion of a state's news that will be about the state. It is derived from the assumption that any station will cover news about the state in direct proportion to the number of state residents living in the station's DMA. A state's "average news mix" is then the weighted average of all stations.

Year is 1992: CODED 1 = THE YEAR IS 1992; CODED 0 FOR 1988 AND 1990

Education: CODED 1-10; 1 = EIGHT GRADES OR LESS; 10 = ADVANCED DEGREE

Interest: "Some people don't pay much attention to political campaigns. How about you? Would you say that you were very much interested, somewhat interested, or not much interested?"

CODED 1 = VERY MUCH INTERESTED; 5 = NOT MUCH INTERESTED. PLEASE NOTE THAT IN PRESENTATION THE SIGN IS SWITCHED SO THAT IT IS INTUITIVELY CLEAR.

Political Knowledge: An additive index (0-4) based on political knowledge. A factor analysis indicates that these variables all load on one factor:

- whether the respondent could name the sitting senator not up for reelection (+1)
- whether the respondent could name the political party of that senator (+1)
- whether the respondent could correctly place the Republicans as conservative on a scale from one to seven (+1 if the respondent said the Republicans were anywhere from a four to a seven on the scale, +0 if the respondent said they did not understand the concept of ideology, didn't know or responded that the Republicans were liberal, from one to three on the scale)
- whether the respondent could correctly place the Democrats as liberal on a scale from one to seven (+1 if the respondent said the Democrats were anywhere from a one to four on the scale, +0 if the respondent said they did not understand the concept of ideology, didn't know or responded that the Democrats were conservative, from five to seven on the scale)

Candidate quality: Based on ANES items measuring each candidate's elective and partisan history. CODED 0 = NO ELECTIVE OR PARTISAN OFFICE; 1 = PARTISAN OFFICE OR CAMPAIGN MANAGEMENT POSITION; 2 = ELECTED TO STATE LEGISLATURE, MAYOR OR OTHER; 3 = ELECTED TO OTHER STATEWIDE OFFICE (NOT GOVERNOR); 4 = ELECTED TO U.S. HOUSE OF REPRESENTATIVES; 5 = ELECTED GOVERNOR; 6 = ELECTED TO U.S. SENATE

APPENDIX B. News Mix Values

State	News Mix
Arizona	0.7888
California	0.9940
Colorado	0.9343
Delaware	0.1457
Hawaii	1.000
Illinois	0.8373
Iowa	0.7766
Kansas	0.7399
Maryland	0.7319
Missouri	0.6952
New Jersey	0.3007
Pennsylvania	0.8198
Rhode Island	0.6639
South Dakota	0.8063
Washington	0.8801
Wisconsin	0.9138
Wyoming	0.4198

Do Differences Matter? Women Members of Congress and the Hyde Amendment

Dena Levy, State University of New York-Brockport
Charles Tien, Hunter College-City University of New York
Rachelle Aved, University of Iowa

SUMMARY. Have women members of Congress made a difference? A handful of studies have answered this "so what" question by looking for differences between male and female legislators. We build on previous research and propose an additional way of answering this question. If women members are making a difference, then they should be changing how men behave in Congress. Specifically, if women members are making a difference, then they should be changing how their male colleagues debate the issues. We content-analyze each House floor debate on the Hyde Amendment to see if women are changing how men debate the abortion issue. We find that men and women frame the abortion debate differently, and we find some evidence that women members of Congress have shifted the debate over time to focus less on the morality of abortion and more on the health of the pregnant women. We hope our research stimulates further work that not only looks for differences between men and women legislators, but also looks to see if the differences cause legislatures to change the way they do business.

[Haworth co-indexing entry note]: "Do Differences Matter? Women Members of Congress and the Hyde Amendment." Levy, Dena, Charles Tien, and Rachelle Aved. Co-published simultaneously in *Women & Politics* (The Haworth Press, Inc.) Vol. 23, No. 1/2, 2001, pp. 105-127; and: *Women and Congress: Running, Winning, and Ruling* (ed: Karen O'Connor) The Haworth Press, Inc., 2001, pp. 105-127. Single or multiple copies of this article are available for a fee from The Haworth Document Delivery Service [1-800-HAWORTH, 9:00 a.m. - 5:00 p.m. (EST). E-mail address: getinfo@haworthpressinc.com].

INTRODUCTION

The 1990s have seen a significant increase in the number of women serving in the U.S. Congress. In the 106th Congress, women made up over 12% (56 of 435) of the House of Representatives and 9% of the Senate. The increase in the House was almost a fourfold increase from the 90th Congress of 30 years ago. As the length of time that women have been in Congress increases and as the number of women in Congress increases, it is natural to ask whether or not they have changed Congress. That is, have women members made a difference? Most studies have answered this "so what" question by looking for differences between male and female legislators on a variety of indicators (see, for example, CAWP 1995). We propose an additional and different way of answering the question. If women members are really making a difference, then they should be changing how men behave in Congress. Specifically, have female members changed how their male colleagues debate the issues? If yes, how has debate been changed by their presence? In essence, have women members changed how men members debate on the floor? Our research hopes to invigorate the literature on women in Congress by proposing a different method of answering the question of "Do differences matter?" In addition to looking for differences between men and women legislators, we attempt to determine if these differences change how men debate on the House floor.

The impact of women representatives we are testing for has been commented on by members of Congress as well. Many members suggest that legislative outcomes would differ substantially if the numerical composition of the membership were to shift between men and women. Representative Elizabeth Holtzman (D-NY) made just this point in the 1977 House floor debate on the Hyde Amendment:

> Mr. Chairman, someone once said that if the membership of this House were different, this decision would not even be before us today. I think that this is very true. After listening to the debate, I would say that if there were 417 women in this House instead of 417 men, and if there were 18 men instead of 18 women in this House, that we would not be faced with this amendment today. (*Congressional Record*, 17 June 1977, 19708)

Representative Joel Pritchard (R-WA) made a similar claim a year earlier, again during the House debate of the Hyde Amendment. "Finally, Mr. Speaker, if we had 17 men and the rest of them were women, then both of us know that there would be a different discussion made today on this decision" (*Congressional Record,* 16 September 1976, 30900).

WOMEN IN LEGISLATURES

Pitkin (1969) argues that in addition to representing the likeness of the general population (descriptive representation), legislators need to represent constituents' desires, views, and interests (substantive representation). An increase in the descriptive representation of women may increase the substantive representation of women. Hawkesworth (1990, 184) argues that because women and men come from different backgrounds, having proportionate numbers of women in Congress will expand the terms of debate in Congress. Burrell (1994, 7) also writes that because men do not encounter the same experiences women do, they may never think to propose certain laws; therefore, women's presence will change what is even considered a political question. The different experiences that legislators bring to the process produce a different definition of issues and mobilization of coalitions. If there is no difference in legislators' experiences (that is, if only men serve), certain issues would never be raised and certain coalitions would never form. Men may not differ from women as to how they vote on proposed legislation, but there would be a difference in the legislation each would choose to sponsor. In essence, having women in Congress should result in better representation of their interests.[1] Former Representative Marjorie Margolies-Mezvinsky (D-PA) offers her own insight into why women matter in political office:

> It is because of our own experiences, and those of our mothers, sisters, daughters, and granddaughters, that we have a vested interest in the outcome of gender-specific issues. Only a woman can viscerally know the nightmarish connotations that accompany the word *mastectomy;* only a woman can truly imagine the very personal ramifications of not having the legal right to make her own reproductive choices. (1994, 90)

In 1989, Representative Les AuCoin (D-OR) (*Congressional Record* H6909) echoed this view as he talked on the House floor about the different experiences men and women have:

> Mr. Speaker, every time we debate this issue on the floor of the House, it is so easy for us to throw out words like "rape" or "incest," as if they were abstractions like "grand larceny" or "petty theft."
>
> We can do that because most of us in this House are male, and, when the debate is over, we can walk off this floor, and go about our business, and forget all that has happened here.
>
> But there are some who can never forget. They are the victims. Of rape. Of incest.

Assume for the moment that women are expanding the debate and introducing bills that otherwise would never be introduced. It is then logical to ask, "Have the outputs of the institution changed as a result of the presence of women in the institution?" In other words, women may bring new proposals to the table, but have they also had a more direct influence on their male colleagues? Do men talk about issues differently when women are present? Has the content of passed legislation changed as more women enter Congress? If women members are making a difference in Congress by their very presence, then not only should they expand agendas and terms of the debate, but more importantly, they should change how men debate and vote on legislation.

As women stay in Congress and as more women enter Congress, their influence should be felt in debates and legislative outcomes. Increasing the number of women in Congress results in better representation of their interests. The effect of having women in office extends beyond just being different than men. We believe that the very presence of women in Congress will alter the behavior of the male representatives. Women are not operating in a vacuum–they must work with their male colleagues to accomplish their goals. Representative Steny Hoyer (D-MD) offers a male perspective on how women affect the institution:

> The fact that we have appreciably increased the number of women has heightened issues of historical concern to women: women's health issues, reproductive rights issues, issues of the working family. Also because you have more women in Congress, there is greater attention to women's issues by men. Just by virtue of their presence, it serves as a reminder and raises the consciousness level on issues of concern to women. (quoted in Margolies-Mezvinsky 1994, 90)

Previous research (outside of the exceptions noted below) on women in legislatures tends to examine the differences between men and women legislators in terms of voting and floor behavior, bill sponsorship, and ideology at the state and federal level. This literature does not ask whether or not male legislators have changed their behavior as women enter the institution. The literature suggests that women are systematically different from their male colleagues (see, for example, Kathlene 1989; Saint-Germain 1990; Hawkesworth 1990). Women have been found to be more liberal than their male colleagues regardless of party (Dodson et al. 1995; Burrell 1994) and women have been found to make more feminist speeches on the floor (Tamerius 1993). Likewise, women are more apt to sponsor and cosponsor feminist legislation (Tamerius 1993) and focus on issues concerning women, children, families, health, and welfare (Thomas 1994). Women legislators in Colorado were found to approach political issues and problems differently than men legislators (Kathlene 1989). However, when it comes to party loyalty, women state legislators were found just as likely as men to vote against their party in an analysis of voting on the Equal Rights Amendment (Hill 1983). Moreover, when researchers of Congress turn to the question of whether the differences between male and female legislators make a difference on legislative outputs, most also seem to focus on differences. Leader (1977) finds that women are somewhat more liberal than men as measured by ADA scores and feminist ratings. Gehlen (1977) compared men and women members of Congress, among other things, on support for ERA, hiring of senior staff, voting attendance, and voting behavior. Welch (1985) also used interest group ratings (Conservative Coalition scores) to show that women vote slightly more in the liberal direction than men, but that the gender gap was narrowing.

Some research at the state level has gone beyond identifying differences between men and women. In Saint-Germain's (1990) study of the Arizona state legislature, she found that women introduced more feminist categorized bills, and that the bills were being passed. Another exception is the committee level analysis by Berkman and O'Connor (1993) that finds that women use their committee assignments to block pro-life bills (especially parent notification bills).

Our research is a natural progression from this previous research. By looking at the interaction between women and men within the institution, we build on earlier studies that find that male and female legislators behave differently. Our ultimate goal is to examine whether or not the presence of women *changes* the behavior of men. O'Connor and Segal (1990) pursued a similar objective in their study of Justice O'Connor's impact on her male colleagues in the Supreme Court on sex discrimination cases. Fox (1997) also investigates how the presence of women in campaigns changes the behavior of their male challengers.

To answer our research question, we content analyze each of the House floor debates on the Hyde Amendment from 1974 through 1997. By examining the behavior of men over time, we empirically determine whether or not the continued presence and increasing presence of women alters the way men talk about abortion. In essence, we are seeing if the behavior of men is changed by the very (continued) presence of women and by the increasing presence of women in Congress.

RESEARCH DESIGN

To analyze our research question, "does the presence of women representatives change the way that men debate issues of concern to women," we analyze debate on the course of the Hyde Amendment. First passed by Congress in 1976, the Hyde Amendment, in its barest form, simply denies federal funding "for abortions except where the life of the mother would be endangered if the fetus were carried to term" (quoted in Rovner 1989, 3064) and has been debated in several Congresses since that time (with each Congress passing some form of the ban on the use of federal funds for abortions).

The funding ban was first proposed in 1974 by Representative Angelo Runcallo (R-NY), but did not become law until 1976 when the House passed an amendment (207-167) sponsored by Representative Henry Hyde (R-IL) to the Health, Education and Welfare (HEW) Appropriations bill. The Hyde Amendment prohibited the use of federal funds from paying for or promoting abortion. In 1977, Congress amended the Hyde Amendment to allow funding for abortions for the "victims of rape or incest, when such rape or incest has been reported promptly to a law enforcement agency or public health service; or . . . in those instances where severe and long-lasting physical health damage to the mother would result if the pregnancy were carried to term when so determined by two physicians" (Rovner 1989, 3064). In 1979, the language on "severe and long-lasting physical health damage to the mother" was dropped (Rovner 1989, 3065). In 1981, Congress tightened the restrictions to abortion by dropping the exceptions for rape and incest, such that federal funding of abortions was only allowed to save the life of the woman. This language remained in place until 1989, when the House again included provisions for abortions in the case of rape and incest. See Rovner (1989) for a more detailed summary of congressional action on the Hyde Amendment.

We content analyzed the debate on the Hyde Amendment for each year that it was debated on the House floor–1974, 1976, 1977, 1978, 1979, 1989, 1993, and 1997. Content analysis allows us to take eight different debates spanning over 24 years, and allows us to make inferences from the debates about the influence of women in Congress. To measure influence, we counted the number of sentences spoken by each member speaking on the floor, and recorded each speaker's name, party, sex, position on the amendment, number of times asked to yield while speaking, number of times yielded, and whether or not the speaker included a personal experience in the speech. Each sentence was then coded for one or more of the following categories:

1. concern for the woman's health
2. concern for the fetus (immorality of aborting fetus)
3. appropriateness of spending public money for abortions
4. objection to using abortion as a method of birth control
5. constitutional right to privacy
6. equal access to abortion
7. cost adding children to welfare rolls
8. whether it is appropriate for Congress to legislate over abortion

Then within each category, each sentence was coded as either pro-life or pro-choice based on the member's stated position. For example, the following sentence was coded as pro-choice concern for the woman's health: "One of the things that concerns me most is the threat this amendment presents to the lives and health and future of millions of America's young women–people already born" (Seiberling 1977, *Congressional Record* 19701). In contrast, the following sentence was coded pro-life (based on the member's stated position) concern for the woman's health, "Mr. Speaker, I believe, for the woman who has been raped, every medical, legal, emotional and compassionate support that can be provided at the time of rape, must be made available" (Smith 1989, *Congressional Record* H6907).

Several issues must be dealt with when using content analysis. The most important, in our opinion, is content validity and reliability. How do we know that we are actually measuring what we claim to be measuring? And how do we know that each of the three researchers coded text the same way? We evaluated our data for face validity and hypothesis validity. Face validity is a comparatively weak measure of validity, but it is necessary to establish. It essentially means that our categories *appear* to measure the concepts we are trying to measure. Hypothesis validity is more difficult to establish, as it requires that the measured variables are related to other measured variables as hypothesized (Weber 1990).

We believe our concern for the fetus category has face validity because the sentences we coded as showing concern for the fetus *appear* to be capturing that concept. We classified sentences that had mentions of the abhorrence of "killing," "slaughtering," or "murdering" of "innocent human beings" into the category of concern for the fetus. For example, Robert Dornan's sentence from the 1977 (*Congressional Record* 19704) debate, "We will have executed in mother's wombs 14 million American citizens" was coded as showing concern for the fetus. We made similar evaluations for the other categories as well. In Appendix A are a few examples that led us to conclude that our data have face validity.

Hypothesis validity was also established, as many of the hypothesized relationships (discussed below) were supported by the data. Our major task was to determine whether the increased presence of women would gradually change the content of debate over time. The data suggest that they did. Also, the data reveal that, as expected, men and women used different arguments. These and other results are presented in detail below. They all support the validity of our data collection method.

Reliability is also an important issue for content analysis. We determined our reliability by all coding the same debate and checking to see how similar our results turned out–intercoder reliability. For each category that we coded for (the pro-life or pro-choice argument for each of the eight categories listed above) we produced correlation coefficients among all three coders. Of the 21 correlations computed, 18 were at .70 or higher, 14 were at .80 or higher, and 11 were at .90 or higher.[2]

RESULTS

By examining the nature of the debate about publicly funded abortion we gain insight into how the presence of women affects the issues that are emphasized in the debate. Our results suggest, on three different levels, that women do make a difference. First, the language that women use when discussing the Hyde Amendment differs considerably from that used by men. Second, men and women differ in terms of their support for the amendment. Third, the participation of women in floor debates on the Hyde Amendment seems to have altered the way men talk about the issue. Women members of Congress have shifted the debate to focus more on how abortion affects a woman's mental and physical health and less on the state of the unborn fetus. Content analysis provides us with the opportunity not only to count words and sentences, but provides us with direct insight into how issues such as the Hyde Amendment are debated and decided.

Language of the Debate

It is necessary to first establish that men and women talk about abortion differently, before testing to see if women have changed how men talk about abortion. Thus, the first question we address is whether men and women discuss the issue of abortion funding differently. Do women use different arguments than men? The simple answer is yes. In debate, women focus on separate issues from their male colleagues. Several examples help illustrate these differences. Representative Henry Hyde (R-IL), one of the strongest opponents of abortion, once argued: "All politicians, when they campaign, they say, I'm for the little guy, I'm for the little guy. There is no one literally littler than an unborn child in the womb, defenseless" (*Congressional Record,* 30 June 1993, 4322). According to Representative Christopher Smith (R-NJ), "Abortion on demand is child abuse" (*Congressional Record,* 30 June 1993, 4325).

In contrast to these men, Representative Gladys Noon Spellman (D-MD) drew on her own experience as a mother and concern for her own daughter:

> I know without question, without giving the matter one second's thought, that if my daughter's life were endangered by a pregnancy I would frantically seek to save her life. Are you different from me? How many of you would choose to let your daughters die? How then can you let the daughters of other mothers and fathers die? (*Congressional Record,* 17 June 1977, 19705)

Table 1 compares the average number of times that different kinds of arguments are used by women and men who participated in the floor debate. In almost every case, the differences between men and women are statistically significant and in the expected direction. Men are much more likely to couch their support of the Hyde Amendment in terms of (1) the morality of killing an unborn child, (2) questioning the appropriateness of using public money to fund abortions, and (3) not being concerned about the inequity of allowing wealthy women to fund abortions privately and preventing poor women from the same opportunity. In contrast, in their opposition to the Hyde Amendment, women are more concerned with (1) the impact of an abortion on the woman's mental

TABLE 1. Average Number of Mentions for Men and Women Floor Speakers by Debate Category

	Male	Female
Constitutional right (pro-choice)	0.70	1.6**
Constitutional right (pro-life)	0.19	0.02**
Equal access (pro-choice)	0.72	2.1***
Equal access (pro-life)	0.28	0.02***
Welfare cost (pro-choice)	0.04	0.12
Welfare cost (pro-life)	0.11	0*
Public funding (pro-choice)	0.14	0.41*
Public funding (pro-life)	0.97	0.15***
Concern for fetus (pro-choice)	0.68	0.32
Concern for fetus (pro-life)	2.1	0.07***
Concern for woman's health (pro-choice)	1.4	3.4***
Concern for woman's health (pro-life)	0.15	0.02*
Appropriate for congressional action (pro-choice)	0.16	0.39
Appropriate for congressional action (pro-life)	0.15	0.03**
Concern for abortion as birth control (pro-choice)	0.19	0.27
Concern for abortion as birth control (pro-life)	0.14	0.02**
N =	116	41

Source: *Congressional Record*
Averages were calculated by dividing the total number of mentions by the total number of speakers in the debate. Asterisks indicate a statistically significant difference in means for men and women.
*$p < .10$
**$p < .05$
***$p < .01$
N = Sample size

and physical health, (2) that all women should have the same access to abortion regardless of income, and (3) that abortion is a constitutional right upheld by the Supreme Court. For example, pro-choice women debaters averaged 3.4 utterances of some concern for the woman's health, while pro-choice men averaged only 1.4 such utterances. Notable differences can be found when comparing men's and women's responses to the issues of equal access, public funding, concern for the fetus and concern for the mother's health. For example, men discussed the immorality of killing an unborn fetus on average 30 times more often than women (2.1 versus .07). Likewise, men were on average 6.5 times more likely to use pro-life public funding arguments (federal money should not be used to finance abortions). In contrast, women were almost three times as likely as men to address questions of unequal access to abortions that stem from successful passage of the Hyde

Amendments. These results provide confirmation of research at the state level that finds that women, when involved in the debate, bring up different issues than men (Kathlene 1990; Tamerius 1993).

The next question we address is whether or not men and women voted differently on the Hyde Amendment. Table 2a looks only at those individuals who spoke in the debates for the years that we examine, and shows that both party and gender are important factors. We find support that women (who debated) regardless of party are slightly more likely to oppose the Hyde Amendment than men. Among Republican debaters, 75% of women opposed the Hyde Amendment, while only 14% of men opposed it. These percentages exceed the expected values under the null hypothesis. The chi-square statistic of 18.4 with one degree of freedom far exceeds the .05 critical value of 3.84, so the null hypothesis of independence is rejected, which provides evidence that Republican women debaters are more likely to oppose the Hyde Amendment than are Republican men debaters. Among debating Democrats, 97% of women opposed the Hyde Amendment, compared to 61% of men. Again, the chi-square statistic of 12.5 far exceeds the critical value, indicating that debating female Democrats are more likely than their male counterparts to oppose the Hyde Amendment. These results correspond with Hill, Burrell, and Thomas, who argue that on some issues, such as abortion and the ERA, women are more likely to act as a group regardless of their party affiliation. In Congress, party clearly matters, but on abortion it appears that gender matters, too.

Of course, it is possible that the results in Table 2a are merely a function of self-selection. In other words, are the women who participate in floor debates systematically different than those who remain silent? We address this concern by comparing how all women and men voted on the Hyde Amendment over time (see Table 2b). The chi-square statistics on gender and vote on the Hyde Amendment for all Democrats and Republicans (31.9 for Democrats and 9.7 for Republicans) far exceed the critical value (3.84) for significance at .05 with one degree of freedom. The results in Table 2a and Table 2b, when examined separately, provide statistical evidence that women are more likely than men to oppose the Hyde Amendment. However, when comparing the results from Table 2a to Table 2b, a more insightful explanation of the Hyde Amendment debates appears. A comparison of the data in these tables suggests that pro-life women and pro-choice Republican men participate less in the Hyde Amendment debates. Almost 85% of all women Democratic representatives opposed the Amendment. But, among the Democratic women debaters, almost all (28 out of 29) opposed the Amendment. The differ-

TABLE 2a. Vote on Hyde Amendment by Gender and Party for All Years (Among Debaters)

		Men	Women
Republican*	Oppose	14.3%	75.0%
	Support	85.7%	25.0%
N		49	12
Democrat*	Oppose	61.2%	96.6%
	Support	34.3%**	3.4%
N		67	29

Source: *Congressional Record*
*chi-squared test of statistical independence $p < .05$
$\chi^2 = 18.4$ (Republicans); 12.5 (Democrats)
**values do not add to 100 due to individuals not voting
N = Sample size

TABLE 2b. Vote on Hyde Amendment by Gender and Party for All Years (All Members)

		Men	Women
Republican*	Oppose	23.0%	41.1%
	Support	77.0%	58.9%
N		1208	56
Democrat*	Oppose	60.1%	84.8%
	Support	39.9%	15.2%
N		1954	132

Source: *Congressional Record*
*chi-squared test of statistical independence $p < .05$
$\chi^2 = 9.7$ (Republicans); 31.9 (Democrats)
N = Sample size

ence between all Republican women and debate participating Republican women is even sharper. Almost 59% of all Republican women supported the Hyde Amendment compared to only 25% of debate participating women. Aggregating Democratic and Republican women together shows that 90% (37 of 41) of debating women were pro-choice compared to 72% (135 of 188) of all women. Juxtaposing Tables 2a and 2b tells us that pro-life women tended to refrain from entering the Hyde Amendment debates. Further comparison of Tables 2a and 2b shows that Republican men who opposed the Hyde Amendment also appear to participate less–only 14% of male Republican debaters opposed the Amendment compared to 23% of all male Republicans.

If we assume that the pro-life women and pro-choice Republican men did not speak on the floor because of electoral concerns, then it is interesting to speculate about from whom they were trying to hide their votes. As a majority of Republicans are pro-life, we speculate that pro-life women legislators were probably concerned about how other women would react to their pro-life position. Otherwise it would have made sense for the pro-life women to publicize rather than remain quiet about their pro-life positions. It is also unlikely that the Republican leadership was silencing the pro-life women, as it would be appealing for Republicans to have women making pro-life arguments for them on the House floor. For the pro-choice Republican men, their desire to keep a low profile on the issue was probably more out of concern for how their core Republican constituency would respond to their pro-choice position. It is also possible that pro-choice Republican men remained quiet because of concerns with their leadership. The data in Tables 2a and 2b give some support to the proposition that women members of Congress work to represent their gender as well as their electoral constituency.

Evolution of the Debate

The previous results provide evidence that men and women debate the abortion issue in different terms, and also tend to vote differently on it. Since the results in Table 1 and Tables 2a and 2b are aggregated and do not control for time, they only bluntly establish that men and women are different. To see if men have changed over time requires time-series analysis, which we turn to below. The next question we address is whether or not women have shaped the floor debate. That is, has their presence in Congress somehow changed the nature of how men argue about abortion funding on the House floor? Though there are only eight years of debate to analyze, some patterns emerge in the data. In general, there is a positive trend in the number of women participating in the debate over abortion funding (see Table 3). In 1977, almost 24% of the speakers were women (8 of 33). By 1989, the percentage of women speakers rose to over 36% (12 out of 33 speakers), and exceeded 58% (14 out of 24) in 1993. The average number of women participants in the 1970s is 2.6, while the average number for 1989 and the 1990s is 9.3. Has the increased presence of women in floor debates changed the kind of arguments made by the men in the debate? If yes, we would expect to find that the issues that men address when debating the Hyde

TABLE 3. The Women's Impact: Comparison of Men and Women Referring to Health Concerns

Year	Number of Men Debating	Number of Women Debating	Ratio of Women to Men Debating	Ratio of Women to Men Referring to Health Concerns
1974	22	2	0.09	1.40
1976	14	2	0.14	3.50
1977	27	8	0.30	2.00
1978	10	0	0.00	*
1979	8	1	0.12	31.00
1989	21	12	0.57	1.80
1993	10	14	1.40	1.10
1997	4	2	0.50	4.70

Ratio of Women to Men Debating was calculated by dividing Number of Women Debating by Number of Men Debating. Ratio of Women to Men Referring to Health Concerns was calculated by dividing number of times women debaters referred to women's health concerns by the number of times men debaters referred to women's health concerns.
* The average number of mentions by men for concern for women's health was 0.2. This figure was the second lowest for all years.

Amendment change over time while women remain relatively constant in their language.

Results from Table 1 showed that men tend to talk about the fetus and the immorality of aborting the fetus, while women tend to talk about the health of the pregnant woman. Thus, if women are changing the debate we should find (1) women talking about women's health issues consistently throughout the eight debates spanning 24 years, and (2) men talking more about women's health issues and less about the fetus over time. Table 3 presents a first look at whether or not women changed how men discuss abortion funding.

The results in Table 3 are not as strong as we would have liked to see. We calculated the ratio of health concern sentences spoken by women to health concern sentences spoken by men, where larger ratios indicate larger differences between men and women and smaller ratios indicate smaller differences (unit of analysis is each sentence). If women are changing how men debate abortion, then we should see more utterances of health concerns by women than men (larger ratio) in the 1970s and relatively equal utterances (smaller ratio) in 1989 and the 1990s. However, no strong pattern of men and women converging in their arguments emerges (last column in Table 3). The results in Table 3, though, do provide some insights at second glance. We do find some evidence of women changing how men debate abortion, especially when more women participate in the floor debate.

In the years with the greatest number of women participating in the debates (1977, 1989, and 1993) the ratio of women to men using the same women's health arguments is the lowest. That is to say, in these three years, women referred to women's health only from 1.1 to 2.0 times more often than men did. However, 1974 runs counter to our expectation, as the ratio of women to men mentioning health issues is the lowest with only two women debating. In the other years where there were considerably fewer women participating on the floor, men were considerably less likely to focus on the mother's health–1979 illustrates this nicely. Eight men and only one woman spoke on the floor. The men made an average of 0.13 remarks about women's health while the one female averaged four such comments (the ratio is thus 4/0.13 = 30.77). Clearly the lone woman legislator did not influence the language of the men participating in the 1979 debates. The year 1976 serves as another example of how difficult it is for only a couple of women to shift the terms of the debate. In this year, there were 14 men and only two women participating. The women pointed to the women's health for an average of six remarks whereas the men used this argument on average only 1.7 times (the ratio is thus 6/1.7 = 3.5). It is usually when there is relative parity between the number of men and women debating that we see less disparity in the kinds of arguments being used to debate the Hyde Amendment. In the 1993 debate, there were actually more women participating in the debate than men (14 versus 10), which coincides with the smallest difference between men and women in the kinds of arguments used. Women referred to the health of the woman only 1.1 times more often than did their male colleagues.

When we aggregate the data by time period and change the level of analysis from individual sentences to individual speakers, a stronger pattern of influence emerges. It may be difficult to see patterns over time with only eight data points, so we combined the 1970s into one observation and 1989, 1993, and 1997 into another observation. The results for the aggregated data with each member as the unit of analysis are presented in Table 4. Three findings in Table 4 deserve mention. First, the changes in what men talk about are much larger than the changes in what women talk about. In the 1970s, 37% (30 of 81) of men talked about the morality of aborting a fetus and in the 1990s only 14.3% (5 of 35) did–a change of 22.7%. Few women talked about the morality of abortion over time, only 7.7% (1 of 13) talked about the fetus in the 1970s and 3.6 (1 of 28) in the 1990s. The same general pattern emerges when we look at changes in the percent of men and women talking about women's health concerns. During the 1970s, 33.3% (27 of 81) of all male speakers talked about women's health issues. The percentage jumps to 68.6 (24 of 35) in the 1990s. The percentage of women talking about health is consistently high–84.6% (11 of 13) in the 1970s and 78.6% (22 of 28) in the 1990s.

Second, the changes in how men talk about abortion are in the expected direction. In the 1990s, 35.3% more men talked about the health of women than in the 1970s (33.3% to 68.6%). And there is a decrease in the percent of men who talked about the morality of abortion from the 1970s (37%) to the 1990s (14.3%). Since most women consistently talked about health issues and few women talked about the morality of abortion over the time series, we expect their influence to increase the percent of men talking about health issues and decrease the percent of men talking about the morality of abortion over time. This pattern of influence is what we find in Table 4.

The last result of note in Table 4 is that the differences in arguments used by men and women have decreased over time. In the 1970s, 37% of men talked about the morality of abortion compared to 7.7% of women. This difference in the 1970s between men and women of 29.3% is statistically significant at the .05 level. The difference in the 1990s drops to 10.7%, and is not statistically significant. Again, the same pattern emerges when looking at health issues. This difference in the 1970s between men and women talking about women's health is 51.3% and statistically significant at the .05 level. The difference in the 1990s for health issues drops to 10%, and is not statistically significant. In sum, women have consistently talked about women's health issues over time and now more men are talking about women's health issues and fewer men are talking about the morality of abortions than before.

When we control for position on the Hyde Amendment, the results also indicate that men have changed how they talk about abortion since the 1970s. Table 5 looks at the percent of debaters who mention morality of abortions and women's health concerns by gender and position on the Hyde Amendment over time. In some cells the sample size is too small to generalize from; however, results indicate that men now talk less about the morality of abortions and more about women's health issues than they did in the 1970s. In the 1970s, of those who supported the Hyde Amendment, 57.1% (24 of 42) of men talked about the morality of abortions. By the 1990s, this percentage drops to 21.7 (5 of 23). When we look at the percent of Hyde supporters who mention women's health issues, we see that in the 1970s only 21.4% (9 of 42) of men did so. By the

TABLE 4. The Women's Impact: Changes in How Men Talk About Abortion

Percent of Debaters Who Mention Abortion Morality		
Decade	Men	Women
1970s*	37.0% (81)	7.7% (13)
1989, 1990s	14.3 (35)	3.6 (28)

Percent of Debaters Who Mention Women's Health Concerns		
Decade	Men	Women
1970s**	33.3% (81)	84.6% (13)
1989, 1990s	68.6 (35)	78.6 (28)

Source: *Congressional Record*
* chi-square significant at .05 (2-tailed)
** chi-square significant at .01 (2-tailed)
Note: some cells < 5
Total sample size in parentheses

1990s, this number increases to 60.9% (14 of 23). Similar changes appear among men who oppose the Hyde Amendment (47.4% and 80.0% respectively). The differences between the men and women over health concerns are statistically significant in the 1970s, indicating that women were using different arguments than their male colleagues. However, by the 1990s the differences have disappeared and men are now just as likely to use the arguments used by the women.

The results in Tables 3, 4, and 5 (though not particularly strong in Table 3) provide some evidence that the continued presence and growing number of women in the House and participating in floor debates may have caused men to change how they talk about abortion. The suggestion in Table 3 that increased participation affects debate deserves further discussion because it indicates that the challenge is not only electing more women to office but also getting women to participate in debates once they are in office. One way to get more women to participate in debates is, of course, to elect more women. The correlation between the number of women in the House and the number of women debating the Hyde Amendment is 0.42. This is not a particularly strong relationship, but the data suggest that having more women in office decreased the number of male debaters–the correlation between number of women in the House and number of men debating is −0.52. We also looked at the relationship between the number of women in the House and the proportion of debaters who are women. This correlation suggests that increasing the number of women in the House may lead to a greater percentage of women debaters on the Hyde Amendment. The

TABLE 5. The Women's Impact: Changes in How Men Talk About Abortion (Controlling for Position on Hyde Amendment)

	Percent of Debaters Who Mention Abortion Morality		
	Decade	Men	Women
Support Hyde	1970s	57.1% (42)	100% (1)
	1989, 1990s	21.7 (23)	33.3 (3)
Oppose	1970s	15.8 (38)	0 (12)
	1989, 1990s	0 (10)	0 (25)

	Percent of Debaters Who Mention Women's Health Concerns		
	Decade	Men	Women
Support Hyde	1970s**	21.4% (42)	100.0% (1)
	1989, 1990s	60.9 (23)	66.7 (3)
Oppose	1970s*	47.4 (38)	83.3 (12)
	1989, 1990s	80.0 (10)	80.0 (25)

Source: *Congressional Record*
*chi-square statistically significant at .05 (2-tailed)
** chi-square statistically significant at .05 (1-tailed)
Note some cells < 5
Total sample size in parentheses

correlation between the number of women in the House and the ratio of women to men debating is 0.76. The data show that electing more women to the House leads to having a greater proportion of women speakers on the Hyde Amendment. We believe that research on why women participate can help us further understand how women affect Congress.

It should be noted that one likely cause for the shift in the debate in 1989 was that Representative Barbara Boxer (D-CA) introduced the Hyde Amendment motion being considered. Her amendment to the Hyde Amendment focused on concern for women and involved funding abortions for victims of rape or incest.[3] This further supports our belief that women do make a difference. The nature of Boxer's amendment to the Hyde Amendment focused on women rather than the unborn child. Her presence allowed the debate to shift simply by changing the agenda. If she were not in office, and therefore had not offered the amendment, Congress could have continued to argue in the same vein as in previous years. Congress did not, however. Instead, the preponderance of participating representatives in the 1989 debate responded to the change suggested by Boxer.

CONCLUSION

A few caveats to our findings must be noted. Because of the rules of floor debate there is always a problem with self-selection into the debate and who controls it. For example, in the beginning of the debate in 1993, Representatives Henry Hyde and Patricia Schroeder (D-CO) each were given 10 minutes of the floor. Each then parceled out how those 10 minutes would be used. Interestingly, Hyde kept the majority of the time for himself whereas Schroeder gave nine others one minute of her 10 minutes. Thus, both Hyde and Schroeder clearly influenced who had access to the debate. Schroeder obviously would avoid yielding her time to someone who was not in support of her position. However, neither representative could dictate the language used by their fellow representatives.

Critics may argue that given the divisive nature of the abortion issue it is necessary to consider change in the general public over the issue of funding for abortions, and that the change in male members of Congress is caused by factors other than the presence of women in Congress. A more complete model of the debate might include public opinion polls to help determine whether the change in types of arguments being made by men is the result of the increasing number of women in office, or whether representatives are reflecting changes in their constituents. Although we do not explicitly include survey data into our analysis, we know from the National Election Studies data that the percentage of the population who are opposed to abortion under any circumstances has remained relatively constant, between 10% to 13% (from 1972 to 1994) during the period under analysis here. This provides at least some evidence that the shift in the terms of floor debates on the Hyde Amendment is not solely a function of changing public opinion.

A related point is that members do not listen to each other on the floor–that members are talking past each other and men are not hearing what women are saying. Watching House floor debates on C-SPAN may give this impression at times, but at other times members are very engaged with each other during floor debate. In a personal interview, one member replied to our question of whether or not he thinks that women and minority members are changing other members' minds on the floor:

> Yeah I do. They change minds and at minimum they make people feel uncomfortable about voting the way that they do. But sometimes I think they instill a little bit of fear in the Republican leadership. If they bring an issue up, ____ will be on the floor ripping their heads off, on C-SPAN live across the country. They're doing something that's going to directly hurt the minority community. They don't want that because they're trying to win votes in that direction. Sometimes the impact that these people have is that they know how to damage the trust. The Republicans would like to do these things but they don't do them because they know the minority Democrat members will recall them. And again minority members of Congress that do that, . . . when I see them on the floor, I thank God that they're part of the party. Because if they weren't, I don't think the passion would be anywhere near what it is when they're on the stage.

Certainly this is the view of just one member and may not be representative of what most members think. It does suggest, however, that members do care what others are saying on the floor, that members do listen to other members, and that some members are influenced by the House floor debate.

In summary, our results suggest that increasing the number of women in Congress will likely result in fuller representation of women's interests. On the most basic level, we find that women use different language than men when discussing abortion. Men are also more likely than women are to vote for the Hyde Amendment. Finally, women appear to influence how their male colleagues talk about abortion. Since the Hyde Amendment first entered the legislative arena, the focus of the debate has shifted from the immorality of abortions to concerns about the health of the woman. We believe this change in focus partially is the result of the continued presence and increased presence of women in Congress. Our findings suggest that the presence of women in Congress does make a difference. The difference women make is not only in the fact that they vote differently and speak differently than men about abortion, but that their differences may be *changing* how men speak about abortion. While the overall results here are not as strong as we would have liked, we hope that they will push forward the debate over whether differences matter. Our research is preliminary and we hope it stimulates further work that not only looks for differences between men and women legislators, but also looks to see if the differences cause legislatures to change the way they do business.

AUTHOR NOTE

A previous version of this paper was presented at the 1997 annual meeting of the American Political Science Association. We thank the editor and anonymous reviewers for helpful comments. Dena Levy thanks the SUNY Brockport Summer Research Grant and Scholarly Incentive Grant for supporting this research. Charles Tien was supported (in part) by a grant from The City University of New York PSC-CUNY Research Award Program, and also Hunter College's Eugene Lang Junior Faculty Development Award.

NOTES

1. The theory that women matter in Congress is based on the assumption that women members of Congress work not only to represent their electoral constituencies, but also their gender.
2. We attempted to settle coding disputes by discussing the sentence in question. Unsettled disputes were ultimately decided by the person who performed the data analysis (Dena Levy).
3. Sentences that expressed support for the Boxer Amendment to the Hyde Amendment were, therefore, coded as pro-choice.

REFERENCES

Berkman, Michael B., and Robert E. O'Connor. 1993. "Do Women Legislators Matter? Female Legislators and State Abortion Policy." *American Politics Quarterly* 21: 102-124.

Burrell, Barbara C. 1994. *A Woman's Place Is in the House*. Ann Arbor: University of Michigan Press.

Carroll, Susan J. 1985. "Political Elites and Sex Differences in Political Ambition: A Reconsideration." *Journal of Politics* 47: 1231-43.

Carroll, Susan J. 1989. "The Personal is Political: The Intersection of Private Lives and Public Roles Among Women and Men in Elective and Appointive Office." *Women & Politics* 9(2): 51-67.

Center for the American Woman and Politics (CAWP). 1995. "Voices, Views, Votes: Women in the 103rd Congress." New Brunswick: Center for the American Woman in Politics.

Congressional Record. Various volumes. Washington, DC: Government Printing Office.

Dodson, Debra L. et al. 1995. *Voice, Views, Votes: The Impact of Women in the 103rd Congress*. New Brunswick: Center for the American Woman and Politics.

Fox, Richard L. 1997. *Gender Dynamics in Congressional Elections*. Thousand Oaks, CA: Sage.

Gehlen, Frieda L. 1977. "Women Members of Congress: A Distinctive Role." In *A Portrait of Marginality: The Political Behavior of American Women*, eds. Marianne Githens and Jewel L. Prestage. New York: David McKay.

Hawkesworth, Mary E. 1990. *Beyond Oppression: Feminist Theory and Political Strategy*. New York: The Continuum Publishing Company.
Hill, David B. 1983. "Women State Legislators and Party Voting on the ERA." *Social Science Quarterly* 64: 318-326.
Kathlene, Lyn. 1989. "Uncovering the Political Impacts of Gender: An Exploratory Study." *Western Political Quarterly* 42: 397-421.
Kathlene, Lyn. 1990. "The New Approach to Understanding the Impact of Gender on the Legislative Process." In *Feminist Research Methods*, ed. Joyce McCarl Nielsen. Boulder: Westview Press.
Leader, Sheilah G. 1977. "The Policy Impact of Elected Women Officials." In *The Impact of the Electoral Process*, eds. Louis Maisel and Joseph Cooper. Beverly Hills: Sage.
Margolies-Mezvinsky, Marjorie. 1994. *A Woman's Place . . . The Freshmen Women Who Changed the Face of Congress*. New York: Crown.
National Election Studies. 2000. Available at www.umich.edu/~nes/nesguide/toptables/.
O'Connor, Karen, and Jeffrey A. Segal. 1990. "Justice Sandra Day O'Connor and the Supreme Court's Reaction to Its First Female Member." *Women & Politics* 10(2): 95-104.
Pitkin, Hannah. 1969. *Representation*. New York: Atherton Press.
Rovner, Julie. 1989. "In Debate on Abortion Funding, Only the Dynamics Are New." *Congressional Quarterly Weekly Reports,* 11 November. Washington, DC: Congressional Quarterly.
Saint-Germain, Michelle. 1990. "Does Their Difference Make a Difference? The Impact of Women and Public Policy in the Arizona Legislature." *Social Science Quarterly* 70: 956-68.
Sapiro, Virginia. 1981. "Research Frontier Essay: When Are Interests Interesting? The Problem of Political Representation of Women." *American Political Science Review* 75: 701-716.
Tamerius, Karin. 1993. "Does Sex Matter?" Presented at the Annual Meeting of the Midwest Political Science Association.
Thomas, Sue. 1994. *How Women Legislate*. New York: Oxford University Press.
Thomas, Sue. 1991. "The Impact of Women on State Legislative Policies." *Journal of Politics* 53: 958-976.
Thomas, Sue, and Susan Welch. 1991. "The Impact of Gender on Activities and Priorities of State Legislators." *Western Political Quarterly* 44: 445-456.
Thompson, Joan Hulse. 1980. "Role Perceptions of Women in the Ninety-Fourth Congress, 1975-76." *Political Science Quarterly* 95: 71-81.
Weber, Robert Philip. 1990. *Basic Content Analysis*. 2nd ed. Sage University Paper Series on Quantitative Applications in the Social Sciences, 07-49. Newbury Park: Sage.
Welch, Susan. 1977. "Women as Political Animals? A Test of Some Explanations for Male-Female Political Participation Differences." *American Journal of Political Science* 21: 711-730.
Welch, Susan. 1985. "Are Women More Liberal Than Men in the U.S. Congress?" *Legislative Studies Quarterly* 10: 125-134.
Young, Louise M. 1976. "Women's Place in American Politics: The Historical Perspective." *Journal of Politics* 38: 295-335.

APPENDIX A

Here are a few examples of our coding decisions that lead us to believe that our data have face validity.

Pro-life concern over spending tax dollars for abortions: "Why should tax payers be forced to pay for any woman's abortion, let alone hundreds of thousands of abortions a year?" (Rudd 1977, *Congressional Record* 19705).

Pro-choice concern over spending of tax dollars for abortions: "Mr. Speaker, these are very difficult situations that must be balanced out, and I think it is very important that we stand up and say that it is all right to have Medicaid funding in the case of rape and incest" (Schroeder 1989, *Congressional Record* H6910).

Pro-life stance on equal access to abortions, and appropriateness of spending public money for abortions: "Women, rich and poor, have the right to seek a face lift solely at their own discretion–but the Equal Protection Clause does not require that tax dollars go to providing face lifts for every indigent who wants one" (Dornan 1977, *Congressional Record* 19703).

Pro-choice stance that there be equal access to abortions: "I am shocked and frankly appalled that my colleague from Illinois laments his inability to control a wealthy woman's reproductive rights, but takes satisfaction in controlling a poor woman's reproductive rights" (Eshoo 1993, *Congressional Record* 4326).

Speaking Out: An Analysis of Democratic and Republican Woman-Invoked Rhetoric of the 105th Congress

Colleen J. Shogan, Yale University

SUMMARY. This study demonstrates that Republican female House members invoke women in their public statements at the same frequency as their Democratic counterparts. Despite this congruency, the specific issues that female partisan legislators emphasize when they invoke women in their statements are quite different. Republican women discuss how tax, business, and pension laws affect working women while Democratic female representatives concern themselves with laudatory tributes and funding for welfare state programs. In addition to controlling for party, the explanatory variable of race is also introduced to explain variation in emphasis, particularly regarding the issue of abortion. *Congressional Record* entries contributed by the female members of the 105th Congress in 1997 serve as the data for this analysis. *[Article copies available for a fee from The Haworth Document Delivery Service: 1-800-HAWORTH. E-mail address: <getinfo@haworthpressinc.com> Website: <http://www.HaworthPress.com> © 2001 by The Haworth Press, Inc. All rights reserved.]*

Most scholarly discourse concerning female legislators asks if women possess different policy interests, leadership styles, or legislative behavior than their male counterparts. This analysis of female House

[Haworth co-indexing entry note]: "Speaking Out: An Analysis of Democratic and Republican Woman-Invoked Rhetoric of the 105th Congress." Shogan, Colleen J. Co-published simultaneously in *Women & Politics* (The Haworth Press, Inc.) Vol. 23, No. 1/2, 2001, pp. 129-146; and: *Women and Congress: Running, Winning, and Ruling* (ed: Karen O'Connor) The Haworth Press, Inc., 2001, pp. 129-146. Single or multiple copies of this article are available for a fee from The Haworth Document Delivery Service [1-800-HAWORTH 9:00 a.m. - 5:00 p.m. (EST). E-mail address: getinfo@haworthpressinc.com].

members examines the legislative behavior of female office holders, but not in comparison to their male colleagues. Instead, partisan and racial differences amongst female members of Congress are explored.

Specifically, this paper analyzes the public statements of female members of the U.S. House of Representatives when they invoke women's specific interests or concerns in *Congressional Record* entries. The goal of this examination is to determine how often female members of Congress talk about women publicly and what policy issues they discuss in relation to women. Furthermore, this analysis seeks to discover if female representatives of a particular party or racial group talk more frequently about women in their political discourse than others.

This research is an exercise in understanding descriptive political representation. When a legislator provides relevant information about a represented population, he or she engages in one type of descriptive representation. In this sense, descriptive representation is not simply "standing for" a particular subset of the population, but also "talking and deliberating" (Pitkin 1967, 83). Many females in the House might feel that as women, they should attempt to represent descriptively the interests of women in some tangible way, such as providing information about women's needs, desires, or special interests. Reingold finds that female legislators accept a link between "being a woman and actively representing women's concerns" (1992, 531). Furthermore, rhetoric is important because the "congressman as position taker is a speaker rather than a doer" (Mayhew 1974, 62). Although the representative as a provider of information is not the only role a legislator plays in the House of Representatives, it is an important facet of the descriptive representation of women. This analysis will explore how often female legislators in the House exercise this role in relation to the specific interests and concerns of women.

PREVIOUS RESEARCH

Since few women served in Congress until the early 1990s, most researchers gathered data from state legislatures. Most of the literature surrounding female legislators attempted to assess the impact, if any, of gender on legislative outcomes and activities (Dolan 1997; Thomas 1991; Welch 1985; Welch and Thomas 1990).

A smaller amount of the literature considers partisan differences. When the concept of party is incorporated, strong comparisons are usually drawn between partisan men and women. Paddock and Paddock's recent study (1997) concluded that slight differences in partisan style exist between male and female state party committee members. Less emphasis is placed on exploring the distinctions or similarities between Republican and Democratic women, though such studies do exist. Leader concluded in 1977 that Democratic women are more supportive of feminist goals and policies than their Republican counterparts. Hill's study of state legislature Equal Rights Amendment (ERA) voting discovered that Republican women are more likely to abandon their party's cues than Democratic women (1983). Vega and Firestone's analysis of roll-call votes from 1981 to 1992 revealed that Democratic women were less cohesive in their voting agreement than Republican women (1995). Sapiro and Farah's study of 1972 delegates to the presidential nominating conventions found that Republican women were more traditional and more interested in party positions than Democratic women (1980). Freeman discussed how Democratic and Republican female partisans argued for distinct versions of "women's issues" at the 1992 presidential nominating conventions (1993). Most recently, Carroll and Casey described how Democratic and Republican female members of Congress distinctively influenced welfare reform in the 104th session (1998).

This review of the scholarly literature surrounding female legislators hints at gaps in the research. First, most research has focused too narrowly on roll-call votes (Dolan 1997). Position-taking is an integral part of congressional behavior that can often remain distinct from roll-call voting (Mayhew 1974). Secondly, although political scientists have studied many legislative behaviors of female representatives (voting records, types of bills introduced, committees joined), they have not studied how women profess to represent women in their political rhetoric. This is an important part of the descriptive representation of women which needs further scholarly examination and attention. Thirdly, most previous research concerning female legislators has concentrated on gender differences. Because the numbers of women in Congress have grown substantially, researchers can begin to study women as an independent group of political actors. Pitting Democrats against Republicans, this study was designed to determine *what issues* female House members talked about on the floor when their arguments concerned women's interests, and also the *frequency* of such discourse. This research aims to contribute to the short list of scholarly work that explores the differences in policy behavior between congressional women of different political parties.

This research does not aim to determine if the special interests of women, claimed by the female members of the House in their public statements, accurately mirror the true desires of a particular female constituency.[1] Throughout this examination, it is important to keep in mind that female members of Congress, regardless of party or other characteristics, profess to know and represent the interests or desires of women. This does not mean female representatives actually know and understand the priorities of women, or female legislators represent female views in any way beyond mentioning them in their public statements as points of information or persuasion.

Furthermore, this empirical endeavor does not attempt to ascertain the motivations of female members of the House when they talk about women's interests in their public statements. Some female members might mention women's special concerns because they genuinely wish to represent the perceived views of their female constituency while other female representatives might mention women's interests for more strategic reasons. For example, a Fact Sheet "The Gender Gap" published by the Center for the American Woman and Politics states that women are more likely to vote for candidates who support publicly women's interests or issues (1996). In 1997, 58 PACs and donor networks gave money predominately to female candidates in the United States (CAWP 1997). More than half of female state legislators report that women's organizations provide "support" for their electoral efforts (Carroll 1991, 44). Perhaps monetary contributions or other electoral concerns motivate female members of Congress to talk about women's special interests. Determining the motivations behind making public statements about women on the House floor is beyond the scope of this specific project. Instead, this research asks how often female representatives speak about the distinct interests of women and what types of policy issues they speak about when invoking women in their statements.

METHODOLOGY

Entries of the 1997 *Congressional Record* serve as the data for this analysis. At the time of data collection, the 1997 session of the 105th Congress provided the most recent *Congressional Record* entries of a legislative session in which substantive numbers of both Democratic and Republican female members served in Congress.[2] Each female House member's entries as recorded in the *Congressional Record*, including extensions of remarks as well as contributions to debates, were read and examined.[3] In total, 16 Republican women and 34 Democratic women were used in this study.[4]

I read and analyzed each entry in the *Congressional Record* for each female representative. Points of parliamentary procedure, public comments, extension of remarks, speeches, and motions executed by a member of Congress constitute entries in the *Congressional Record.* First, I determined whether or not an entry was "substantive." A "substantive" entry was defined as an argument concerning a bill, resolution, amendment, or previous speaker's comment. Actions not termed "substantive" for purposes of this analysis were as follows: those concerning leaves of absence, additional sponsors of bills, motions to adjourn, recorded votes, personal explanations, special orders, and notations of reports submitted. In short, if a representative argued a point or offered an opinion in a *Congressional Record* entry, her remarks were deemed "substantive" while entries serving as procedural instructions or requests were not defined as "substantive." Although most of the *Congressional Record* entries analyzed were reactions or opinions regarding legislation, "substantive" remarks were not confined to legislative debates. Tributes made by female members lauding outstanding female accomplishments were also termed "substantive." *Congressional Record* inserts were included.

As I analyzed the entries of each representative, I determined how many substantive entries each member contributed to the *Congressional Record* in 1997. In this respect, some members were more active than others. For example, Representative Sheila Jackson Lee (D-TX) was credited with 234 substantive entries while Sue Myrick (R-NC) only managed 24 such entries.

After determining an entry was "substantive," I then examined it to discover if women's issues or concerns were invoked in the argument.[5] To determine if an entry was an example of "woman-invoked rhetoric," I carefully scanned all substantive remarks for feminine words or pronouns such as "women," "mothers," "girls," or "daughters." If the speech contained such words, I analyzed the entry to determine if the representative invoked the interests or welfare of females in their argument, making this determination by reading the entire entry at hand. The substantive *Congressional Record* entry had to claim, in some way (even in only one or two sentences), that the legislation or issue at hand affects females. Merely mentioning the word "women" or another feminine noun was not enough for inclusion; the representative had to profess concern with women's well-being, specific interests, or desires within the substantive remark for it to be coded as "woman-invoked rhetoric." For example, on November 9, 1997, Representative Patsy Mink (D-HI) argued that the Small Business Reauthorization Act would help women and minorities who owned businesses. On October 28, 1997, Representative Nita Lowey (D-NY) asked Congress for more money for breast cancer research because such research affects the health of women. A September 22, 1997 speech given by Representative Nancy Johnson (R-CT) discussed the issue of sexual misconduct in the military. Johnson never mentioned how sexual misconduct specifically harms women or females. Instead, Johnson spoke broadly about the "victims" of sexual misconduct with no specific reference to how harassment hurts females in the military. As a result, Johnson's speech *was not* coded as "woman-invoked rhetoric."

The speech concerning a particular bill or subject did not have to concern wholly women's interests or concerns. If only one part of the *Congressional Record* entry mentioned the impact of the legislation, amendment, or policy on women, then I included it as "woman-invoked rhetoric." On June 26, 1997, Representative Nydia Velázquez (D-NY-12) spoke against the Taxpayer Relief Act of 1997. She stated that the Republican tax plan would "punish two million working, middle-class women" by not providing them with appropriate tax relief. Within her speech, the interests of women were not Velázquez's only expressed concern. However, in at least part of her remarks, Velázquez claimed that this piece of legislation affected the interests of women.

After an entry was categorized as "woman-invoked rhetoric," I noted down a description of the remarks. This description consisted of a short paragraph that explained what policy, legislation, or issue was being discussed, how the representative specifically invoked women in her argument or statement, and the date of the entry. Although an individual *Congressional Record* entry might have contained several claims involving women, each entry only counted as one instance of "woman-invoked rhetoric."

Upon completion of the data collection, I subsequently developed eight nonexclusive policy categories for coding and grouping purposes.[6] The eight policy areas were as follows: abortion, personal economics, welfare state, safety, health, equality, foreign policy, and tributes. Each instance of "woman-invoked rhetoric" was placed in only one category. Specific distinctions between the categories are outlined as follows.

"Personal economics" policy issues claim to affect the financial well-being of working women. These arguments refer to changes in tax laws, labor laws, pension laws, IRA provisions, and programs for women-owned businesses. "Welfare state issues" refer to rhetoric endorsing the continuation, expansion, or revision of traditional welfare programs such as Woman, Infants, and Children (WIC) and child care programs for mothers receiving federal subsidies. This category also includes arguments that discuss changes in welfare reform, such as provisions that would allow continuing education to count as work. "Safety" refers specifically to criminal issues such as domestic violence, sexual harassment, and repeat sexual offender laws, while "health" concerns breast cancer research funding, teen pregnancy, HIV/AIDS research for women, and other female health problems. In this data set, no speeches argued for issues that could be classified as both "safety" and "health." Both "safety" and "health" refer to domestic policy issues rather than international concerns. "Equality" is comprised of ideological arguments surrounding gender equity or civil rights. Examples include arguments for the continuation of Title IX and speeches discussing the unequal treatment of women in the military. "Foreign policy" refers to comments that criticize or applaud proposed policy that affects the condition or status of foreign women. If the statement mentioned the health or safety of foreign women, it was placed in the "foreign policy" category. Countries addressed in these foreign policy remarks were China, Bosnia, Ecuador, India, Ethiopia, Israel, and Afghanistan. "Tributes" are dedications made to women who are said to have significantly impacted the lives of women. The tribute had to mention that the person or organization receiving commendation affected the lives of females. Finally, the category of "abortion" includes remarks on "partial-birth" abortion legislation and funding foreign population planning programs. Even if they referred to policies that affect foreign women, all references to abortion were placed in the "abortion" category only. Additionally, all arguments concerning the funding of abortion were placed in the abortion category. For examples of entries in each issue category, see Appendix A.

It is important to note that the rhetoric examined for this study includes arguments on both sides of any given issue. For example, arguments characterized as pro-life as well as pro-choice were counted equally in the "abortion" category. The focus of this research is to discover *how often* female House members invoke women in their remarks and *what issues* this rhetoric concerns. Data collection was completed to include both sides of controversial issues that result in "woman-invoked rhetoric."

RESULTS

Democratic and Republican female House members invoked women in their arguments at similar frequencies. To compare these two groups, a woman's rhetoric score (WRS) was calculated for each member. This percentage is the number of times the representative invoked women divided by her total number of substantive remarks. For example, Representative Connie Morella (R-MD) was credited with 131 substantive entries. Of these 131 substantive remarks, I coded 26 as including "woman-invoked rhetoric." As a result, her WRS score was 26/131, or .198. According to Table 1, Republican and Democratic female legislators invoked women in their arguments at strikingly similar rates. Almost 12% of the substantive remarks made by Republican women in 1997 contained woman-invoked rhetoric of some sort while 9% of Democratic women's substantive remarks included woman-invoked speech.[7]

Democratic and Republican female House members both considered women in their arguments. Although the *frequency* of woman-invoked rhetoric was similar across political parties, it is important to remember that the overall amount of rhetoric is dramatically unequal because Democratic women greatly outnumber their GOP counterparts. In 1997, Republican females as a group invoked women in substantive remarks 110 times in the *Congressional Record* while their Democratic counterparts invoked women 221 times. Even if their woman-invoked rhetoric ratios are similar, Democratic women simply generated more aggregate rhetoric about women than Republican females.

What kinds of issues motivated female House members to employ woman-invoked rhetoric in their substantive remarks? As demonstrated by Figure 1, abortion remained a salient issue for female members of the 105th Congress. Nearly a third (29.3%) of the speeches invoking

TABLE 1. All Women Members–Frequency of Woman-Invoked Rhetoric

	WRS	Instances	Cases
Republicans	.119	110	16
Democrats	.090	221	34

women were arguments, either pro-choice or pro-life, about abortion policy. Surprisingly, tributes to female achievements consumed 17% of the total woman-invoked rhetoric. Health related issues were also mentioned with high frequency (18.4%). Rhetoric referring to gender-equity or civil rights only comprised 3.3% of the total woman-invoked rhetoric sampled. Foreign policy issues, such as Most Favored Nation status for China, also constituted a scant 3.3% of woman-invoked rhetoric.

A comparison between Republican and Democratic women on policy issues produces interesting results. While female representatives of the two parties invoked women in their substantive remarks at similar rates, Table 2 shows that issues emphasized by female partisans were dissimilar.

The most important issue for Republican and Democratic women is abortion. Health issues affecting women are also mentioned frequently by women of both parties. However, Democratic women pay more attention to tributes of women. Almost 20% of their woman-invoked rhetoric is spent on tributes while Republicans spend considerably less time (11%) on this activity. Additionally, Republican women discuss the effects of personal economics on women at a higher frequency (18.2% versus 8.6%) than Democratic women.

However, it is important to note once again that the overall amount of rhetoric greatly favors Democratic women. This observation is particu-

FIGURE 1. Percentage of Substantive Comments by All Women Members

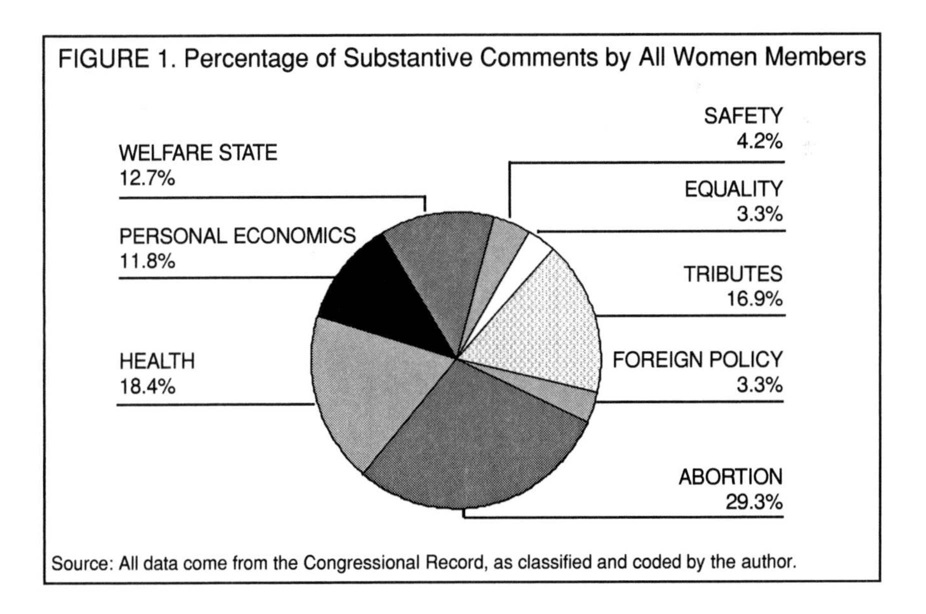

Source: All data come from the Congressional Record, as classified and coded by the author.

TABLE 2. Issues Discussed in Woman-Invoked Rhetoric, Partisan Differences

	Dem. Women N = 34	Repub. Women N = 16
Abortion	27.1% (60)	33.6% (37)
Economics	8.6% (19)	18.2% (20)
Equality	4.5% (10)	.9% (1)
Foreign Policy	3.6% (8)	2.7% (3)
Health	15.4% (34)	24.5% (27)
Safety	4.5% (10)	3.6% (4)
Tributes	19.9% (44)	10.9% (12)
Welfare State	16.3% (36)	5.5% (6)

larly instructive in the issue categories of abortion, personal economics, and tributes. Although abortion ranks highly for women in both parties, Democratic women spoke about the issue 60 times while Republican women discussed it 37 times. Republican women focus more on personal economics for women, but only spoke one more time (20 versus 19) about this issue in 1997 than their Democratic counterparts. Additionally, the number of tributes offered by Democratic women greatly outnumber the amount offered by Republican females (44 versus 12).

Female representatives of color might not spend as much time as white female representatives speaking about women because perhaps part of their time is spent addressing racial issues or concerns. In a study of state legislators, Barrett discovered that black women are similar to nonblack women in their strong support for "pro-women policies" but also similar to black men in their support of minority policies (1995). According to Barrett, the most pressing policy issues among black female state legislators are education, health care, economic development, and employment issues. Swain explains that black members of Congress have a broader view of constituency that includes "all blacks and disadvantaged people within the United States" (1993). When considering the policy interests of nonwhite female legislators, we must ask if racial priorities conflict with gender priorities or if the two merge into a unique position (Barrett 1995, 224).

Possibly Democratic women of color lowered the Democratic mean WRS because of this phenomenon. To test this hypothesis, I compared the mean women's rhetoric scores of Democratic white women and Democratic women of color.[8] (See Table 3.) No negligible difference exists between women of color and white women. These data suggest that women of color did not substantially lower the Democratic mean women's rhetoric score.

Even if Democratic women of color invoked women at the same frequency as Democratic white female House members, did they address the same policy issues in their woman-invoked rhetoric? Furthermore, controlling for race, did white Republican women address different policy issues than white Democratic women? (See Table 4.)

When it comes to policies or legislation that claims to affect women, Democratic women of color professed different concerns than did

TABLE 3. Democratic Women

	WRS	**Cases**
Women of Color	.0896	13
White Women	.0903	21

TABLE 4. Issues Discussed in Woman-Invoked Rhetoric, Racial Differences

	Democratic White Women N = 21	**Democratic Women of Color N = 13**	**Republican White Women N = 15**
Abortion	36.1% (48)	13.6% (12)	32.7% (32)
Economics	4.5% (6)	14.8% (13)	20.4% (20)
Equality	1.5% (2)	9.1% (8)	1.0% (1)
Foreign Policy	4.5% (6)	2.3% (2)	2.0% (2)
Health	14.3% (19)	17.0% (15)	24.5% (24)
Safety	5.3% (7)	3.4% (3)	4.1% (4)
Tributes	17.3% (23)	23.9% (21)	9.2% (9)
Welfare State	16.5% (22)	15.9% (14)	6.1% (6)
Total	100% (133)	100% (88)	100% (98)

Democratic white women. While Democratic white women talked about abortion frequently (36.1%), women of color devoted much less time to this issue (13.6%). If Democratic women of color spoke about abortion at the same rates as Democratic white women, we would expect them to discuss abortion approximately 32 times during 1997. However, Democratic women of color mentioned this issue only 12 times during the legislation session.

Finally, it is interesting to note that this data partially confirms Barrett's findings regarding pressing policy issues for nonwhite female legislators. Speeches concerning economics, employment, and health issues all ranked highly for Democratic women of color, although discourse about education was scant for all female members in 1997.

Comparing Republican white women to Democratic white women also yields notable results. A great deal of the white Republican woman-invoked rhetoric concerned economic policy and its effect on women (20.4%). Democratic white women spent only 4.5% of their woman-invoked rhetoric time on this issue. Additionally, health issues ranked higher for Republican women in comparison to Democratic white women (24.5% versus 14.3%). The issue of abortion consumed roughly the same portion of woman-invoked rhetoric time for white female House members of both parties.

CONCLUSION

The results of this empirical investigation are important to political scientists for several reasons. Although political scientists previously investigated how legislators represent women's interests or causes, an analysis of how often female representatives discuss this topic on the House floor has never been completed prior to this examination. Almost 11% of the public 1997 *Congressional Record* statements of female members of Congress mentioned the specific concerns of women. Female representatives do not forget the concerns of women when they engage in discussion on the House floor. This finding indicates that female representatives often utilize the "talking and deliberating" activity associated with descriptive representation to promote women's issues, interests, and concerns.

More surprisingly, this data demonstrates that Democratic and Republican women do not differ in the rates in which they mention women on the House floor. Although Democratic women are frequently considered the symbolic representatives of women's causes, Republican women actually speak about women at the same frequency as their liberal counterparts. Despite this unanticipated finding, this analysis also explains, in part, why Democratic women are still largely perceived as the leaders of women's causes. Because Democratic female representatives greatly outnumber Republican females, Democratic women talk much more about women in the aggregate. Republican women do not avoid discussion about women's interests and concerns, but their contributions are greatly outweighed by Democratic efforts. This finding is particularly instructive to the Republican Party. If the GOP wants to alter this large disparity, either more Republican women must win election to the House or the already-elected female GOP partisans must speak more frequently about women to compensate for this deficit. The large partisan difference in aggregate woman-invoked rhetoric is important for the perceived images of the two major political parties. The continued appearance of the Democrats as the "party of women" is undoubtedly related to the continued persistence of electoral phenomena such as the gender gap.[9]

Democratic and Republican women talk about different issues when they discuss women's interests. Although female representatives from both parties are concerned about abortion policy, Democrats concentrate on welfare policy and laudatory tributes to women while Republicans talk more about economic policy. Once again, the small number of Republican women legislators limits the ability of the GOP contingent to direct discussion about women. If Republicans hope to change the types of issues discussed in relation to women's interests, the party might consider trying to increase their aggregate output of woman-invoked rhetoric. These data suggest that Republican women talk about different issues affecting women than their Democratic counterparts, but the small number of Republican female legislators perhaps limits the GOP's ability to challenge the traditional Democratic agenda of women's issues to address more conservative causes, such as economic policy.

Finally, these numbers suggest that the issue of abortion is complicated. While Republican and Democratic white women address abortion at the same rates, Democratic women of color talk about this issue much less on the House floor. Although abortion was mentioned 92 times in 1997 by all female legislators, Democratic women of color, who comprise approximately one-fourth of all female House members, only discussed this issue 12 times. This empirical evidence implies that among female House members, the issue of abortion is dominated by the discourse of white women. Further research on the issue of abortion is needed to confirm these findings.

Additional scholarship is needed to provide a more robust picture of the "talking and deliberating" function of female descriptive representation. Analyzing *Congressional Record* entries beyond the first legislative session of the 105th Congress would provide a broader outlook of how female representatives invoke women in their political rhetoric. A longitudinal study might decrease variability, making inferential analysis more readily applicable. Although content analysis of *Congressional Record* entries is time-consuming and tedious, an enlarged sample size would help determine the validity of these findings. This examination has included two independent variables in its analysis, namely party identification and race. Including demographic district characteristics such as mean income level might explain some of the differences in policy concerns amongst female House members. Further content analysis of this rich source of empirical data is warranted as more scholars pursue research in the growing field of female representation.

AUTHOR NOTE

The author would like to thank Professor David Mayhew of Yale University for his helpful assistance on this project. This material is based upon work supported under a National Science Foundation Graduate Fellowship.

NOTES

1. For a discussion of the connection between public opinion of congressional districts and voting records of House members, see Benjamin Page, Robert Shapiro, Paul Gronke, and Robert Rosenberg's article entitled "Constituency, Party, and Representation in Congress" published in 1984 in *Public Opinion Quarterly,* Volume 48. The authors discover that issues involving women's rights and ERA display a high degree of correlation (.59) between a district's opinion and a member of Congress's voting record.

2. The following is a listing of female members elected to the House of Representatives with reference to party affiliation. 102nd Congress–19D, 9R; 103rd Congress–35D, 12R; 104th Congress–31D, 17R. 105th Congress–35D, 16R; 106th Congress–39D, 17R. Because of the small number of Republican women in the House in the 102nd and 103rd Congresses, the 105th Congress provided the most recent data for comparison across parties. Source: Center for the American Woman and Politics Fact Sheet, Elected Women in 2000, http://www.rci.rutgers.edu/~cawp.

3. I used the Internet resource called "Thomas" for my analysis of the *Congressional Record.* "Thomas" is maintained by the Library of Congress and can be located at http://thomas.loc.gov.

4. Because they are non-voting delegates rather than full members of the House, I did not include Representatives Donna Christian-Green (U.S. Virgin Islands) or Eleanor Holmes Norton (District of Columbia). Due to her absence from the House in 1997 because of heart bypass surgery, I also did not include Representative Julia Carson (D-IN) in this sample. Health problems greatly diminished Carson's activity in the House; according to my analysis, she only produced six substantive entries in the *Congressional Record* in 1997. I did include Representative Susan Molinari (R-NY) since she was present and active for over three-quarters of the 1997 session, although she resigned from the House on August 2, 1997.

5. In my research, I found 3100 "substantive remarks" in total. All of these speeches or remarks were read to determine if arguments concerning females were present in the text.

6. All of my instances of "woman-invoked rhetoric" fit into one of these eight categories. In total, I found 331 instances of "woman-invoked rhetoric" in 1997's *Congressional Record.* Although eight categories might seem like a small number of policy areas, keep in mind that this data only represents entries from one year's (1997) *Congressional Record* entries. I re-checked my data twice for accuracy in categorization. I did not choose "education" as an analytical category because I found very few references to education in the entries I coded. Educational advances by women were mentioned in three speeches invoking the 25th Anniversary of Title IX. Those three speeches [given by Representatives Kilpatrick (D-MI), Pelosi (D-CA), and Mink (D-HI)] were coded as examples of "gender equity" because they lauded the increased opportunities for women due to the prohibition of sex discrimination in Title IX. Additionally, Representative Lynn Woolsey (D-CA) discussed educational opportunities for women on welfare twice in the month of May. Since both comments endorsed amending existing welfare law to provide more educational opportunities for women receiving public assistance, I placed these two remarks in the "welfare state" category.

7. I have not performed any inference tests (such as a t-test) to compare the means between Republican and Democratic women. In this instance, statistical tests are not appropriate since I am examining the entire population of female members of the 105th Congress. If an entire population is analyzed, no sampling variance exists, thus making it inappropriate to use significance tests to assess the probability of sampling error.

8. Since I am not treating my data as a sample but as a population, the small size of the Democratic women of color category (N = 13) is not a hindrance. I am not drawing statistical inferences from the data set.

9. See the 1999 Center for American Women and Politics (CAWP) Fact Sheet entitled "Gender Gap Evident in Numerous 1998 Races." In 1998, the Voter News Service estimated the gender gap, or the number of percentage points between the proportion of men's and women's votes garnered by the winner, at 4%.

REFERENCES

Barrett, Edith J. 1995. "Gender and Race at the State House: The Legislative Experience." *Social Science Journal* 34: 131-144.

Carroll, Susan J. 1991. "Taking the Lead." *Journal of State Government* 64: 43-47.

Casey, Kathleen, and Susan J. Carroll. 1998. "Wyoming Wolves and Dead-Beat Dads: The Impact of Women Members of Congress on Welfare Reform." Presented at the annual meeting of the American Political Science Association.

Center for American Women and Politics (CAWP). 1996. "The Gender Gap." CAWP Fact Sheet available at http://www.rci.rutgers.edu/~cawp/Facts.html.

Center for American Women and Politics (CAWP). 1997. "Women's PACs and Donor Networks." CAWP Fact Sheet available at http://www.rci.rutgers.edu/~cawp/Facts.html.

Center for American Women and Politics (CAWP). 1999. "Gender Gap Evident in Numerous 1998 Races." CAWP Fact Sheet available at http://www.rci.rutgers.edu/~cawp/Facts.html.

Congressional Record. 1997. Washington, DC: Government Printing Office.

Dolan, Julie. 1997. "Support for Women's Interests in the 103rd Congress: The District Impact of Congressional Women." *Women & Politics* 18(4): 81-94.

Freeman, Jo. 1993. "Feminism vs. Family Values: Women at the 1992 Democratic and Republican Conventions." *PS: Political Science & Politics* 26: 21-28.

Hill, David B. 1983. "Women State Legislators and Party Voting on the ERA." *Social Science Quarterly* 64: 318-326.

Leader, Shelah Gilbert. 1977. "The Policy Impact of Elected Women Officials." In *The Impact of the Electoral Process,* eds. Louis Maisel and Joseph Cooper. Beverley Hills: Sage.

Mayhew, David. 1974. *The Electoral Connection.* New Haven: Yale University Press.

Paddock, Joel, and Elizabeth Paddock. 1997. "Differences in Partisan Style and Ideology Between Female and Male State Party Committee Members." *Women & Politics* 18 (4): 41-56.

Pitkin, Hanna. 1967. *The Concept of Representation.* Berkeley: University of California Press.

Reingold, Beth. 1992. "Concepts of Representation Among Female and Male State Legislators." *Legislative Studies Quarterly* 17: 509-535.

Sapiro, Virginia, and Barbara Farah. 1980. "New Pride and Old Prejudice: Political Ambition and Role Orientations Among Female Partisan Elites." *Women & Politics* 1(1): 13-35.

Swain, Carol. 1993. *Black Faces, Black Interests.* Cambridge, MA: Harvard University Press.

Thomas, Sue. 1991. "The Impact of Women on State Legislative Policies." *Journal of Politics* 53: 958-976.

Thomas, Sue, and Susan Welch. 1990. "The Impact of Gender on Activities and Priorities of State Legislators." *Western Political Quarterly* 44: 445-456.

Vega, Arturo, and Juanita M. Firestone. 1995. "The Effects of Gender on Congressional Behavior and Substantive Representation of Women." *Legislative Studies Quarterly* 20: 213-222.

Welch, Susan. 1985. "Are Women More Liberal Than Men in the U.S. Congress?" *Legislative Studies Quarterly* 10: 125-134.

APPENDIX A

Health:

March 10, 1997–We must standardize Medicare coverage for bone density testing–80% of those suffering from osteoporosis are women (Representative Connie Morella, R-MD).

April 29, 1997–Heart disease is the number one cause of death and disability among American women (Representative Maxine Waters, D-CA).

Abortion:

February 13, 1997–Approving the Presidential Finding Regarding the Population Planning Program–family planning funding is good for women and children but using taxes for abortion is inappropriate (Representative Jennifer Dunn, R-WA).

February 13, 1997–Family Planning Facilitation and Abortion Funding Restriction Act of 1997–United States has provided money for thirty years to organize family planning abroad; this funding has helped poor women (Representative Sheila Jackson Lee, D-TX).

Safety:

May 6, 1997–Housing Opportunities and Responsibilities Act of 1997–amendment introduced to ban sexual predators from public housing because these offenders have "stalked women and children" previously (Representative Nancy Johnson, R-CT).

June 19, 1997–Proving for Consideration of National Defense Authorization Act–we need a better review of the entire military justice system because women in the military are routinely subjected to harassment (Representative Carolyn Maloney, D-NY).

Personal Economics:

March 19, 1997–Working Families Flexibility Act of 1997–This bill does not help women because women who work to support their families need to know they have the security to depend on overtime pay (Representative Loretta Sanchez, D-CA).

July 31, 1997–Conference Report on HR 2014–For the first time in sixteen years, American women are getting a tax cut–women are starting businesses today at twice the rate of men–a lower capital gains tax helps women (Representative Jennifer Dunn, R-WA).

Equality:

November 4, 1997–Dismantling of Equal Opportunity–disapproval of allowing affirmative action ban in California to stand because it will reverse the gains made by African Americans, women, and other minorities (Representative Eva Clayton, D-NC).

February 5, 1997–Response to General Dennis Reimer's suggestion that sex-segregated training return to the military–we cannot use human nature and sexuality as an excuse for gender discrimination–women must be treated equally (Representative Eddie Bernice Johnson, D-TX).

Welfare State Funding:

April 30, 1997–Congressional Black Caucus Opposes an Appropriations Bill Which Throws Women and Children off WIC–WIC allows hundreds and thousands of women and children to avoid the disaster of hunger (Representative Maxine Waters, D-CA).

May 6, 1997–Housing Opportunities and Responsibilities Act–need this act to address the plight of working mothers who have jobs and/or take educational classes (Representative Diana DeGette, D-CO).

Foreign Policy:

June 24, 1997–Disapproval of Most-Favored Nation (MFN) Status for China– one of the many reasons not to support MFN status for China is the "outrageous abuse and neglect of baby girls" in China (Representative Tillie Fowler, R-FL).

July 30, 1997–Foreign Operations, Export Financing, and Related Programs–need to address concerns about Ethiopia's treatment of women, including practices surrounding genital mutilation and maternal care (Representative Sheila Jackson Lee, D-TX).

Tributes:

October 21, 1997–20th Anniversary of the Congressional Caucus for Women's Issues–this caucus has worked to insure the well being of women, children, and families (Representative Connie Morella, R-MD).

June 17, 1997–Recognition of the Michigan Women's Historical Center–this center has enabled the people of Michigan to learn more about its outstanding women (Representative Debbie Stabenow, D-MI).

"How Does She Have Time for Kids and Congress?" Views on Gender and Media Coverage from House Offices

David Niven, Florida Atlantic University
Jeremy Zilber, College of William and Mary

SUMMARY. According to previous studies, women political leaders often are cast by the media as focused narrowly on matters of significance to their gender, and as being less weighty players in government than their male counterparts. This research explores the degree to which the press offices of women members of Congress perceive this to be the case, and the degree to which women representatives' communication efforts contribute to this pattern of coverage. Interviews with press secretaries to House members reveal that press secretaries find the media to be less fair in their treatment of women members, and that they believe women members are subject to sex role stereotyping. Contrary to the media's depiction, however, Congressional press secretaries and House member Web sites reveal that women members portray themselves, and seek to be portrayed, as having diverse interests and significant influence in Washington. Thus, it appears that the media, rather than the members and their staffers, are responsible for the stereotyped coverage that women representatives receive. *[Article copies available for a fee from The Haworth Document Delivery Service: 1-800-HAWORTH. E-mail address: <getinfo@haworthpressinc.com> Website: <http://www.HaworthPress.com> © 2001 by The Haworth Press, Inc. All rights reserved.]*

[Haworth co-indexing entry note]: " 'How Does She Have Time for Kids and Congress?' Views on Gender and Media Coverage from House Offices." Niven, David and Jeremy Zilber. Co-published simultaneously in *Women & Politics* (The Haworth Press, Inc.) Vol. 23, No. 1/2, 2001, pp. 147-165; and: *Women and Congress: Running, Winning, and Ruling* (ed: Karen O'Connor) The Haworth Press, Inc., 2001, pp. 147-165. Single or multiple copies of this article are available for a fee from The Haworth Document Delivery Service [1-800-HAWORTH, 9:00 a.m. - 5:00 p.m. (EST). E-mail address: getinfo@haworthpressinc.com].

INTRODUCTION

The offices of members of Congress often serve as the tail wagged by the media dog. Congressional offices are communication centers geared to respond to media requests for interviews, comments, and information, with the ultimate goal of ensuring that a positive message reaches the voters back home (Cook 1989; Dewhirst 1983; Miller 1976). Scholars have found good reason for such a commitment. To wit, media coverage of congressional candidates has been found to influence recognition, emotional connections, evaluations, and ultimately, vote choice (see, for example, Goidel and Shields 1994; Herrnson 1995; Niven and Zilber 1998; Parker 1981; Payne 1980).

Though the media are a crucial link between candidates and office holders and voters, many would argue that the media abuse this power by employing stereotypes in political coverage (for example, Witt, Paget, and Matthews 1995). Specifically, women candidates seem to be portrayed quite differently and in some cases quite dismissively (Devitt 1999; Kahn and Goldenberg 1991). The scope and origins of this gender difference in coverage are explored here to determine if female members of the U.S. House of Representatives and their staffs are concerned with media stereotyping, and if women members perhaps contribute to this pattern by cultivating different images than their male colleagues.

A number of studies reveal differences in media coverage of women and men political leaders. Scholars have found women candidates and legislators are taken less seriously (Braden 1996; Devitt 1999; Kahn and Goldenberg 1991; Witt, Paget, and Matthews 1995) and receive less general coverage (Clawson and Tom 1999), but receive more attention on "women's issues" such as abortion and family leave (Carroll and Schreiber 1997) while being ignored on most other matters of substance (Braden 1996; Clawson and Tom 1999). News coverage of women more frequently mentions their family situations and is more likely to invoke matters of a more superficial nature, highlighting personality, appearance, and fashion decisions (Braden 1996; Devitt 1999; Gidengil and Everitt 1999; Witt, Paget, and Matthews 1995). Men, meanwhile, can expect greater media attention to their experience and accomplishments, as well as greater attention to their position on particular issues (Davis 1982; Devitt 1999; Jamieson 1995).

Not only do male candidates receive more vis-à-vis their position on the issues, but that coverage is more likely to suggest that men are prepared, qualified, and understand the logic and evidence of the issue at hand (Devitt 1999). Ultimately, the portrait of women that emerges from the press suggests that they are less powerful and less weighty players in the political game (Carroll and Schreiber 1997; Clawson and Tom 1999; Devitt 1999).

Startlingly, some women politicians report that the media's portrayal of women has stagnated since the 1960s. For example, Elizabeth Holtzman (D-NY), who served in the House in the 1970s and ran unsuccessfully for the Senate in 1992, found that the same damaging stereotypes she experienced in the 1970s still existed 20 years later (Braden 1996, 73). Holtzman became fond of quoting Eleanor Roosevelt's warning: "If you're going to be a woman in public life, you've got to have a skin as thick as a rhinoceros" (quoted in Braden 1996, 73).

The implications of negative coverage are great. Koch (1999) reports that better informed voters have more rigid stereotypes of women candidates, presumably because of their constant exposure to media stereotyping. Indeed, Kahn and Goldenberg (1991) argue, and experimental research has shown (Dayhoff 1983; Kahn 1992), that typical media coverage of women candidates can serve to undermine their credibility with voters. According to advisors to Senator Barbara Boxer (D-CA) and former Senator Carol Moseley-Braun (D-IL), media-fed perceptions that women are out of the loop, cannot get things done, are insubstantial, and are concerned only about some people's problems, are major factors that negatively affect the popularity of women leaders.[1] Even some potentially benign stereotypes, such as the portrayal of women as concerned about women's issues, may not be particularly useful. Leeper (1991) argues that women already have the edge in regard to women's issues, and instead need to shore up their credentials in other areas.

Despite the well-documented and important differences in media treatment of women and men leaders, one vital question that generally has been overlooked is: Where does this emphasis originate? In other words, do the media create and perpetuate stereotypic images of women leaders? Or, are the actions and words of women feeding this pattern in coverage?

Some scholars argue that the primary method by which the media attempt to be objective is by reporting the range of what politicians do and say, not what media members themselves think (Bennett 1990; Zaller and Chiu 1996). As such, a gender emphasis in reporters' coverage need not reflect any bias on their part, but merely the reality of what the candidates are doing and saying (Kahn and Gordon 1997). One could argue that suggesting most women politicians are committed to issues involving women is merely stating the obvious (see, for example, Berkman and O'Connor 1993; Saint-Germain 1989), and that other differences in coverage are simply a product of differences in personal presentation by men and women politicians.

Skeptics of this perspective, however, note the media's general willingness to be influenced by stereotypes in political coverage. For example, because of Congress's large size and its attention to a wide array of issues, those who cover the House and Senate develop a stable of spokespersons on whom to rely depending on the events of the day (Cook 1989; Miller 1977). The complexity of the media's task thus necessitates categorizing members, and categorizing members encourages the media to portray certain members as concerned about agriculture, taxes, and/or women's issues. In the process, members often receive coverage only concerning "their" issue. Members can quickly be stereotyped as knowing or caring only about one or two issues. Further entrenching this process is the cycle of information on Congress, which often begins in the specialty congressional publications (such as *Roll Call*), then appears in the national papers of note (*The New York Times, The Washington Post*), and then filters down to other outlets (Cook 1989). Thus, as reporters pay attention to each other's work for story ideas and information, they are exposed to each other's stereotypes. It is not surprising, then, that despite the variety of issues individual members may care about and work on, many members have trouble drawing media attention outside of their reputed areas of expertise or interest (Cook 1989).

This process is not, of course, limited to gender, but it may be rather acute because of the predominance of men in the newsroom. At *The New York Times,* for example, articles by male authors outnumber articles by female authors by five to one (Mills 1997), while more generally, male reporters outnumber women two to one nationwide (Weaver 1997). Based on these figures and the coverage that results, Norris (1997, 6) concludes that "journalists commonly work with gendered frames to simplify, prioritize, and structure the narrative flow of events when covering women and men in public life."

OVERVIEW OF METHODS

To address the perspective of congressional offices on the media, and to assess what role, if any, women legislators' media presentations have in creating an imbalance in coverage, press secretaries to women members of the House were interviewed. Interviews explored the media relations efforts made by women representatives, the images they and their staffs try to cultivate, and their views of the process.

Congressional press secretaries are the ideal source for such information, according to Cook (1989), who finds that press secretaries are the media arm of House offices. Press secretaries not only map out media strategy, they also implement it. In fact, more so than the members themselves, it is their press secretaries who have media expertise and experience. It is the press secretary's responsibility to gain positive attention for the member in the media (Miller 1976).

Thus, the press secretaries of all women representatives were initially called and asked to participate. To make conclusions about women members' media goals relative to other representatives, two comparison samples were created. In the first group, 20 male members of the House whose ideology and tenure in office were similar as a group to the women legislators were selected.[2] This "women comparison group" was complemented by a second group of 20 male representatives who were roughly representative of men in the House, which is to say, largely Republican and conservative.[3] Through the use of these three groups (women members, the women comparison group, and the overall comparison group), the responses from women's offices can be understood in context.

Interviews were obtained by calling each representative's office and asking to speak with the press secretary.[4] Respondents were informed that their office had been selected to take part in a research project on "media coverage of Congress"; they were not made aware of either the reason their office was chosen or any of our specific concerns.[5] Respondents were assured that their answers would not be attributed to them or to their respective offices.

All interviews were conducted between late June and mid-August of 1998. While many press secretaries were receptive to our request, several declined to be interviewed. By far the most common explanation for refusing to participate was a standing office policy against responding to surveys of any kind. Others rejected our request on the grounds that they were serving as "acting" press secretary or simply felt they had too little experience to be of assistance. Some interviews could not be completed because of time constraints and schedule conflicts or because the press secretary could not be reached at all. In such cases, press secretaries were sent a letter requesting a written response to the interview questions. We received a total of 19 written responses, which were assimilated into the pool of 40 completed telephone interviews.[6] Overall, our sample contains responses from 28 of 68 press secretaries working for women representatives and 31 working for men (16/20 in the women comparison group, and 15/20 from the overall comparison group).[7]

VIEW OF THE MEDIA FINDINGS

The interview questionnaire (Appendix A) contained several items designed to tap the general level of satisfaction with media coverage and to allow respondents to express their feelings about the prominence of gender stereotypes in news reporting. Press secretaries were asked whether the member had been treated fairly by the media; whether the member's coverage accurately reflected his or her priorities and accomplishments; what specific disappointments they had encountered with media coverage; and whether the member was subject to any media stereotypes.

Overall, the interviews provide support for the contention that press secretaries for female members believe that the media define women members of Congress by their gender. These press secretaries also believe that this poses a significant problem for women members.[8]

Relative to both comparison groups, press secretaries working for women members were considerably more likely to complain about unfair coverage. Whereas almost every respondent in both male comparison groups stated that the media generally treated their bosses fairly, only 32% of the press secretaries for women members agreed with that sentiment (see Table 1). Similar results were obtained with respect to whether media coverage accurately reflected members' priorities and accomplishments.

Moreover, when asked about specific disappointments concerning media coverage, there was a tendency for press secretaries to men and women representatives to emphasize different concerns. For the most part, press secretaries to men complained about a particular story or issue (see Table 2). For example, one press secretary felt that his boss was not getting enough credit for his efforts on issues such as economic assistance. Another complained that the media had not paid enough attention to a particular bill that the member had been instrumental in getting through the House. One press secretary was livid that the media had chosen to focus on only certain aspects of his boss's education proposal (specifically its beneficial effect on private schools) and ignored much of what he thought was the bill's true importance. Another bemoaned a specific newspaper's inability to understand the intricacies of foreign policy.

TABLE 1. General Perceptions of Media Treatment

	Women Representatives Group	Women Comparison Group of Men	Overall Comparison Group
Generally, do you think the media treat your representative fairly? (% yes)	32	88*	93*
Is media coverage commensurate with your representative's priorities and accomplishments? (% yes)	46	81*	93*

Source: Authors' survey of congressional press secretaries.
* $p < .05$
N = 59

TABLE 2. Disappointments with Media Coverage

What, if any, disappointment has your office experienced in dealing with the media?	Women Representatives Group	Women Comparison Group of Men	Overall Comparison Group
Wanted more coverage of specific issue or event	28	44*	46*
Unfair coverage of specific issue or event	32	25*	33
Wanted more coverage generally	46	19*	20*
Unfair coverage of service in office/lack of respect of member	43	6*	7*

Source: Authors' survey of congressional press secretaries.
Note: Respondents could give multiple responses.
* $p < .05$
N = 59

In contrast, press secretaries to women were more likely to cite a general lack of press coverage as their greatest disappointment. Many suggested that the reason their representative received less coverage is that the media afford women lawmakers less respect. One press secretary to a woman member said "time and again, she is underestimated by the media." Another added that her boss "might as well be invisible for all the attention they pay to her leadership on issues."

Striking differences also emerged in response to the question about stereotypes (see Table 3). It should be emphasized that, to this point in the interviews, respondents had no indication of our project's true purpose. That is, there had been no direct or indirect references to gender. Nevertheless, when asked if their representative had been subject to any media stereotypes, the vast majority (75%) of press secretaries to women complained specifically about categorizations having to do with gender (press secretaries to female African American members typically decried stereotypes of both their gender and race). Indeed, we received several strong reactions to this line of inquiry:

> They see her as a woman, and they come to us when they think they have a "woman's issue" and need to hear a woman's view.
>
> She's a woman first to the media, and it's always as if she was elected to be in some kind of special woman's seat, like her job is somehow different from that of the men in the delegation.

Others focused on the media's fascination with women members' family situations:

> The next time [our local paper] puts together a story that doesn't mention she's a mom with young children it will be a first.
>
> A reporter once asked me, "How does she have time for kids and Congress?" I asked him if he had ever posed the same question to a man.

TABLE 3. Media Stereotypes

Is your member subject to any media stereotypes?	**Women Representatives Group**	**Women Comparison Group of Men**	**Overall Comparison Group**
Gender Stereotypes	75	0*	0*
Political/Ideological Stereotypes	28	50*	40*
Not Subject to Stereotypes	7	44*	53*

Source: Authors' survey of congressional press secretaries.
Note: Respondents could give multiple responses.
* $p < .05$
N = 59

In stark contrast, press secretaries to male members were often hard pressed to think of stereotypes that applied to them. Indeed, some seemed confused by the question and asked for clarification. Many paused before answering. Some press secretaries to men flatly stated that their members had not been subject to *any* media stereotypes. Of those who did mention any stereotyping, virtually all complained about either a political characterization ("liberal," "right wing," "Clinton supporter," "Washington bureaucrat," "Gingrich Clone," etc.) or an unflattering personality trait ("hot-tempered," "confrontational," "nerdy," etc.). In *not one* case did a press secretary for a male representative complain about gender stereotyping. Indeed, one press secretary to a woman pointed directly to an example of what she saw as an overwhelming and indefensible double standard:

> Our opponent in the last campaign was a man running on family values. He portrayed himself with his granddaughter as the paragon of what a family man should be. We had reason to believe he was not what he seemed, and eventually he admitted his "granddaughter" was in fact his out-of-wedlock biological daughter, who he had never acknowledged as his own, or even admitted to his affair with her mother. We expected to have a field day with this–to really tear him apart for his hypocrisy. Instead, the media turned right back at us, and basically said, well your candidate is a single mother, so it's really the same thing.

IMAGES CULTIVATED

Press secretaries to women certainly argue that women receive different treatment. We wondered to what extent they actually might seek different treatment, that is, attempt to cultivate an image different from men. We asked what type of image they were trying to create, what types of stories they generally found most satisfying, and what an "ideal" story might look like. We also asked whether they preferred to be portrayed as "important in Washington" or "caring about the district," and the extent to which they preferred national versus local media exposure. Finally, we asked whether specific constituent groups were being targeted for media messages.

Here, the responses from women's offices were virtually indistinguishable from those of men's. Naturally, we encountered a number of personal idiosyncrasies on both the "image" and "story" items, but the same general themes emerged from both women's and men's offices. Press secretaries to women and to men wanted their bosses to be seen as "intelligent," "hardworking," "in touch with the people," "respected," etc. And, of course, both coveted stories in which their member was seen as "effective," "getting things done," "helping the district," and "solving problems." Given our specific interests, however, what is most noteworthy about these answers is the degree to which press secretaries to women did *not* talk about an image centered on serving the interests of women (see Table 4). Nor did women's offices suggest in any way that they sought coverage on matters of family or appearance.

Moreover, when directly asked if they were trying to reach specific constituent groups with their media efforts, press secretaries to women representatives infrequently mentioned women voters as a target. Indeed, only 18% mentioned women, which was less than the frequency of their references to a number of non-gender related groups, including senior citizens, taxpayers, and veterans. Groups targeted by women representatives were substantially similar to targets of the male comparison groups. Both comparison groups and women members were most likely to highlight senior citizens and taxpayers (see Table 5).

Interestingly, despite media coverage often suggesting women are outsiders to the workings of Washington, press secretaries to women professed no less interest in generating Washington-centered stories than did press secretaries in either comparison group. Specifically,

TABLE 4. Images Members Try to Convey

Could you list a few words that capture the image of your representative that you are trying to communicate?	**Women Representatives Group**	**Women Comparison Group of Men**	**Overall Comparison Group**
Intelligent/respected	54	62	66
In touch/caring	46	56	59
Effective/getting things done	61	50	53
Serving the interests of women	0	0	0
Family person/appearance	0	0	0

Source: Authors' survey of congressional press secretaries.
Note: Respondents could give multiple responses.
N = 59

TABLE 5. Groups Targeted in Media Messages

What groups, if any, do you target in your communication efforts?	Women Representatives Group	Women Comparison Group of Men	Overall Comparison Group
Senior Citizens	32	37	40
Taxpayers	28	25	40
Veterans	22	19	33
Women	18	6*	0*

Source: Authors' survey of congressional press secretaries.
Note: Respondents could give multiple responses.
N = 59

when asked to choose between the two, 18% of the press secretaries to women said their boss preferred being seen as politically important in Washington over being seen as caring about the district, while 12% of the women comparison group of men and 7% of the male overall comparison group chose that option (see Table 6). Similarly, when asked about the value they placed on national coverage versus local coverage, press secretaries to women gave no less weight to national coverage than did members of either comparison group (see Table 6).

An Independent Look at Images Cultivated

These responses reveal that congressional press secretaries believe that women in the House receive significantly different, indeed worse, coverage than men, despite trying to cultivate much the same image. To assess the images congressional offices proffer, independent of what those offices say they try to do, we also analyzed the congressional Web sites of women and comparison sample members to determine what issue areas members most often touted.

The value of these Web sites as a source of information is that they represent a forum of communication under the complete control of the congressional office. Members' Web sites can mention as many or as few issues as they want and present the members in any terms desired. This method does not rely upon a subject's recall, nor is it vulnerable to problems of hindsight. These sites represent the actual messages members circulate (Owen, Davis, and Strickler 1999).

TABLE 6. Type of Coverage Sought

	Women Representatives Group	Women Comparison Group of Men	Overall Comparison Group
If you had to choose, would you rather gain coverage for the representative's importance in Washington, or the representative's caring for the home district? (% Washington)	18	12	7
Generally, would you rather get coverage in the national media or the local media? (% national)	14	12	13

Source: Authors' survey of congressional press secretaries.
N = 59

While the Web is undoubtedly a developing medium for congressional communication, its significance as an outlet for members' messages should not be ignored (see, for example, Dulio, Goff, and Thurber 1999; Owen, Davis, and Strickler 1999). Indeed, as of December 1999, over 97% of House offices had Web sites. Some House Web sites receive as many as 1,000 visits per month.[9] The Web sites tend to feature substantially similar content as the traditional congressional newsletters that are sent to all constituents.[10] Owen, Davis, and Strickler (1999, 26) find that "Web sites have become another institutional tool, much like news releases and press releases, for members to use to communicate with their constituents and exhibit their home style." Finally, Web sites are considered significant enough that, just as franking privileges are suspended during the two months preceding an election, House members are not allowed to update their Web sites during the two months prior to an election.

WEB SITE ANALYSIS

All member-created material within each site was read, and all mentions of issues–and the amount of space dedicated to each issue–were recorded by two coders who were unaware of the concerns being explored.[11] At the time of the analysis in the summer of 1998, 47 male members maintained Web sites, 18 members in the women comparison group of men sample, and 18 in the male overall comparison sample. All 83 of those sites are included in the analysis.

While we find the vast majority of women members (84%) highlight their record on "women's issues" on the Web,[12] the majority of men also highlight these areas (70% of the male comparison group of men and 63% of men overall mention women's issues).

Women's issues, however, are only a small part of what women legislators articulate as their concerns. Moreover, most women members did not feature women's issues prominently on their Web pages. In fact, 88% of women legislators dedicated more space to an issue that falls outside of the definition of a women's issue, and *all* women legislators dedicated most of their total space to areas that fall outside of the rubric of women's issues.

To determine what the members considered their most significant accomplishment in office, we looked for synonymous direct labels, and in the absence of those, determined what legislative achievement was afforded the most space on each Web site. Consistent with the previous findings, when it comes to listing their top accomplishment in office, only 17% of women legislators featured women's issues as an area in which they have enjoyed their greatest legislative success. In fact, bringing home dollars for economic development was listed most frequently by women legislators as their most significant achievement in Congress (see Table 7). Their focus on economic development is not at all unique–as the overall comparison sample and the women's comparison group of men sample both highlight economic development as one of their biggest areas of achievement.[13]

This examination of Web sites offers additional support for the press secretaries' contention that the portrayal of women members is not the product of differences in the images sought or the presentation made by women. Rather, the results are consistent with the conclusion that media coverage of women in Congress is more the product of the media than of the women.

CONCLUSION

The media's gender-centered view of women politicians is a subject of concern to women in Congress. Compared with those who work for male members of Congress, the press secretaries to women members are less likely to believe their members are treated fairly, less likely to believe that their member's priorities and accomplishments are covered adequately, and more likely to believe that there is a general problem in media coverage.

In sum, press secretaries to women agree with the scholarly conclusions on this matter, such as Devitt (1999, 12) who argues that the media

TABLE 7. Top Accomplishment of House Members Listed on Web Site

Women Representatives Group	Women Comparison Group of Men	Overall Comparison Group
Economic Development (47%)	Poverty Legislation (22%)	Taxes/Budget (33%)
Women's Issues (17%)	Economic Development (22%)	Economic Development (27%)

Source: House members' Web sites.
N = 83.

are "diminishing the pipeline of women's leadership." Press secretaries to women believe that their members are subject to being viewed by the media as a woman representative, rather than as a representative who happens to be a woman.

The media's depiction of women representatives as being narrowly focused on gender, operating outside the wheels of power, does not appear to originate with the members themselves. This does not mean that women legislators are indifferent to women's issues. Instead, it means that for women legislators, if gender issues define them to the exclusion of all other beliefs and concerns, this will deny them credit for the breadth of their interests and efforts.

These media coverage patterns paint a picture of women representatives as out of touch, out of influence, and often belonging out of office. And while some of the "cheerleader," "motherhood," and "fashion" coverage women representatives garner may appear innocuous, this coverage is completely inconsistent with the image women need to project to compete successfully for the highest offices in this country (see Huddy and Terkildsen 1993).

Instead, what women legislators want from the media is a chance to speak for themselves and present the true nature of their agendas. As one press secretary remarked, "The day the media spend as much time pointing out that [Senate Majority Leader] Trent Lott was a cheerleader in college, spend as much time worrying about how the men in this body take care of their young kids while they're in office, and start asking why these men don't care about family issues instead of why we [women Representatives] do, then you can ask me if the media are fair and I won't have to laugh out loud."

NOTES

1. See, for example, Collins 1998.

2. Both groups had a median year elected of 1992. The women legislators had an average ADA score (Americans for Democratic Action ideology measure from 0 to 100, with 100 being most liberal) of 63, while the comparison group had an average ADA of 64. Members in the women comparison sample are: Edward Royce (R-CA), Dan Miller (R-FL), James Greenwood (R-PA), Peter Hoekstra (R-MI), Rick Lazio (R-NY), James Talent (R-MO), Martin Meehan (D-MA), Maurice Hinchey (D-NY), Thomas Barrett (D-WI), Ted Strickland (D-OH), Jim McDermott (D-WA), Frank Pallone (D-NJ), Neil Abercrombie (D-HA), Jerry Costello (D-IL), Patrick Kennedy (D-RI), Sherrod Brown (D-OH), Jerrod Nadler (D-NY), Bob Filner (D-CA), John Olver (D-MA), and Eliot Engel (D-NY).

3. The sample was chosen to mirror the experience and ideology of white males in the House. Both the population and the sample had a median year elected of 1992, while the ADA score for the population and the sample were 31 and 33 respectively. Members of the overall comparison group are Stephen Horn (R-CA), Bob Franks (R-NJ), Jack Quinn (R-NY), Michael Castle (R-DE), Spencer Bachus (R-AL), John Mica (R-FL), Mac Collins (R-GA), Michael Crapo (R-ID), Joe Knollenberg (R-MI), Bob Inglis (R-SC), Bob Goodlatte (R-VA), Donald Manzullo (R-IL), Paul McHale (D-PA), Cal Dooley (D-CA), Collin Peterson (D-MN), Robert Andrews (D-NJ), Chet Edwards (D-TX), Tim Roemer (D-IN), James Barcia (D-MI), and Ron Klink (D-PA).

4. While position titles vary slightly from office to office, our calls were invariably directed to individuals whose primary duties involved regular contact with the media. Each subject was asked to provide a brief description of his or her position, and in all cases respondents offered some variant of "press relations" as his or her principal role. A few respondents' duties also included tasks such as legislative assistance, speech writing, "Webmaster," etc., but in every instance it was clear the individual considered him or herself the office's primary media contact.

5. When pressed for more information regarding the nature of the study, we offered only that our research was looking into issues such as "accuracy in media coverage of Congress." If asked how the member's office came to be included in the sample, we revealed only that our sample had been designed to include members with certain demographic and political backgrounds, and that their office happened to meet our criteria. In short, every effort was made to assure that our specific interests were not revealed, i.e., that gender would not be artificially injected into a respondent's thoughts.

6. Our mail instrument produced results that were generally consistent with our interviews.

7. There are no statistically significant differences between our respondents and our full samples on ideology, party, or experience. There were 51 women serving full terms in the House at the time of the study, giving us a response rate of 55%.

8. There are men and women press secretaries in our sample working for male members and for female members. Significant differences based on the gender of the press secretaries did not emerge.

9. Most House Web sites did not feature a counter noting how many visits the site has received. Among those that did, Representative Constance Morella's (R-MD) site reported receiving 12,800 visits in just over one year (www.house.gov/morella/), and Representative Bob Goodlatte's (R-VA) site counted over 7,000 visitors in its seven months online (www.house.gov/goodlatte/).

10. For example, Representative Jerold Nadler's (D-NY) Web site (www.house.gov/nadler/) features a complete copy of his latest newsletter. The issues and Nadler's role in them are quite consistent in the newsletter and on the Web site.

11. A subsample of sites (10%) was coded by both coders, producing an intercoder reliability over .9.

12. The definition of "women's issues" used in this research encompasses initiatives that exclusively affect women (such as funding for women's health research), initiatives that primarily affect women (such as sexual harassment laws), and initiatives that fall at the intersection of family, children, and compassion (including education, family leave, child care, safe gun laws). This is consistent with the usage in a number of scholarly studies (for example, Thomas 1994), and is thought to be what voters have in mind when they think in these terms (Alexander and Andersen 1993; Rosenwasser and Seale 1988). Moreover, 1998 candidates, including Representative Scotty Baesler (D-KY) have explicitly campaigned on their record of "women's issues" by highlighting these varied concerns. Nevertheless, the analysis presented and the conclusions derived would be substantially similar if a more constricted definition of "women's issues" were used.

13. It is possible that women legislators have understated their commitment to women's issues, and that the media's focus on this area reflects the reality of their political agenda, if not the image the members have sought. To investigate this possibility, the legislation introduced by each member of the sample during this session of Congress was categorized by topic. Most women legislators were indeed active in women's issues (78% introduced legislation in a women's issue area), but again, the vast majority of their attention was directed elsewhere. Specifically, 73% of the legislation women introduced was not directed toward a problem of women, children, or families.

REFERENCES

Alexander, Deborah, and Kristi Andersen. 1993. "Gender as Factor in the Attribution of Leadership Traits." *Political Research Quarterly* 46: 527-545.

Bennett, W. Lance. 1990. "Toward a Theory of Press-State Relations in the United States." *Journal of Communication* 40: 103-125.

Berkman, Michael B., and Robert O'Connor. 1993. "Do Women Legislators Matter? Female Legislators and State Abortion Policy." *American Politics Quarterly* 21: 102-124.

Braden, Maria. 1996. *Women Politicians and the Media.* Lexington: University of Kentucky Press.

Carroll, Susan, and Ronnee Schreiber. 1997. "Media Coverage of Women in the 103rd Congress." In *Women, Media, and Politics,* ed. Pippa Norris. New York: Oxford University Press.

Clawson, Rosalee, and Ryan Tom. 1999. "Invisible Lawmakers: Media Coverage of Black and Female State Legislators." Unpublished manuscript. Purdue University.

Collins, Gail. 1998. "Why the Women Are Fading Away." *New York Times Magazine,* October 25.

Cook, Timothy. 1989. *Making Laws and Making News.* Washington, DC: Brookings.

Davis, Junetta. 1982. "Sexist Bias in Eight Newspapers." *Journalism Quarterly* 59: 456-460.
Dayhoff, Signe. 1983. "Sexist Language and Person Perception: Evaluation of Candidates from Newspaper Articles." *Sex Roles* 9: 527-539.
Devitt, James. 1999. "Framing Gender on the Campaign Trail: Women's Executive Leadership and the Press." Report for the Women's Leadership Fund.
Dewhirst, Robert. 1983. "Patterns of Interaction between Members of the U.S. House of Representatives and Their Home District News Media." Ph.D. diss. University of Nebraska.
Dulio, David, Donald Goff, and James Thurber. 1999. "Untangled Web: Internet Use During the 1998 Election." *PS: Political Science and Politics* 32: 53-59.
Gidengil, Elisabeth, and Joanna Everitt. 1999. "Metaphors and Misrepresentation: Gendered Mediation in News Coverage of the 1993 Canadian Leader's Debates." *Harvard International Journal of Press/Politics* 4: 48-65.
Goidel, Robert, and Todd Shields. 1994. "The Vanishing Marginals, the Bandwagon, and the Mass Media." *Journal of Politics* 56: 802-810.
Herrnson, Paul. 1995. *Congressional Elections: Campaigning at Home and in Washington.* Washington, DC: Congressional Quarterly.
Huddy, Leonie, and Nayda Terkildsen. 1993. "The Consequences of Gender Stereotypes for Women Candidates at Different Levels and Types of Office." *Political Research Quarterly* 46: 503-525.
Jamieson, Kathleen Hall. 1995. *Beyond the Double Bind: Women and Leadership.* New York: Oxford University Press.
Kahn, Kim Fridkin. 1992. "Does Being Male Help?" *Journal of Politics* 54: 497-517.
Kahn, Kim Fridkin, and Edie Goldenberg. 1991. "Women Candidates in the News: An Examination of Gender Differences in U.S. Senate Campaign Coverage." *Public Opinion Quarterly* 55: 180-199.
Kahn, Kim Fridkin, and Ann Gordon. 1997. "How Women Campaign for the U.S. Senate." In *Women, Media, and Politics,* ed. Pippa Norris. New York: Oxford University Press.
Koch, Jeffrey. 1999. "Candidate Gender and Assessments of Senate Candidates." *Social Science Quarterly* 80: 84-96.
Leeper, Mark. 1991. "The Impact of Prejudice on Female Candidates: An Experimental Look at Voter Inference." *American Politics Quarterly* 19: 248-261.
Miller, Susan. 1976. "Congress and the News Media: Coverage, Collaboration and Agenda-Setting." Ph.D. diss. Stanford University.
Miller, Susan. 1977. "News Coverage of Congress: The Search for the Ultimate Spokesman." *Journalism Quarterly* 54: 459-465.
Mills, Kay. 1997. "What Difference Do Women Journalists Make?" In *Women, Media, and Politics,* ed. Pippa Norris. New York: Oxford University Press.
Niven, David, and Jeremy Zilber. 1998. " 'What's Newt Doing in *People* Magazine?' The Changing Effect of National Prominence in Congressional Elections." *Political Behavior* 20: 213-224.
Norris, Pippa. 1997. "Introduction: Women, Media, and Politics." In *Women, Media, and Politics,* ed. Pippa Norris. New York: Oxford University Press.
Owen, Diana, Richard Davis, and Vincent James Strickler. 1999. "Congress and the Internet." *Harvard International Journal of Press/Politics* 4: 10-29.

Parker, Glenn. 1981. "Interpreting Candidate Awareness in U.S. Congressional Elections." *Legislative Studies Quarterly* 6: 219-234.

Payne, James. 1980. "Show Horses and Work Horses in the United States House of Representatives." *Polity* 12: 428-456.

Rosenwasser, Shirley M., and Jean Seale. 1988. "Attitudes Toward a Hypothetical Male or Female Presidential Candidate." *Political Psychology* 9: 591-598.

Saint-Germain, Michelle. 1989. "Does Their Difference Make a Difference? The Impact of Women on Public Policy in the Arizona Legislature." *Social Science Quarterly* 70: 956-968.

Thomas, Sue. 1994. *How Women Legislate*. New York: Oxford University Press.

Weaver, David. 1997. "Women as Journalists." In *Women, Media, and Politics,* ed. Pippa Norris. New York: Oxford University Press.

Witt, Linda, Karen Paget, and Glenna Matthews. 1995. *Running as a Woman: Gender and Power in American Politics*. New York: Free Press.

Zaller, John, and Dennis Chiu. 1996. "Government's Little Helper: U.S. Press Coverage of Foreign Policy Crises, 1945-1991." *Political Communication* 13: 385-405.

APPENDIX A

Telephone interviews followed these general questions, although respondents were encouraged to elaborate and in many cases spoke to multiple questions in one response. Written questionnaires presented these questions in an open-ended format with space provided for responses.

Generally, do you think the media treat your representative fairly?

Is media coverage commensurate with your representative's priorities and accomplishments?

What, if any, disappointment has your office experienced in dealing with the media?

Is your member subject to any media stereotypes?

Could you list a few words that capture the image of your representative that you are trying to communicate?

What types of stories generally produce the most satisfying media coverage?

What would an ideal story on your member be?

What groups, if any, do you target in your communication efforts?

If you had to choose, would you rather gain coverage for the representative's importance in Washington, or the representative's caring for the home district?

Generally, would you rather get coverage in the national media or the local media?

What advice would you give to the media to improve the content of congressional news coverage?

Research on Women in Legislatures: What Have We Learned, Where Are We Going?

Michele Swers, Mary Washington College

SUMMARY. Media commentators, political activists, and feminist scholars all express the belief that the election of more women to public office will result in greater attention to the needs of women, children, and families and will change the very process by which public policy is made. This review essay examines the progress made by scholars towards answering these questions. I evaluate the major findings in three significant areas of research: the experience of women as candidates, the policy impact of women as legislators, and the relationship of women to the institutions in which they serve. Finally, directions for future research are suggested. *[Article copies available for a fee from The Haworth Document Delivery Service: 1-800-HAWORTH. E-mail address: <getinfo@haworthpressinc.com> Website: <http://www.HaworthPress.com> © 2001 by The Haworth Press, Inc. All rights reserved.]*

Even before women secured the right to vote, members of Progressive Era women's groups demanded the appointment of women to public offices ranging from the school board to the labor bureau because they believed that female officeholders would consider the needs of children and the family and they would eliminate corruption in government (Baker 1984; Skocpol 1992). Similarly, the rise of feminism led to the creation of numerous political action committees (PACs) that raise

[Haworth co-indexing entry note]: "Research on Women in Legislatures: What Have We Learned, Where Are We Going?" Swers, Michele. Co-published simultaneously in *Women & Politics* (The Haworth Press, Inc.) Vol. 23, No. 1/2, 2001, pp. 167-185; and: *Women and Congress: Running, Winning, and Ruling* (ed: Karen O'Connor) The Haworth Press, Inc., 2001, pp. 167-185. Single or multiple copies of this article are available for a fee from The Haworth Document Delivery Service [1-800-HAWORTH, 9:00 a.m. - 5:00 p.m. (EST). E-mail address: getinfo@haworthpressinc.com].

money to support women candidates who pledge support to specific issues including abortion rights and the Equal Rights Amendment (Burrell 1994; Nelson 1994). These feminist groups believe that electing women will lead to a "feminization of politics" in which female legislators will make the interests of women, children, and families a central part of the national agenda and they will reform the very process by which public policy is made. To evaluate these long-held beliefs about women's impact on the political process, scholars of women in the state legislatures and Congress have focused their research on three broad areas: the experience of women as candidates, the policy impact of women as legislators, and the relationship of women to the institutions in which they serve. In this paper I review the major research findings in each of these three areas and I suggest directions for future research.

WOMEN AS CANDIDATES

In the early years, particularly before World War II, the most common way for a woman to attain elective office was by inheriting the seat of her deceased husband (Gertzog 1995; Werner 1966). Despite the recent publicity dedicated to the Senate election of Jean Carnahan (D-MD), the widow of former governor and Senate candidate Mel Carnahan, the phenomenon of the congressional widow is largely a relic of the past as women, like men, compete as individuals for party nominations and political office.

The fact that women currently constitute only 13.6% of the House of Representatives, 13% of the Senate, and 22.3% of state legislatures raises the question of why more women are not elected to public office (Center for the American Woman and Politics 2000). Research reveals that the single greatest obstacle to the election of women is the "incumbency factor." Since incumbents are reelected at a rate of more than 90%, it is very difficult for challengers to gain legislative seats (Jacobson 1997; Palmer and Simon 2001). Studies comparing men and women in similar races, including open seat contestants, challengers, and incumbents, find that women win just as often as men (Darcy and Schramm 1977; Deber 1982; Darcy, Welch, and Clark 1994; Carroll 1994; Burrell 1994; Seltzer, Newman, and Voorhees Leighton 1997; Gaddie, Hoffman, and Palmer 2001). Additionally, research demonstrates that there is no gender gap in fundraising (Uhlaner and Schlozman 1986; Biersack and Herrnson 1994; Burrell 1994; Darcy, Welch, and Clark

1994), although Herrick (1996) suggests that male challengers receive a larger benefit from each dollar raised than do female challengers.

Given the fact that women who run win, scholars must focus more attention on the stages before the campaign to understand why more women do not run for office. Does the paucity of women candidates reflect the underrepresentation of women in the occupations that lead to political careers (Nechemias 1987; Carroll 1994; Darcy, Welch, and Clark 1994; Duerst-Lahti 1998; McGlen and O'Connor 1998), the dearth of women in the local and state government positions that provide the necessary political experience to run for higher levels of office (Carroll and Strimling 1998; Darcy, Welch, and Clark 1994; Carroll 1994), the uneven distribution of and expectations concerning family responsibilities (Nechemias 1985; Dodson 1997; Duerst-Lahti 1998), or the recruitment patterns of political parties (Rule 1981; Bledsoe and Herring 1990; Carroll 1994; van Assendelft and O'Connor 1994; Niven 1998)?

While the studies of election outcomes indicate that men and women are equally successful in attracting votes, research on gender stereotypes demonstrates that voters view male and female candidates differently and these differences may impact their votes. Voter stereotypes generally fall into two categories, trait stereotypes and issue/belief stereotypes. With regard to personality traits, voters view women candidates as more compassionate and willing to compromise, while men are seen as more assertive and self-confident. On issues, voters view female candidates as more ideologically liberal than men and they favor women on such issues as education, health care, and welfare while they perceive men as more capable of handling the economy, military crises, and crime (Huddy and Terkildsen 1993a, 1993b; Burrell 1994; Alexander and Anderson 1993; Sapiro 1981-82; McDermott 1997).

Although numerous studies document the existence of voter stereotypes, scholars must illuminate more carefully the conditions in which these stereotypes affect actual votes. Since many of these studies are conducted as experiments in college classrooms (for example, Sapiro 1981-82; Huddy and Terkildsen 1993a, 1993b), it is not clear how much gender stereotypes influence voters' decisions in the electoral arena. For instance, knowledge of the candidate's party affiliation may overshadow the use of gender stereotypes. Alternatively, voters may only rely on gender stereotypes in "low-information" elections, when little is known about the candidates (Alexander and Anderson 1993; McDermott 1997). Thus, researchers should examine whether voters are more likely to rely on gender stereotypes in primary elections when party affiliation is held constant, rather than in the general election (King and Matland forthcoming). Similarly, voters may be more likely to utilize gender stereotypes in races that do not garner as much media attention, such as in a local election rather than a highly publicized U.S. Senate race (McDermott 1997) or for offices that draw on traditional male characteristics, such as attorney general, or female characteristics, such as superintendent of schools (Oxley and Fox 2000).

It is also possible that the damaging effects of gender stereotypes increase at higher levels of office. Dolan (1997) suggests that there is a glass ceiling, in which support for women candidates declines at higher levels of office, particularly among male voters. On the other hand, in the right electoral environment, voter stereotypes can favor women candidates. For example, analyses of the 1992 election indicate that the primary role of women's issues in the presidential and congressional campaigns and the media's combined focus on women's issues and the underrepresentation of women in office helped women candidates, particularly those who emphasized gender issues in their campaigns (Biersack and Herrnson 1994; Jelen 1994; Schroedel and Snyder 1994; Chaney and Sinclair 1994; Wilcox 1994; Plutzer and Zipp 1996; Fox 1997; Dolan 2001).

Beyond analyses of voter choice, more research is needed on the experience of women in campaigns, particularly their treatment by their opponents, the political parties, and the media. For example, Fox (1997) found that women candidates in California ran a different kind of campaign than men, in which they used a more personal style of campaigning and were more likely to emphasize their credentials to compensate for the assumption that a woman is less qualified. Additionally, he found that male candidates running against women changed their strategies to place greater emphasis on women's issues than they would if they were running against a male opponent.

The role that political parties play in encouraging or discouraging the candidacies of women for state-level and national office is still unclear. Baer (1993) calls the political parties the missing variable in women and politics research. Research conducted in the 1970s and early 1980s highlighted the tendency of parties to run women as sacrificial lambs in contests the parties had little chance of winning (Gertzog and Simard 1981; Deber 1982). However, the increased attention to the gender gap since the early 1980s has led both the Republican and Democratic parties to create committees and structures within their national party institutions to facilitate efforts to recruit, train, and fund women candidates for Congress (Jennings 1990; Burrell 1994). Studies that focus on the fundraising patterns of male and female candidates do not indicate any partisan bias against women candidates (Biersack and Herrnson 1994; Burrell 1994; Herrick 1995).

While numerous scholars view the political parties as a positive force for increasing the presence of women in Congress and the state legislatures (Bernstein 1986; Bledsoe and Herring 1990; Burrell 1994; Carroll 1994; Darcy, Welch, and Clark 1994; Thomas 1994), a recent study by David Niven (1998) cautions against the assumption that the parties are no longer biased against women candidates. Surveying party chairs and female local legislators in four states, Niven found that male party chairs do discriminate against women in their recruitment patterns. He attributed this biased treatment to an outgroup effect in which party leaders relate positively to those potential candidates seen as being similar to themselves, while candidates viewed as dissimilar are thought to be part of a homogeneous and less valued group. Therefore, Niven concludes that the "old boys network" is still a powerful deterrent to women's candidacies, since a predominantly male party elite is less likely to recognize the merits of a potential female candidate.

While the political parties remain a significant force in legislative elections, the rise of the candidate-centered campaign highlights the importance of the media. The growing influence of the media in electoral campaigns requires a better understanding of the media's impact on women candidates and their campaigns. Kahn (1992, 1994a, 1994b, 1996) finds that the media does discriminate against women in the amount of coverage they receive in their Senate and gubernatorial races, in the quality of that coverage, and in the extent to which that coverage reflects the messages issued by the campaign. Other scholars maintain that the media portrays women as less viable candidates than men and reporters focus a disproportionate amount of attention on their family situation, their appearance, and their position on women's issues (Witt, Piaget, and Matthews 1995; Braden 1996; Smith 1997; Vavrus 1998; Rausch, Rozell, and Wilson 1999; Kropf and Boiney 2001). This discriminatory coverage of female politicians continues once they reach elective office (Braden 1996; Carroll and Schreiber 1997; Niven and Zilber 2001). Future research must continue to investigate the differences in the ways men and women conduct their campaigns and the ways in which the media and the electoral environment impact the success of women candidates.

THE POLICY IMPACT OF WOMEN IN CONGRESS AND THE STATE LEGISLATURES

The overarching question facing those who study the policy impact of women in legislatures is whether descriptive representation, the election of women, leads to substantive representation–legislation on behalf of women's interests (Pitkin 1967). To answer this question, we first must demonstrate that women have distinct interests that require representation as members of a group and not just as individuals. Scholars focusing on representational theory assert that women do have distinct interests, which are based both on their private sphere responsibilities and the tension of integrating their private and public sphere roles (Sapiro 1981; Phillips 1991, 1995, 1998; Mansbridge 1999). Additionally, women's concerns are relatively new to the public agenda and have largely been ignored by politicians. Finally, since women as a group have historically been excluded from the political arena, women must be elected to provide role models for other women and to demonstrate that politics is not only a male domain (Sapiro 1981; Mansbridge 1999).

Evidence from the States

Scholars interested in delineating the policy impact of electing women originally focused their attention on the state legislatures because more women have served in the state legislatures than in Congress. Studies of women in state legislatures in the 1970s found differences in the attitudes of female legislators, but few differences in their policy priorities. For example, female state legislators expressed more liberal attitudes than men on feminist issues such as support for the ERA, public funding of day care, and the liberalization of abortion laws (Diamond 1977; Johnson et al. 1978). However, when asked to rank their policy priorities, these priorities were not significantly different from the legislative focus of their male colleagues (Mezey 1978; Thomas 1994). Thomas (1994) asserts that the slow acceptance of women into the political arena discouraged women from translating their more liberal policy attitudes into legislative priorities, since women were not willing to risk their standing in the legislature to pursue issues that were not viewed as legitimate by their male colleagues.

Additionally, women serving in the state legislatures in the 1970s were not fully integrated into the institutions in which they served. Women were disproportionately concentrated on committees that incorporate the traditional concerns of women, such as education, health, and welfare. Compared to their male colleagues, female legislators devoted more attention to constituency service and reported lower levels of activity in areas including speaking in committee and on the floor, working with colleagues, and bargaining with lobbyists (Kirkpatrick 1974; Diamond 1977; Thomas 1994). The focus on constituency service reflected women's background in community service, while women's lower rates of participation in the substance of legislative work was attributed to feelings of inefficacy that stemmed from the difficulty of adapting to the norms of a male-dominated institution (Kirkpatrick 1974; Diamond 1977; Thomas 1994).

As the number of women in state legislatures increased throughout the 1980s and the role of women in the public sphere became increasingly accepted, female state legislators became full participants in all legislative activities and began to pursue distinctive agendas. The evidence from studies since the 1980s demonstrates that women serving in the state legislatures exhibit unique policy priorities, particularly in the area of women's issues. In her comprehensive study of sex differences in legislative behavior across twelve legislatures, Thomas (1994) found that women held more liberal attitudes on policy issues than did their male colleagues. Additionally, women were more likely than their male counterparts to include legislation concerning women, children, and families among their top priorities and they were more successful in their efforts to pass these bills into law. These gender-related differences persisted across legislative bodies that differed by region of the country, political culture, and the proportion of women in the legislature.

In multi-state analyses and longitudinal studies of single legislatures, scholars have found that in comparison to men, female legislators are more liberal in their policy attitudes and they exhibit a greater commitment to the pursuit of feminist initiatives and legislation incorporating issues of traditional concern to women, including education, health, and welfare (Saint-Germain 1989; Dodson and Carroll 1991; Berkman and O'Connor 1993; Thomas 1994; Dolan and Ford 1995). Women are more likely to see their women's issue proposals passed into law (Saint-Germain 1989; Thomas 1994). In addition to differences in policy behavior, researchers found that women display a unique view of their representational role. Female legislators expressed a sense of responsibility to represent the interests of women, and they were more likely than men to view women as a distinct part of their constituency (Reingold 1992; Thomas 1994, 1997). Some scholars maintain that women exhibit a distinctive way of thinking about policy problems; thus, in her analysis of crime policy, Kathlene (1995) notes that women favored rehabilitative initiatives while men preferred proposals concerning punishment.

By examining legislative behavior across time and in different states, scholars found that the sex differences in the policy priorities of members gained strength as the proportion of women in the legislature approached a "critical mass" (Saint-Germain 1989; Berkman and O'Connor 1993; Thomas 1994). Drawing on the theories of Rosabeth Moss Kanter (1977) concerning the impact of proportions on groups, these researchers noted that as women increase their numbers in the legislature, they feel more free to pursue policy preferences based on gender.[1] Additionally, Thomas (1994) and Saint-Germain (1989) maintain that the presence of a women's caucus provides women with additional resources beyond their numbers, thus reducing the negative effects of tokenism.

Congressional Research

The paucity of women in Congress before the 1992 Year of the Woman election made it difficult to evaluate the policy impact of electing women. Early works catalogued the backgrounds, committee assignments, and legislative priorities of individual congresswomen (Werner 1966; Leader 1977; Gertzog 1984). The first systematic efforts to delineate the policy impact of women in Congress focused on roll-call voting behavior (Gehlen 1977; Leader 1977; Frankovic 1977). Over time, studies that examine whether women are more liberal than their male colleagues have had mixed results (Leader 1977; Gehlen 1977; Frankovic 1977; Welch 1985; Burrell 1994; McCarty, Poole, and Rosenthal 1997). However, other research indicates that gender does exert a significant effect on voting for specific women's issues such as abortion (Tatolovich and Schier 1993) or a set of women's issues (Burrell 1994; Dolan 1997; Swers 1998).

Yet analyses of roll-call voting only scratch the surface of potential gender differences in legislative participation, since the position a legislator takes on a roll-call vote does not reveal the depth of the member's commitment to women's interests, nor does it indicate the process by which a bill advanced through the legislative process (Hall 1996; Swers 2000). Beginning in the early 1990s, scholarly efforts to examine women's influence on the entire legislative process demonstrate that, like their counterparts in the state legislatures, women in Congress have had a unique influence on the congressional policymaking process, particularly in the area of women's issues. Congresswomen are opening the national agenda to women's issues by sponsoring and cosponsoring more legislation concerning feminist issues and issues that reflect women's traditional role as caregiver than their male colleagues do (Tamerius 1995; Vega and Firestone 1995; Swers 2000, forthcoming; Wolbrecht forthcoming). Congresswomen utilize their committee positions to advocate for the incorporation of women's interests into committee legislation (Gertzog 1995; Dodson et al. 1995; Dodson 1998, forthcoming; Bratton and Haynie 1999; Norton forthcoming; Swers 2000, forthcoming). Female legislators also demonstrate higher rates of participation in floor debates on women's issues (Tamerius 1995; Swers 2000; Cramer Walsh forthcoming) and speak with a distinctive voice on these issues (Dodson et al. 1995; Swers 2000; Levy, Tien, and Aved 2001; Cramer Walsh forthcoming). Finally, Congresswomen do view women as a distinct portion of their constituency and they express a commitment to representing women's interests in their legislative activities (Margolies-Mezvinsky 1994; Boxer 1994; Dodson et al. 1995; Gertzog 1995; Foerstel and Foerstel 1996; Bingham 1997; Molinari 1998; Carroll forthcoming).

Clearly, the research on the policy impact of female officeholders at the state and national levels has revealed important differences in the legislative priorities of individual legislators. Additionally, the research on state legislatures highlights the influence of the proportion of women in the legislative body and the presence of a women's caucus on a legislator's ability to express unique preferences based on gender. However, scholars need to devote more attention to the ways in which the political and institutional contexts shape the decision calculus of legislators concerning what policies to pursue. A new frontier of women and politics research focuses on illuminating how institutional and political context factors, such as a member's position within the committee structure and the agenda of the majority party in the legislature, shape the range of choices available to members regardless of their abstract policy preferences (for example, see Norton 1994; Dodson et al. 1995; Rosenthal 1998; Swers 2000).

THE RELATIONSHIP OF WOMEN TO THE INSTITUTION

The new institutional research illuminates the ways in which women are adapting to legislative norms as well as the ways in which the institutional and political contexts can inhibit legislators' efforts to advance their policy priorities. For example, Dodson (1995, 1998, forthcoming) demonstrates how Democratic and Republican women in the 103rd Congress used their positions on key committees and within the party leadership to ensure that legislation concerning violence against women, reproductive rights, and women's health gained a place on the national agenda and did not fall victim to issues of time and funding on their way to becoming law. By contrast, in her work on congressional action on reproductive issues, Norton (1994, 1995, 1999, forthcoming) reports that between 1969 and 1992, the members of key committees and subcommittees were able to impose their preferences on reproductive policy regardless of the will of the majority in Congress. The absence of women from these key committees inhibited their efforts to change policy regardless of their commitment to pro-choice initiatives. Similarly, Berkman and O'Connor (1993) maintain that state legislative committees with higher percentages of Democratic women were the most successful in blocking pro-life legislation. Demonstrating the importance of political context and majority vs. minority party status, Swers (2000, forthcoming) found that moderate Republican women changed their bill sponsorship patterns between the 103rd and 104th Congresses as they increased their sponsorship of social welfare bills and decreased their advocacy of more controversial feminist proposals in order to capitalize on their majority power and avoid antagonizing important party constituencies, particularly social conservatives. This new institutional research indicates that we must further investigate how the positions of members within the institution and changes in the external political environment alter the priorities of legislators regardless of their abstract policy preferences.

Beyond investigating the impact of institutional factors on the ability of members to pursue their policy priorities, scholars are also examining whether women are transforming the nature of the institutions in which they serve. These scholars start from the premise that institutions are gendered, meaning, "gender is present in the processes, practices, images, and ideologies, and distributions of power in the various sectors of social life" (Acker as quoted in Kenney 1996). Thus, male behavior is regarded as the norm in legislative institutions and women feel pressure to adapt to those expectations (Kenney 1996; Kelly and Duerst-Lahti 1995a, 1995b; Thomas 1997; Rosenthal 1998). Research on male-female differences in leadership style demonstrates that women exhibit an alternative method of leadership, which is challenging institutional norms. For example, Rosenthal (1997, 1998, 2000) finds that female committee chairs exhibited a more integrative leadership style than their male counterparts. As a result of gender role socialization and their distinctive paths to leadership, women's integrative style emphasizes consensual, cooperative, and inclusive decision-making rather than the transactional and competitive bargaining styles employed by their male colleagues. Similarly, in her analysis of crime legislation, Kathlene (1995) found that women focused more on community-based solutions such as prevention and rehabilitation proposals while men concentrated on abstract rights and expanding punishment.

Since women's integrative leadership style challenges established masculine legislative norms, women cannot easily incorporate this alternative style in all institutional settings. For example, Rosenthal (1998) found that integrative leadership behavior is less likely to occur in the more professionalized legislatures in which legislating is a full-time job and members have access to staff to develop policy expertise. She also notes that more states are trending toward the model of the professional legislature in which both male and female legislators eschew an inclusive, collaborative leadership style in favor of a more competitive model of leadership. Additionally, Kathlene (1989, 1994) reports that in committee hearings in the Colorado legislature, women entered the debate later, spoke less often than their male colleagues did, and interrupted witnesses less frequently than male legislators did. The aggressive behavior of men in committee hearings actually increased as the number of women in the committee room rose. This tension between the new methods of leadership introduced by women and the established institutional norms demonstrates that political activists cannot assume that increasing the number of women in office will lead to reform of the political process.

DIRECTIONS FOR FUTURE RESEARCH

The existing research on women in Congress and the state legislatures has greatly expanded our understanding of the experience of women as candidates and legislators. However, significant gaps remain. Future scholarship on women as candidates must continue to investigate why more women do not run for office. This line of inquiry requires us to expand our perspective from the focus on candidates and voters to include psychological and sociological factors such as gender role socialization and occupational trends as well as a more careful examination of candidate recruitment patterns. Those scholars who study the impact of gender role stereotypes must illuminate the conditions in which voters utilize those stereotypes. Does voter reliance on stereotypes vary with the type of election or the prestige of the office? Do these stereotypes help women in certain races and hurt them in others? Do voter stereotypes affect Republican and Democratic women differently? For example, gender stereotypes may help Republican women draw independent voters, while hurting Democratic women who may be perceived as too liberal.

With regard to research on women as legislators, current research at the state and national levels demonstrates that female legislators do perceive women as a distinct part of their constituency, and they do bring different policy priorities to the legislative agenda, particularly in the area of women's issues. Future research must investigate the ways in which female legislators incorporate women's interests into the policy discussion on issues that are not obviously women's issues. Scholars should also examine whether the increasing presence of female officeholders is influencing the policy priorities of male representatives. Additionally, we must devote more attention to the intersections of race and gender (Barrett 1995; Darling 1998). How does being an African-American or Hispanic woman impact a legislator's policy priorities and her relationship with white female legislators, white male legislators, and male legislators of her own race?

Finally, scholars must devote more attention to the influence of the institutional and political contexts on the legislative activity of members. A focus on institutions allows us to move beyond the testimony of legislators concerning their policy interests to an understanding of how the positions members occupy within the institution shape their willingness to pursue policy preferences based on gender. Future research on institutions must also more carefully delineate the ways in which institutions are gendered and how these hidden norms influence the behavior of male and female legislators. Thus, more research is needed to expand our understanding of the ways in which gender considerations mediate the experience of women as candidates and officeholders.

NOTE

1. In her study of skewed groups, Kanter (1977) found that the more numerous "dominants" set organizational norms and treat members of the minority as "tokens" who represent their category as symbols rather than as individuals. Minorities do not escape the constraints of tokenism until the groups become "balanced" at approximately 35%.

REFERENCES

Alexander, Deborah, and Kristi Anderson. 1993. "Gender as a Factor in the Attribution of Leadership Traits." *Political Research Quarterly* 46: 527-545.

Baer, Denise. 1993. "Political Parties: The Missing Variable in Women and Politics Research." *Political Research Quarterly* 46: 547-576.

Baker, Paula. 1984. "The Domestication of Politics: Women and American Political Society, 1780-1920." *American Historical Review* 89: 620-647.

Barrett, Edith. 1995. "The Policy Priorities of African-American Women in State Legislatures." *Legislative Studies Quarterly* 20: 223-247.

Berkman, Michael B., and Robert E. O'Connor. 1993. "Do Women Legislators Matter? Female Legislators and State Abortion Policy." *American Politics Quarterly* 21: 102-124.

Bernstein, Robert. 1986. "Why Are There So Few Women in the House?" *Western Political Quarterly* 39: 155-63.

Biersack, Robert, and Paul S. Herrnson. "Political Parties and the Year of the Woman." In *The Year of the Woman: Myths and Realities,* eds. Elizabeth Adell Cook, Sue Thomas, and Clyde Wilcox. Boulder, CO: Westview Press.

Bingham, Clara. 1997. *Women on the Hill: Challenging the Culture of Congress.* New York: Time Books.

Bledsoe, Timothy, and Mary Herring. 1990. "Victims of Circumstances: Women in Pursuit of Political Office." *American Political Science Review* 84: 213-223.

Boxer, Barbara. 1994. *Strangers in the Senate.* Washington, DC: National Press Books.

Braden, Maria. 1996. *Women Politicians and the Media.* Lexington: University Press of Kentucky.

Bratton, Kathleen A., and Kerry L. Haynie. 1999. "Agenda Setting and Legislative Success in State Legislatures: The Effect of Gender and Race." *Journal of Politics* 61: 658-679.

Burrell, Barbara C. 1994. *A Woman's Place is in the House: Campaigning for Congress in the Feminist Era.* Ann Arbor: University of Michigan Press.

Carroll, Susan J. Forthcoming. "Representing Women: Congresswomen's Perception of Their Representational Roles." In *Women Transforming Congress,* ed. Cindy Simon Rosenthal. Norman: University of Oklahoma Press.

Carroll, Susan J. 1994. *Women as Candidates in American Politics,* 2nd ed. Bloomington: Indiana University Press.

Carroll, Susan J., and Ronnee Schreiber. 1997. "Media Coverage of Women in the 103rd Congress." In *Women, Media, and Politics,* ed. Pippa Norris. New York: Oxford University Press.

Carroll, Susan, and Wendy S. Strimling. 1983. *Women's Routes to Elective Office: A Comparison with Men's.* New Brunswick: Center for the American Woman and Politics, Rutgers, The State University of New Jersey.

Center for the American Woman and Politics (CAWP). 2000. "Election 2000: Summary of Results for Women." New Brunswick: Center for the American Woman and Politics, Rutgers, The State University of New Jersey.

Chaney, Carole, and Barbara Sinclair. 1994. "Women and the 1992 House Elections." In *The Year of the Woman: Myths and Realities,* eds. Elizabeth Adell Cook, Sue Thomas, and Clyde Wilcox. Boulder, CO: Westview Press.

Cramer Walsh, Katherine. Forthcoming. "Resonating to Be Heard: Gendered Debate on the Floor of the House." In *Women Transforming Congress,* ed. Cindy Simon Rosenthal. Norman: University of Oklahoma Press.

Darcy, Robert, Susan Welch, and Janet Clark. 1994. *Women, Elections, and Representation.* 2nd ed. Lincoln: University of Nebraska Press.

Darcy, Robert, and Sarah Slavin Scramm. 1977. "When Women Run Against Men." *Public Opinion Quarterly* 41: 1-12.

Darling, Marsha L. 1998. "African-American Women in State Elective Office in the South." In *Women and Elective Office: Past, Present, and Future,* eds. Sue Thomas and Clyde Wilcox. New York: Oxford University Press.

Deber, Raisa. 1982. "The Fault Dear Brutus: Women as Congressional Candidates in Pennsylvania." *Journal of Politics* 44: 463-479.

Diamond, Irene. 1977. *Sex Roles in the State House.* New Haven: Yale University Press.

Dodson, Debra L. Forthcoming. "Representation, Gender and Reproductive Rights in the U.S. Congress." In *Women Transforming Congress,* ed. Cindy Simon Rosenthal. Norman: University of Oklahoma Press.

Dodson, Debra L. 1998. "Representing Women's Interests in the U.S. House of Representatives." In *Women and Elective Office: Past, Present, and Future,* eds. Sue Thomas and Clyde Wilcox. New York: Oxford University Press.

Dodson, Debra L. 1997. "Change and Continuity in the Relationship Between Private Responsibilities and Public Officeholding: The More Things Change, the More They Stay the Same." *Policy Studies Journal* 25: 569-584.

Dodson, Debra L., and Susan J. Carroll. 1991. *Reshaping the Agenda: Women in State Legislatures.* New Brunswick: Center for the American Woman and Politics, Rutgers, The State University of New Jersey.

Dodson, Debra L. et al. 1995. *Voices, Views, Votes: The Impact of Women in the 103rd Congress.* New Brunswick: Center for the American Woman and Politics, Rutgers, The State University of New Jersey.

Dolan, Julie. 1997. "Support for Women's Interests in the 103rd Congress: The Distinct Impact of Congressional Women." *Women & Politics* 18(4): 81-94.

Dolan, Kathleen. 2001. "Electoral Context, Issues, and Voting for Women in the 1990s." *Women & Politics* 23(1/2): 21-36.

Dolan, Kathleen. 1997. "Gender Differences in Support for Women Candidates: Is There a Glass Ceiling in American Politics?" *Women & Politics* 17(2): 27-41.

Dolan, Kathleen, and Lynne Ford. 1995. "Women in the State Legislatures: Feminist Identity and Legislative Behaviors." *American Politics Quarterly* 23: 96-108.

Duerst-Lahti, Georgia. 1998. "The Bottleneck: Women Becoming Candidates." In *Women and Elective Office: Past, Present, and Future,* eds. Sue Thomas and Clyde Wilcox. New York: Oxford University Press

Duerst-Lahti, Georgia, and Rita Mae Kelly. 1995. "On Governance, Leadership, and Gender." In *Gender Power, Leadership, and Governance,* eds. Georgia Duerst-Lahti and Rita Mae Kelly. Ann Arbor: University of Michigan Press.

Foerstel, Karen, and Herbert Foerstel. 1996. *Climbing the Hill: Gender Conflict in Congress*. Westport, CT: Praeger.

Fox, Richard Logan. 1997. *Gender Dynamics in Congressional Elections*. Thousand Oaks, CA: Sage.

Frankovic, Kathleen A. 1977. "Sex and Voting in the U.S. House of Representatives 1961-1975." *American Politics Quarterly* 5: 315-330.

Gehlen, Freida. 1977. "Women Members of Congress: A Distinctive Role." In *A Portrait of Marginality: The Political Behavior of the American Woman*, eds. Marianne Githens and Jewell Prestage. New York: McKay.

Gertzog, Irwin. 1984. *Congressional Women: Their Recruitment, Integration, and Behavior*. Westport, CT: Praeger.

Gertzog, Irwin. 1995. *Congressional Women: Their Recruitment, Integration, and Behavior* 2nd ed. Westport, CT: Praeger.

Gertzog, Irwin, and M. Michele Simard. 1981. "Women and 'Hopeless' Congressional Candidacies: Nomination Frequency, 1916-1978." *American Politics Quarterly* 9: 449-466.

Herrick, Rebecca. 1996. "Is There a Gender Gap in the Value of Campaign Resources?" *American Politics Quarterly* 24: 68-80.

Herrick, Rebecca. 1995. "A Reappraisal of the Quality of Women Candidates." *Women & Politics* 15(4): 25-38.

Hoffman, Kim U., Carrie Palmer, and Ronald Keith Gaddie. 2001. "Candidate Sex and Congressional Elections: Open Seats Before, During, and After the Year of the Woman." *Women & Politics* 23(1/2): 37-58.

Huddy, Leonie, and Nayda Terkildsen. 1993a. "Gender Stereotypes and the Perception of Male and Female Candidates." *American Journal of Political Science* 37: 119-147.

Huddy, Leonie, and Nayda Terkildsen. 1993b. "The Consequences of Gender Stereotypes for Women Candidates at Different Levels and Types of Offices." *Political Research Quarterly* 46: 502-525.

Jacobson, Gary C. 1997. *Politics of Congressional Elections*. 4th ed. New York: Longman.

Jelen, Ted G. 1994. "Carol Moseley-Braun: The Insider as Insurgent." In *The Year of the Woman: Myths and Realities*, eds. Elizabeth Adell Cook, Sue Thomas, and Clyde Wilcox. Boulder: Westview.

Jennings, M. Kent. 1990. "Women in Party Politics." In *Women, Politics, and Change*, ed. Louise Tilly and Patricia Gurin. New York: Russell Sage Foundation.

Johnson, Marilyn, and Susan J. Carroll, with Kathy Stanwyck and Lynn Korenblit. 1978. *Profile of Women Holding Office II*. New Brunswick, NJ: Center for the American Woman and Politics.

Kahn, Kim Fridkin. 1996. *The Political Consequences of Being a Woman: How Stereotypes Influence the Conduct and Consequences of Political Campaigns*. New York: Columbia University Press.

Kahn, Kim Fridkin. 1994a. "The Distorted Mirror: Press Coverage of Women Candidates for Statewide Office." *Journal of Politics* 56: 154-173.

Kahn, Kim Fridkin. 1994b. "Does Gender Make a Difference? An Experimental Examination of Sex Stereotypes and Press Patterns in Statewide Campaigns." *American Journal of Political Science* 38: 162-195.

Kahn, Kim Fridkin. 1992. "Does Being Male Help? An Investigation of the Effects of Candidate Gender and Campaign Coverage on Evaluations of U.S. Senate Candidates." *Journal of Politics* 54: 497-517.

Kanter, Rosabeth Moss. 1977. "Some Effects of Proportions on Group Life: Skewed Sex Ratios and Responses to Token Women." *American Journal of Sociology* 82: 965-990.

Kathlene, Lyn. 1995. "Alternative Views of Crime: Legislative Policymaking in Gendered Terms." *Journal of Politics* 57: 696-723.

Kathlene, Lyn. 1994. "Power and Influence of State Legislative Policymaking: The Interaction of Gender and Position in Committee Hearing Debates." *American Political Science Review* 88: 560-576.

Kathlene, Lyn. 1989. "Uncovering the Political Impacts of Gender: An Exploratory Study." *Western Political Quarterly* 42: 397-421.

Kelly, Rita Mae, and Georgia Duerst-Lahti. 1995. "The Study of Gender Power and Its Link to Governance and Leadership." In *Gender Power, Leadership, and Governance,* eds. Georgia Duerst-Lahti and Rita Mae Kelly. Ann Arbor: University of Michigan Press.

Kenney, Sally. 1996. "New Research on Gendered Political Institutions." *Political Research Quarterly* 49: 445-466.

King, David C., and Richard E. Matland. Forthcoming. "Partisanship and the Impact of Candidate Gender in Congressional Elections: Results of an Experiment." In *Women Transforming Congress,* ed. Cindy Simon Rosenthal. Norman: University of Oklahoma Press.

Kirkpatrick, Jeane. 1974. *Political Woman.* New York: Basic Books.

Kropf, Martha E., and John Boiney. 2001. "The Electoral Glass Ceiling? Gender, Viability, and the News in U.S. Senate Campaigns." *Women & Politics* 23(1/2): 79-103.

Leader, Shelah Gilbert. 1977. "The Policy Impact of Elected Women Officials." In, *The Impact of the Electoral Process,* eds. Joseph Cooper and Louis Maisel. Beverley Hills: Sage.

Levy, Dena, Charles Tien, and Rachelle Aved. 2001. "Do Differences Matter? Women Members of Congress and the Hyde Amendment." *Women & Politics* 23(1/2): 105-127.

Mansbridge, Jane. 1999. "Should Blacks Represent Blacks and Women Represent Women? A Contingent 'Yes.' " *Journal of Politics* 61: 628-657.

Margolies-Mezvinsky, Marjorie, with Barbara Feinman. 1994. *A Woman's Place . . . : The Freshmen Women Who Changed the Face of Congress.* New York: Crown Publishers.

McCarty, Nolan M., Keith T. Poole, and Howard Rosenthal. 1997. "Income Redistribution and National Politics." Monograph. Washington, DC: AEI Press.

McDermott, Monika L. 1997. "Voting Cues in Low-Information Elections: Candidate Gender as a Social Information Variable in Contemporary U.S. Elections." *American Journal of Political Science* 41: 270-283.

McGlen, Nancy, and Karen O'Connor. 1998. *Women, Politics, and American Society.* 2nd ed. Upper Saddle River, NJ: Prentice Hall.

Mezey, Susan Gluck. 1978. "Support for Women's Rights Policy: An Analysis of Local Politicians." *American Politics Quarterly* 6: 485-497.

Molinari, Susan, with Elinor Burkett. 1998. *Representative Mom: Balancing Budgets, Bill, and Baby in the U.S. Congress*. New York: Doubleday.

Nechemias, Carol. 1987. "Changes in the Election of Women to U.S. State Legislative Seats." *Legislative Studies Quarterly* 12: 125-142.

Nechemias, Carol. 1985. "Geographic Mobility and Women's Access to State Legislatures." *Western Political Quarterly* 38: 119-131.

Nelson, Candice. 1994. "Women's PACs and the Year of the Woman." In *The Year of the Woman: Myths and Realities,* eds. Elizabeth Adell Cook, Sue Thomas, and Clyde Wilcox. Boulder, CO: Westview Press.

Niven, David. 1998. *The Missing Majority: The Recruitment of Women as State Legislative Candidates*. Westport, CT: Praeger.

Niven, David, and Jeremy Zilber. 2001. " 'How Does She Have Time for Kids and Congress?' Views on Gender and Media Coverage from House Offices." *Women & Politics* 23(1/2): 147-165.

Norton, Noelle H. Forthcoming. "Transforming Congress from the Inside: Women in Committee." In *Women Transforming Congress,* ed. Cindy Simon Rosenthal. Norman: University of Oklahoma Press.

Norton, Noelle H. 1999. "Committee Influence Over Controversial Policy: The Reproductive Policy Case." *Policy Studies Journal* 27: 203-216.

Norton, Noelle H. 1995. "Women, It's Not Enough to Be Elected: Committee Position Makes a Difference." In *Gender Power, Leadership, and Governance,* eds. Georgia Duerst-Lahti and Rita Mae Kelly. Ann Arbor: University of Michigan Press.

Norton, Noelle H. 1994. "Congressional Committee Power: The Reproductive Policy Inner Circle, 1969-1992." Dissertation Manuscript.

Oxley, Zoe M., and Richard L. Fox. 2000. "Gender Stereotypes, Candidate Sex, and Success in Statewide Elections." Presented at the annual meeting of the Midwest Political Science Association. Chicago, IL.

Palmer, Barbara, and Dennis Simon. 2001. "The Political Glass Ceiling: Gender, Strategy, and Incumbency in U.S. House Elections, 1978-1998." *Women & Politics* 23 (1/2): 59-78.

Phillips, Anne. 1991. *Engendering Democracy*. University Park: Pennsylvania State University Press.

Phillips, Anne. 1995. *The Politics of Presence*. Oxford: Oxford University Press.

Phillips, Anne. 1998. "Democracy and Representation: Or, Why Should It Matter Who Our Representatives Are?" In *Feminism and Politics,* ed. Anne Phillips. New York: Oxford University Press.

Pitkin, Hanna Fenichel. 1967. *The Concept of Representation*. Berkeley: University of California Press.

Plutzer, Eric, and John Zipp. 1996. "Identity Politics, Partisanship, and Voting for Women Candidates." *Public Opinion Quarterly* 60: 30-57.

Rausch, John David, Mark Rozell, and Harry L. Wilson. 1999. "When Women Lose: A Study of Media Coverage of Two Gubernatorial Campaigns." *Women & Politics* 20 (4): 1-22.

Reingold, Beth. 1992. "Concepts of Representation Among Female and Male State Legislators." *Legislative Studies Quarterly* 17: 509-537.

Rosenthal, Cindy Simon. 2000. "Gender Styles in State Legislative Committees: Raising Their Voices in Resolving Conflict." *Women & Politics* 21(2): 21-45.

Rosenthal, Cindy Simon. 1998. *When Women Lead: Integrative Leadership in State Legislatures*. New York: Oxford University Press.

Rosenthal, Cindy Simon. 1997. "A View of Their Own: Women's Committee Leadership Styles and State Legislatures." *Policy Studies Journal* 25: 585-600.

Rule, Wilma. 1981. "Why Women Don't Run: The Critical Contextual Factors in Women's Legislative Recruitment." *Western Political Quarterly* 34: 60-77.

Saint-Germain, Michelle A. 1989. "Does Their Difference Make a Difference? The Impact of Women on Public Policy in the Arizona Legislature." *Social Science Quarterly* 70: 956-968.

Sapiro, Virginia. 1981. "Research Frontier Essay: When Are Interests Interesting? The Problem of Political Representation of Women." *American Political Science Review* 75: 701-716.

Sapiro, Virginia. 1981-82. "If U.S. Senator Baker Were a Woman: An Experimental Study of Candidate Images." *Political Psychology* 2: 61-83.

Schroedel, Jean, R., and Bruce Snyder. 1994. "Patty Murray: The Mom in Tennis Shoes Goes to the Senate." In *The Year of the Woman: Myths and Realities,* eds. Elizabeth Adell Cook, Sue Thomas, and Clyde Wilcox. Boulder, CO: Westview Press.

Seltzer, Richard, Jody Newman, and Melissa Voorhees Leighton. 1997. *Sex as a Political Variable: Women as Candidates and Voters in American Elections*. Boulder: Lynne Rienner.

Skocpol, Theda. 1992. *Protecting Soldiers and Mothers: The Political Origins of Social Policy in the United States*. Cambridge, MA: Harvard University Press.

Smith, Kevin B. 1997. "When All's Fair: Signs of Parity in Media Coverage of Female Candidates." *Political Communication* 14: 71-82.

Swers, Michele L. Forthcoming. "Transforming the Agenda? Analyzing Gender Differences in Women's Issue Bill Sponsorship." In *Women Transforming Congress,* ed. Cindy Simon Rosenthal. Norman: University of Oklahoma Press.

Swers, Michele L. 2000. "From the Year of the Woman to the Republican Ascendancy: Evaluating the Policy Impact of Women in Congress."

Swers, Michele L. 1998. "Are Congresswomen More Likely to Vote for Women's Issue Bills Than Their Male Colleagues?" *Legislative Studies Quarterly* 23: 435-448.

Tamerius, Karin L. 1995. "Sex, Gender, and Leadership in the Representation of Women." In *Gender Power, Leadership, and Governance,* eds. Georgia Duerst-Lahti and Rita Mae Kelly. Ann Arbor: University of Michigan Press.

Tatalovich, Raymond, and David Schier. 1993. "The Persistence of Ideological Cleavage in Voting on Abortion Legislation in the House of Representatives, 1973-1988." *American Politics Quarterly* 21: 125-139.

Thomas, Sue. 1997. "Why Gender Matters: The Perceptions of Women Officeholders." *Women & Politics* 17(1): 27-53.

Thomas, Sue. 1994. *How Women Legislate*. New York: Oxford University Press.

Thompson, Joan Hulse. 1980. "Role Perceptions of Women in the Ninety-fourth Congress, 1975-76." *Political Science Quarterly* 95: 71-81.

Uhlaner, Carole, and Kay Schlozman. 1986. "Candidate Gender and Congressional Campaign Receipts." *Journal of Politics* 48: 30-50.

van Assendelft, Laura, and Karen O'Connor. 1994. "Backgrounds, Motivations, and Interests: A Comparison of Male and Female Local Party Activists." *Women & Politics* 14(2): 77-92.

Vavrus, Mary. 1998. "Working the Senate from the Outside In: The Mediated Construction of a Feminist Political Campaign." *Critical Studies in Mass Communication* 15: 213-235.

Vega, Arturo, and Juanita M. Firestone. 1995. "The Effects of Gender on Congressional Behavior and the Substantive Representation of Women." *Legislative Studies Quarterly* 20: 213-222.

Welch, Susan. 1985. "Are Women More Liberal Than Men in the U.S. Congress?" *Legislative Studies Quarterly* 10: 125-134.

Werner, Emmy E. 1966. "Women in Congress 1917-1964." *Western Political Quarterly* 19: 16-30.

Wilcox, Clyde. 1994. "Why Was 1992 the 'Year of the Woman'?: Explaining Women's Gains in 1992." In *The Year of the Woman: Myths and Realities,* eds. Elizabeth Adell Cook, Sue Thomas, and Clyde Wilcox. Boulder: Westview Press.

Witt, Linda, Karen Paget, and Glenna Matthews. 1995. *Running as a Woman: Gender and Power in American Politics.* New York: Free Press.

Wolbrecht, Christina. Forthcoming. "Female Legislators and the Women's Rights Agenda." In *Women Transforming Congress,* ed. Cindy Simon Rosenthal. Norman: University of Oklahoma Press.

About the Contributors

RACHELLE AVED is a PhD candidate in Political Science at the University of Iowa.

JOHN A. BOINEY is Assistant to the Executive Director of the San Gabriel Valley Council of Governments, a 30-city Joint Powers Authority representing 1.6 million residents of eastern Los Angeles County. He also provides management services to cities and nonprofit organizations throughout California. Prior to taking his current position, Boiney was Assistant Professor of Government in the School of Public Affairs at American University. He taught and conducted research on public opinion, political communication, and news media politics. Boiney holds a BA from Dartmouth College, and an MA and PhD from Duke University.

KATHLEEN DOLAN is Associate Professor at the University of Wisconsin-Milwaukee. Her research interests include voting behavior and elections, gender and politics, women political candidates, mass political participation, and public opinion. Her publications have appeared in *American Journal of Political Science*, *Political Research Quarterly*, *American Politics Quarterly*, *Political Behavior*, *Political Psychology*, and *Women & Politics*.

PETER L. FRANCIA is a research fellow at the Center for American Politics and Citizenship at the University of Maryland-College Park. His research interests include interest groups, political parties, congressional elections, and campaign finance. He recently received his PhD from the University of Maryland.

RONALD KEITH GADDIE is Associate Professor of Political Science at the University of Oklahoma. His latest book is *Elections to Open Seats in the US House: Where the Action Is* (2000, Rowman and Littlefield Press, with Charles S. Bullock III).

KIM U. HOFFMAN is Visiting Assistant Professor of Political Science at University of Central Arkansas and a PhD candidate at the University of Oklahoma. Her research has previously appeared in *Social Science Quarterly*.

MARTHA E. KROPF is Assistant Professor of Political Science at the University of Missouri-Kansas City. Dr. Kropf conducts research in the area of public opinion, voting behavior and political participation. She is currently involved in a national study of campaign communications coordinated by David Magleby at Brigham Young University. Her focus is on the Missouri Senate elections in 2000. Her work also focuses on "norms of cooperation" and how community expectations affect collective action problems. Her dissertation is about why people contribute to public broadcasting. She has published her work in *Political Psychology* and *PS: Political Science and Politics*.

DENA LEVY is Assistant Professor of Political Science at SUNY-Brockport College. She is a recipient of the Nuala McGann Drescher Affirmative Action/Diversity Leave and is spending this academic year in Washington, DC.

DAVID NIVEN teaches Women and Politics and American Government' courses at Florida Atlantic University. He is the author of *The Missing Majority: The Recruitment of Women as State Legislative Candidates* and co-author of *Racialized Coverage of Congress: The News in Black and White* with Jeremy Zilber.

KAREN O'CONNOR is Professor of Government and Director of the Women & Politics Institute in the School of Public Affairs at American University. Professor O'Connor writes in the areas of judicial politics and women and politics. She currently serves as the editor of *Women & Politics*.

BARBARA PALMER is Academic Director of the Women & Public Policy Semester and Assistant Professor in the Washington Semester Program at American University. Her research interests are in the areas of women and politics, sex-discrimination law, and judicial process. She has published in the *American Political Science Review, Political Research Quarterly*, and the *American University Journal of Gender, Social Policy and the Law*.

CARRIE PALMER is a research fellow in the Institute of Public Affairs and a doctoral student in political science at the University of Oklahoma. Her research has also appeared in *Social Science Quarterly*.

COLLEEN J. SHOGAN is a doctoral candidate at Yale University in Political Science. Her primary research interests include the American presidency, women in Congress, and Catholic hospital mergers. She is currently a Graduate Research Fellow with the National Science Foundation.

DENNIS SIMON is Associate Professor of Political Science at Southern Methodist University and teaches courses on the Presidency, American Politics, Campaigns and Elections, and Public Opinion. His research interests are in the areas of presidential and executive process, public opinion, women and congressional elections, and methodology. He has published in the *American Political Science Review*, *Journal of Politics*, and *Public Opinion Quarterly*.

MICHELE SWERS is Assistant Professor of Political Science at Mary Washington College. She earned her PhD in Political Science from Harvard University. Her research interests include legislative behavior, political parties, and women and politics. Her analysis of roll call voting on women's issues appears in *Legislative Studies Quarterly*. Her book, *The Difference Women Make: Evaluating the Policy Impact of Women in Congress*, is forthcoming from the University of Chicago Press.

CHARLES TIEN is Assistant Professor of Political Science at Hunter College, CUNY. He spent the last academic year as a Fulbright Scholar Lecturer in Beijing, China.

JEREMY ZILBER teaches Media and Politics and American Government courses at Yeshiva University. He is the co-author of *Racialized Coverage of Congress: The News in Black and White* with David Niven. His research on media coverage of politics has also appeared in *Political Behavior* and the *Harvard International Journal of Press/Politics*.

Index